The Crazy Lives of Police Wives

Written and Compiled by:

Carolyn Whiting

Carolyn LaRoche

Dedications

To my husband Bob- for all of his love and support with this book and in all that I do. And to my cat Ollie, who sat next to me during the writing process and persistently tried to add his thoughts with more than a few jaunts across the keyboard.

Carolyn Whiting

To my husband Eric- without him I never would have had the privilege of experiencing all the joys of the police wife life and to my boys Alex and Logan for making it all worth it.

Carolyn LaRoche

Two by two I listened to 12 snaps as 6 belt keepers snapped in place this morning -- even though he tried his best to be as quiet as he could -- not to wake me until the last minutes before he leaves -- I still could hear them just as if they were gun shots. He kisses me softly and I can smell him near me. I open my eyes to see him smiling. We walk to the door and I make sure his gear's in place, make sure he has money for the day, and hug him tight. We exchange I love you(s) and I watch him walk to his car for his shift. Lord I pray that you keep him safe. He's now only in your sight. Bring him home safe to me. Amen.

Angela Machell Robinson

Acknowledgements

Book cover by Bob Buchanan Photography
Further information is available on his Facebook page,
www.facebook.combobbuchananphotography and at www.bobbuchanan.com

We would like to thank the police wives from across the United States and Canada, too numerous to mention by name, for sharing their thoughts, experiences, memories and advice and without whom this book would not be possible. Police wives responded to email questions and social media posts in an effort to help the sisterhood of police wives. The questions and answers come primarily from police wives. In some sections of the book their children and police officer husbands have voiced their thoughts and we are grateful for their assistance. Names and identifying information have been changed. We have kept the casual social media question and answer style to share the true sisterhood of the police wives of this project. Many topics were chosen based on interests shown in LEOW Facebook group postings.

We thank our law enforcement husbands for giving us this crazy life of a police wife. We face joys, sorrows, laughter, tears, loneliness, independence, fears, struggles and challenges that civilian wives do not but, we wouldn't trade our lives for anything… well, most of the time we wouldn't.

Disclaimer

Please bear with us as we get some general housekeeping out of the way. At no point does any product, company, author, organization, owner of rights to any books or movies or any government website or any other website mentioned in this book endorse this book or any content herein. Those who have contributed to this book do not endorse any answers or information given beyond their own answers. This book is meant to share experiences and what has worked for other wives but is not meant to be the sole solution nor represent expert opinion to any issue or problem. This book is not meant to be a substitute for professional advice when circumstances warrant it. Please, if you are feeling overwhelmed or need advice beyond the general life / shared experience knowledge of your sister police wives, give yourself the gift of professional help.

Resources and information mentioned in this book are not meant to suggest that other resources are not available and helpful. We urge you to do your own further research on topics of specific interest to you.

The authors reserve the rights to all material written by them and the people who have shared their advice reserve all rights to their written material.

Law enforcement officer: LEO

Law enforcement officer wife: LEOW

You are cordially invited to join us in our
Conversations with police wives as they share their
lives, wisdom, experience and the always present, when police
wives are talking, laughter.

Time: When it's most convenient for you
Location: Where ever you feel most comfortable
Cost: Great value and well worth it.

The authors decided to write this book with the purpose and
intent of helping other police wives and it is with this purpose in
mind that all profits from the book will be donated to a police
related charity.

Table of Contents

A Life Like No Other

"Hi Honey, Is it all right if I go pick up hookers tonight?"

"Is it overtime?"

"Of course."

"O.K. Have fun."

Yes, this really happened- an actual conversation I had with my husband. I should mention that this call came in as I sat in the teacher's cafeteria having lunch between classes…surrounded by several of my colleagues.

I can still see the look on my friend's face as she heard every word through my cell phone.

Such is the life of a police officer's wife.

Just so you know, it's not like I planned to marry a cop.

Who really does?

I suppose the "Badge bunnies" might. But I don't really think so. They usually aren't interested in marriage…

Nope. If anyone had asked me when I was young and full of dreams for the future if I wanted to be a cop's wife I probably would have asked them if they were on drugs.

Yet, here I sit, a decade and a half later with the alarm set, the dog at my feet and a loaded gun on the dresser beside me because my neighbor called and said she saw someone creeping around our back yard in the dark. And the man I married, who ideally should have been the protector of his home and family in that moment was off somewhere acting as protector for people who didn't even know his name let alone how much I wished he were home with me right then.

With two little ones sleeping in the next room, and a creeper out in the dark, I am tasked with the job of protector and defender against all things that go bump in the night.

Had I known this was going to happen, would I still have said "I do" all those years ago?

ABSOLUTELY.

I can't imagine any other life. I have my very own superhero living right here under my roof.

Understand though- just as it takes a certain kind of man (or woman) to be called to the duty of wearing the badge, it takes a certain kind of person to marry them.

It is not for the faint of heart.

It is not for the weak.

It is not for the co-dependent or frail of self-confidence.

The law enforcement officer's wife's (LEOW as it is sometimes referred to) life is a calling all of its own. It can't be avoided...Like they say, you can run but you can't hide. A police officer in need of the love and support of a LEOW will find you.

Mine found me and he wasn't even a cop yet.

But someone knew...some higher power with a bigger plan than all of us, knew his calling on this Earth and decided it was going to be my duty- my calling-to be the one keeping the home-fires burning and the creepers at bay while he fulfilled his duty. A duty he was born with.

And I wouldn't have it any other way.

However, let's just go ahead and thank that higher power I call God that I am not afraid to protect my home and family should the need arise.

In case you were wondering, the creeper disappeared when the neighbor's dog went after him. He should be thanking his lucky stars he didn't try to get into my home.

It would have been his last creeping experience.

I am woman and I am strong.

I am the wife of a police officer and I am not afraid of things that go bump in the night. I do however wonder how many times I will fall asleep-finally- with the television on or how often I will use a roll of finger print lifting tape to wrap my niece's birthday gift before my call to duty expires and my husband finally sleeps at home every single night for the rest of our lives.

I wish that someone had given me a heads up all those years ago- a little warning of what the law enforcement officer (often referred to as LEO) life was going to be like. I wish there had been a resource, a support group, anything that would have let me know that the things I experienced were a normal part of being a law enforcement family. It was my continuous search that led me to a fellow LEOW who shared the same desire I did to help other law enforcement wives and families make some sense out of this crazy life we all live.

And so here we are.

This book is our shared dream, realized with the help of many amazing wives who willingly shared their tears, heartbreak, sorrow, frustration, happiness, strength, pride and joy with us so that we may share it with you.

In The Beginning

What little girl doesn't dream of being a princess at least once in their young lives? Locked away in a tower or put to sleep by a poison spindle just waiting for her Prince Charming to ride up on his strong, white steed and rescue her from her plight.

As we grew into our teenage years, Prince Charming may have morphed into a crush on some famous music or movie star. By high school, it might have been the star of the football team or even the captain of the debate club who swept us off our feet.

At what point did the prince suddenly show up in a white Chevy Impala with blue lights flashing and sirens blaring?

WOW. Talk about a twisted fairy tale.

Some of us never intended to marry. Others among us may have had our eye on the dashing lawyer or successful business man. Every one of us had a vision and although he probably no longer resembled a fairy tale prince or teen dream rock star, he probably didn't wear Kevlar and polyester- together.

But then, maybe he did.

Everyone has a story. Some more unique than others maybe but they all bring us a smile when we think about the day we met our beloved.

Meeting your LEO is only a short part of the story though. Some of you might not have even known that the man you were falling in love with would one day become his own type of rock star. Others may have been well aware of his calling and so you fought it all the way to the altar. It's a good bet that pretty much all of us had no idea how it would affect our lives. Either way, we all have a story to tell and they may not be as inherently different as you might think.

How did you meet your husband? If he was LEO when you met, did it impact your decision to date him in a positive or negative way?

My husband's ex-girlfriend introduced us. She thought we would have a lot in common because he wanted to be a cop and I was about to start grad school for a master's in forensic science. I didn't like him at all but apparently after we met he asked her for my number. He called me every day for nearly a month before I slipped up and actually answered the phone without checking the caller ID. Somehow in that conversation he managed to convince me to go out with him. We were less than an hour into our date when I knew I would one day marry him. Some might say he was a bit of a stalker but he likes to claim he was persistent!

Maggie F.

My husband and I met through working at the Court House, where I had seen him in passing. I took a volunteer job with his Sheriff's Office and began to go on ride alongs on prisoner transport. We soon became inseparable.

Ashley B

My husband was very persistent in asking me for our first date, which I did not accept immediately. Our first date is one for the books. I had just graduated from college, was working full time and living at home. Between his schedule and mine, it was hard to find a time to go out together. He asked me for a Friday night date but I was a volunteer EMT with an ambulance and was on duty after 10 PM. He asked about an early dinner and I said that I could not because I had dinner plans with my parents. My LEO said "I'm new here, where is a good place to eat?" Figuring I would get a "no," and be rid of him for another week, I said would you like to meet us for dinner?" Wouldn't you know, he said "Yes." Yes, our first date was dinner with my parents that lasted three hours. My parents immediately adored him and I knew I was in trouble if I wanted to get rid of him. He came back to my parent's house after dinner. It was now after 10 PM and I was called to an EMT emergency. Next thing I know, I was doing CPR on an older gentleman and when I looked up, I saw my LEO. He was a volunteer EMT himself and apparently the call was almost across the street from where he lived. So our first date was a three hour dinner with my parents topped off with doing CPR. Very Romantic.

Denise N.

I met my husband back in High School when he was seventeen and I was fifteen. He was a young and charismatic football player. I laugh now as I remember him pulling up in his red sports car and my mother coming out to regulate his speed with a "gentle reminder that she knew where he lived." Never did the thought cross my mind that one day he would become a LEO. He was a mischievous teenager who was well known by the small town officers as a polite young man who liked to hotrod.

Angela L.

I met my husband while working at a bank and he worked there off duty for security. He had already been a cop for eight years. After twelve years now and a promotion for him, we have settled into a pretty good routine. And the fact that he was a LEO didn't affect whether I dated him. The man in a uniform is just a bonus.

Susan M.

I met my husband at a club in Oklahoma in nineteen ninety five. I was working as a dispatcher for a local police department and some friends and I had gone out to a club after work. Greg, my now husband, and his friend had just come into the bar when we walked past him, I heard him make a comment. It is funny because I can still remember what he was wearing. Jeans, boots, a brush popper shirt and a black cowboy hat. A little later on I was sitting at the tables by the dance floor watching my friends dance, when he approached me. He tipped his black hat to me and said "Pardon me ma'am, but could I have a dance with you on the next slow song?" When the next song came on he came over to me, took my hand and we went out and danced. This is when we started talking about ourselves, and I found out that he was a police officer in a town about 30 minutes away. We talked for the rest of the evening, exchanged phone numbers and left. I really did not think that he would call me, but he did. At first he had lost my phone number and called the department that I was a dispatcher for asking for my phone number. The Sgt. at the time refused to give him my number, even though Greg said that he was a cop. Greg finally found my number and called me at 4 AM! It was love from then on. I think knowing he was a police officer when I met him had a positive effect on me because I was involved in law enforcement as well and who could not feel safe with a police officer?

Cathy L

I met my husband of twenty eight years at a restaurant/ bar. I wasn't thrilled that he was a cop but he had just started an office day job at his police department so I did not have to deal with a crazy schedule or worry about him being hurt in the beginning of our relationship.

Elarie S.

I met my husband at a restaurant where he was working as a waiter. He tried to take my order and suddenly started stuttering. Later, after I received my order, we started chatting and instantly hit it off. We were dating a little later, were engaged three months after starting to date and married five months after becoming engaged. He became a dispatcher for a police department while we were engaged and wanted to further his love for law enforcement so he became a police officer three years after we were married.

Becky N.

I met my husband while working dispatch. He was a new deputy and as soon as I heard his voice on the radio, I knew I had to meet him. I asked around and to my joy, the new deputy was single. We began talking, then he began to bring me treats, which turned into us dating and then we became engaged.

Claire D.

I met my husband on a ride along when he was just out of the police academy. He was twenty four and I was twenty two. When we met I told him I wouldn't seriously date an officer due to bad past experiences. I felt all police officers were cheaters. I soon found out that my husband (and I) is a Christian and so cheating will never be an issue in our marriage.

Cassie S.

If he was not a LEO when you met, did you support his decision to become one or was it a difficult career choice for you to accept?

I embraced the career choice my husband made in becoming an officer as I have always thought it to be a respectable position. It is a hard pill for me to swallow these days as he has faced danger so many times. I just remind myself that it would be selfish to keep him from doing what he loves, especially since he does so well at it. I will always 100% support him in any venture he chooses because I don't feel it's my decision to make. I just remember to pray every time he leaves home that he comes home safe.

Angela L.

I was behind his decision one hundred percent, as we both took the written exam at the same time. He beat me by one point and went on to the next step in the process.

Jessica B.

We met in graduate school and at the time his goal was to become an agent with the FBI. He recognized early on that he would need local law enforcement experience to make himself a better candidate. As we were in the same graduate school program, we had the same interests and I didn't think twice about his decision to apply for a local police department. Many of our friends were seeking jobs with federal agencies. This was his first step to get there. Of course, since he got to the local department, he has had no desire to leave and go to a federal job.

Meredith K.

He didn't become interested law enforcement until he met a Sheriff's deputy while he was working as a personal trainer in a gym. I supported his decision to pursue law enforcement. I wish I had had someone to talk to me about the journey we were about to begin.

Tanya D.

I have supported my husband in every decision he has made for our family one hundred and ten percent. I have encouraged him that much more for him to further his love to be a law enforcement officer.

Becky N.

I supported my husband one hundred percent in his desire to become a LEO. However, I did not know what I / we were getting into. I think a lot more thought and discussion would have gone into the decision had I known what I know now.

Maggie D.

"The Road not taken." At times the decision is to not become a LEO, despite the inner voice calling. Were there regrets or was it the right choice?

I can't count how many times someone approached me while I was in uniform and told me that they used to think about becoming a cop but that they were too old now. They often said they regretted their decision and wanted me to tell them all about the job, wondered if I liked it and was it worth it. Yes, it was worth it. I hurt my back and retired after a few years on the job but I absolutely do not regret the decision to become a cop. I would have spent my life wondering "what if" had I not done it.

Terri W.

My grandfather, father and I were all police officers. My oldest brother, Michael served in the army for a few years and went into construction upon his return home from the army. He liked the work and was making a lot of money but he wanted to become a police officer. He was single at the time and when he told my father about his desire to become a police officer my father told him to "stay single because I wouldn't put my worst enemy through what your mother has gone through." Michael joined the Police Department and a short time later he met his wife, Doris. Not long after they were married, Doris realized that being married to a cop was not always easy. She especially didn't like the hours. In the end, Michael decided to leave the job. He drove a taxi for a while and eventually he became a long haul trucker. However, he soon found that driving out to Cleveland in one day and returning at eleven P.M. the next day was not an easy way of life. After a few years, Michael was able to get a job in a Corrections department where he remained until he died from cancer at the age of forty three.

I also had a friend who I worked with as a summer auxiliary police officer. My friend John often said he wanted to be a police officer full time. He served in Vietnam as an army Ranger, was street smart and would have made a great cop. His girlfriend Cecilia was not happy with his decision to become a police officer and it became a major sticking point in their relationship and their plans for a future together. One night, John and Cecelia were watching a movie on television. One scene in the movie involved a police officer being shot and killed during a traffic stop. During this scene, Cecelia screamed and John had to spend considerable time consoling her. She feared that someday, the cop being shot could be John. John realized that Cecelia could not deal with the stress of being a cop's wife and he had to decide if he wanted the police job or Cecelia. He chose Cecelia and they married sometime later. John got a job driving a truck for a freight carrier. Not becoming a cop seemed to be the right decision for John and Cecelia's relationship but I often wonder if John thinks about what might have been had he become a police officer.

Nick F.

Not all women can or want to be a LEOW. They may not have the right personality to navigate the challenges of LEOW life or are intimidated by the lifestyle. What LEOW traits make for a successful marriage? While a LEOW needs a special ability to see humor in situations civilians may not, that's not all that is needed. Patience, flexibility, compassion, understanding, strength, the list goes on. Being married to a cop is a life like no other, and although all people are unique, most spouses can agree that there are certain things that are absolutely required. At the top of the list you might find the following traits, but there are so many more as expressed by fellow LEO wives.

Sense of humor, a little on the warped side.

A law enforcement spouse must have a special kind of sense of humor. She can't be offended easily, she can't be too uptight and she needs to roll with the punches and laugh.

> "I don't smell like dead guy do I?" Ummm, I really don't think this is a normal question asked by husbands when they come home ...LEOW life.
> Meghan B.

Flexibility.

You plan your son's birthday for two in the afternoon knowing that your LEO's shift will be over for a good six hours. You just forgot that he is on the dive team and a car has just gone over the side of a bridge. The party goes on. Everyone else has Thanksgiving dinner on Thanksgiving. You serve a full turkey dinner two days later when your LEO finally has a whole day off.

Understanding

Your LEO comes home agitated and sharp tongued, itching to fight with anyone who is game. Your first instinct is to fall into the cycle and have a good yelling brawl. Instead you let him yell, kick his boots around or whatever he needs to do because you recognize all the signs of a bad call. And then you hug him and tell him you are there for him if he needs to talk about it.

Tolerance

He just worked a fourteen hour shift and comes home exhausted. Kicks his boots off by the front door, drops his duty belt on a chair, loses his uniform somewhere between that chair and the couch he drops onto. Picking up the remote control, he turns on some useless program and proceeds to study it with the intensity of a surgeon repairing a heart valve. All of this without even saying hello to you. Should the wife of a police officer have to put up with this behavior? No. Will you? Probably. From time to time at least. Why? Because you know from experience that the last fourteen hours probably drained every last ounce of anything from him and you understand the effort it took for him to get to that couch. This doesn't mean you should put up with his stuff all over the house, but it might mean you can ignore it for an hour or two while he recovers some of his conscious brain function. Tolerance goes hand in hand with extreme patience, something true LEO wives have been gifted with.

Strength

LEOWs are a little different than their civilian counterparts. Are they born that way or do they get that way after spending a few years with their LEO? The instincts of inner strength, situational awareness and fight vs. flight, stand strong and not cry and curl into a protective ball are often there and may be a part of what attracts their LEO in the first place but marriage to a LEO hones these LEOW instincts.

Wallflowers we are not!

My husband and I are in Walmart and he has to use the bathroom. I'm waiting in the cereal aisle and notice a couple of guys at the other end. I turned around, back to my business and I don't know if it's our natural instinct because of our lifestyles but I felt someone coming up on me. I just had the feeling to look down at my purse and sure enough, a hand goes to snatch my purse. Without thinking, I grab the guys hand, pulled his arm up and back (never seeing his face) and just as I was drawing up, about to put an elbow to his throat.. It's my guy. He comes to the front of me wide eyed and says, "I had no idea you were that fast!" My response was, "I have a family to feed and my iPhone was in there" Moral of the story, don't screw with a LEOW.
Wendy A.

What are the three most important personality traits for a LEOW? Why?

A LEOW has to be strong, independent and patient. I enjoy the days that I have with my husband when he is not working, but I also enjoy my alone time. I have built a solid base of friends and spend time with them when he is working. I see a lot of women who complain that they never see their husbands, but that's the job. My husband and I make it work when he's off and when he's working I get to watch The Real Housewives or whatever without judgment. It's perfect!
Meredith K.

You must have a sense of humor because cops tend to tell weird stories. You must be able to be independent because you may be alone a lot. And you must have self-confidence and be secure in your relationship because your spouse will encounter others that may be flirtatious.
Susan M.

Flexibility: This is probably the number one on the list. You can always count on plans changing, usually when you least expect it or when you least want it to. That arrest your LEO has been after or even a happy call where our LEO finds a lost child coming in at the end of a shift. Holidays will never be on a regular schedule and if your LEO's department works rotations, flexibility is number one!
Self-sufficient: Depending on your LEO's shift and the department he works in, he may be gone for long stretches of time and the LEOW will need to be able to fend for herself. If you are someone who is not very resourceful or dare I use the words "are needy," then you may not do well as a LEOW.
Discreet: There may be times as a LEOW you happen to find yourself in the know with some important or sensitive information. This can happen, even unintentionally so it's just important to be careful of what we say and not be part of the gossip circles.
Denise N.

Patience is vital because you never know what your husband will deal with and how long it will take. Courage is needed because when you kiss him goodbye every day you never know what he may encounter and whether or not he may even come home and you have to be prepared to deal with whatever happens. You also need courage to handle any unexpected situations that may arise from your husband being a LEO because there are crazies out there who want to get even. In my opinion, flexibility is the most important trait for a LEOW. You have to be flexible to account for your LEO's crazy schedule and getting called in on a day off or having to work late and not being able to make dinner or a party or a family activity. Getting mad and upset at your LEO will not make things go smoothly.

Patty R.

Flexibility is a must because there can be a lot of inconsistency with schedules, moods etc. You also need to be consistent yourself because they need stability at home. You need to be understanding and know when to question and when to leave him alone. With my husband's large department, he sees a lot. In almost seven years he's seen more than most do in an entire career.

Cassie S.

Loving, understanding and for us... humor. Any time my husband came home after dealing with losing a child the only thing I could do is listen to him and hold him. And then there is the frustration of not being able to "fix" the criminal.

Elarie S.

Understanding, patience, supportive, flexible, strong, independent and unconditional love are the traits most important to being a LEOW. There will be times (more so than not) that they are late or plans get changed due to work so a LEOW needs to understand that the LEO would much rather be with them but due to their job, it's not always possible. As a LEOW there will be times you feel like a single parent because they will be working while you are at school functions and family events alone so you need to be okay with that and be independent enough to be able to do things alone. They may tell you they will be home for dinner but on their way they get a call; so you have to be patient and understanding to know they will be there when they can because duty called. Instead of getting upset, wrap the food up and put it aside for your LEO to enjoy when he finally makes it home. There will be times they want to talk about their day and times they don't, so be understanding of that. They will have days that things they deal with is more than they can handle and haunts them so be supportive and loving to let them know you are there for them. They will have people that do not like them just because of their profession and you may hear things about them but before you jump to conclusions or assume it is true, ask your LEO. Just remember they are not always the big tough officer and have feelings too. They carry a lot on their shoulders so love them and be understanding.

Vicky C.

A LEO gives his thoughts:

I was called to the hospice center that my wife was a patient in at around 11 PM the day she passed away. I spent a large part of the day there with my children but had to leave because I had pressing business so the late night call was not a surprise. When my children and I arrived at hospice late that night, we saw an amazing sight. Laura, who was an RN and about 26 years old was holding my wife's hand. Needless to say we were deeply moved by the sight. My wife had only been in hospice for about ten days. She had spent the previous eight weeks at a local hospital. The idea that this woman who sees death and horrible suffering on a daily basis and still had the compassion to show this level of care to a stranger touched me greatly. We thanked Laura and she left the room. Having worked in law enforcement for most of my adult life, I have witnessed many people die. As my wife was nearing her final moments she went into Cheyne stokes breathing. From experience, I told my kids what was happening and that my wife would soon pass, which she did. I have since thought about Laura and the compassion she showed to my wife. I don't know her last name but there is one thing I can bet about her: A woman who is smart enough to get through RN training in college, physically tough enough to care for patients who cannot care for their own needs, work the rotating shifts, have the emotional strength to witness the horrible suffering at her workplace every day and in spite of this she has the kindness, compassion and good heartedness to hold the hand of a dying woman who she does not even know is a very unique person to say the least. I have come to the conclusion that Laura would most likely be an excellent wife for a LEO. However, my father who was a LEO, long ago warned when speaking of LEOWs, "I wouldn't wish that on my worst enemy."

My own wife worked in a very bad neighborhood school for many years. She went into neighborhoods that most people would be afraid to go into even in an army tank. She had stories to rival any LEO story. One time a child came to school on Monday after missing school for several days. The girl was about eight and presented an excuse note which stated "Please excuse Maria from school. She was absent because her sister was murdered." Another time my wife and several other teachers observed one of the young girls coming to school dressed in the same rags of clothing every day and no overcoat during the winter. My wife and the other teachers chipped in and bought a coat and some new cloths for the child. The next day the child returned to school wearing the same old rags. The mother sold the new cloths for drugs. While tough enough to work in a crime ridden neighborhood, my wife never lost her compassion for others. Important when married to a LEO.

Early in our dating relationship, my wife and I were coming home on the train in a not so great section of town. When we got off the train we noticed six men at the end of the platform. Three of the men jumped up on top of the roof of the platform and we heard them walking in our direction while and the other three started to walk along the platform in our direction. I knew we might be in trouble and my wife instinctively knew too. Without my asking, she immediately took the bags from my hands that I was holding, thus leaving my hands free to reach for my off duty gun. Fortunately, the men approaching us also noticed what my wife did and must have assumed it would be best for them to leave. I knew then that my wife who had relatives who were LEO and Firefighters, was tough enough to be a LEOW.

Nick F.

A willingness to "go against the grain" is also an important trait for a LEOW.

It's no shock to hear that most people don't like cops. Generally, if one shows up at your door, you have done something to bring them there or the officer is bringing bad news. If those blue lights are flashing in your rear view, there is a reason. Ironically, those same people that make a habit of cursing the thin blue line are also the first ones to hit 9-1-1 on their cell phones in a time of need.

Family and friends may "forget" to keep hurtful words about LEOs to themselves, often couching their hurtful words with "Well, I don't mean your husband of course, but those other LEOs are..." They may have always disapproved of your husband's job but you thought their feelings about LEOs would change as they got to know your husband in his role as a LEO. After all, he's a great guy and what's not to love? Why can't people see that whether off or on duty, he is still the same great guy he has always been?

When I met the man that would one day become my husband, I was a graduate student studying Forensic Science. We share a love of criminal justice so I was excited and supportive of my LEO's goal to become a police officer. So supportive in fact, I moved halfway down the east coast for him to pursue his life's dream. What was most shocking to discover was that I was the only one. No one else in his circle of family or friends realized just how important it was to him and when he had difficulty finding a job in his home state they just told him to find something else. It was obvious to me- and still is- that the general population has no idea that law enforcement is a calling.

Over the years we have lost friends and been shunned by strangers because of his profession. On the other hand, he has also been thanked for his service and commended for being the one who runs in when everyone else runs out and that makes me so proud to be married to a true hero. The rest doesn't really matter.

Did you find that you had issues with family and friends when dating or marrying a LEO?

The hardest part with family has been getting them to understand the schedule. His department is short staffed and scheduling is erratic. My husband is the only LEO in the family so they aren't used to not having control over the schedule. When he gets called in unexpectedly, they do not understand. They feel like he flakes on them, like he does it on purpose.

Theresa K.

Since my husband has become a LEO many of our friendships were kept but in the same token, kept at a distance. Our family/friends are proud of him and do not bring things around us that could be harmful to his career. Most people are respectful of the boundaries that we have set.

Angela L.

My parents were not thrilled that I was dating and eventually married a LEO. They knew guns were there and that people owned them but when I started seeing him they realized he was carrying his weapon constantly and they have an issue with that. Most of my family and friends don't have an issue with his job but I did lose a few friends over him being in that particular career and that was fine because he was more important than some petty friends. When I became pregnant my family had a lot more issues with my husband's job because you never know if he'll come home at the end of his shift. My parents kept insisting that we write a will to make sure we had things in place for our daughter.

Patty R.

My parents were very supportive. I did have issues with friends who tried to make him feel like he was not good enough for me. "What could he offer me? He doesn't make enough money. These relationships never last, there is a high divorce rate." I even had one girlfriend criticize the way he dressed off duty. My LEO wore a bullet proof vest and hot uniform day after day, off duty he was and is partial to a t-shirt and jeans. The girlfriend who criticized my LEO because of his clothes and income, she's history. Married and divorced, I might add.

Denise N.

I have to say that my mom has been pretty supportive. She once tried out her "cop lingo" with hilarious results. My husband's job refers to calling out sick as "Bang'em " or "bang in sick." While out to dinner with the entire family, my mom tried out her cop lingo by asking my husband if he was "Whacking off sick." We all broke out laughing and gently corrected her as she laughed at her mistake too.

Coleen J.

I had issues with my family members at first and some of my friends because I was dating a LEO. Even when I went to get married, my so-called best friend, who was supposed to be my maid-of-honor, called it quits a week before our wedding because she did not like my husband. Even in the present, I have a hard time keeping friends that are not related to a law enforcement because they do not understand or they are intimidated to have a friend that is married to a law enforcement officer.

Cathy L.

My mother had a major problem with him being a cop... but she got over it as she got to know him and realized how he loved his job.

Elarie S.

I haven't had anyone come right out and say they had an issue with my husband's job. They are mostly proud to say that he is a part of the family or their friend.

Becky N.

How do you deal with LEO bashing family and friends on social media, parties or at family gatherings?

This always makes me intensely uncomfortable. I mostly see LEO bashing on Facebook as the people we hang out with are cops or the significant others of cops. Someone recently posted this video about how "You should never talk to cops." It was a friend's husband that I don't know very well. I just stared at it fingers hovering over the keyboard, wanting to say something but not wanting to engage in a battle I wouldn't win. I pick my battles. Sometimes people can hear what I have to say about this type of stuff, sometimes people are so stuck in their opinions they refuse to listen to any other opinion. It scares me, frankly. It makes me feel small. Who wouldn't want to talk to my husband? He's awesome!

Meredith K.

I delete them from Facebook and as far as gatherings/parties, I honestly haven't been in that position. They know my stance on it and know that I am a strong enough person to tell them what I think about them.

Bjae K.

I have no tolerance for this. I usually "hide" this stuff from my newsfeed. Try vocalizing my support if it's a close family member but I don't like negativity in my life so I have no problem "unfriending."

Annemarie J.

For Facebook: I used to engage with people in an attempt to let them know how wrong their post is and why. I soon realized it was a no win for me so I no longer engage. If it's someone I don't know well, I'll just hide that post. If it's someone I know well, I hide all of their posts. I no longer consider them a close friend and keep them at arm's length. I have had family bash LEOs on Facebook and I tell them the post is offensive and I hide it from my newsfeed. If they continue, I hide all of their posts from my newsfeed and just check on their status from time to time. And yes, I think less of them and keep a little more distance between us. Sorry to feel that way and it hurts to not have the support of my friends and family but there isn't a good solution to the problem. For family gatherings and parties with friends, they don't usually say hurtful things to my face but I know their positions so I keep my heart less open. I have had to "discuss" with people the latest LEO shooting and explain why the LEO was right in their actions. I don't think I have changed any opinions but I can't help myself from defending LEOs.

Gail K.

I ask them to politely keep their inappropriate comments to themselves and if they don't, then I remove them from my Facebook list or we graciously leave the gathering and decline any further invitations until the individual can learn to not bash my LEO when he risks his life daily for others.

Patty R.

I normally try to ignore it especially if it's someone I don't know because it will only irritate you more. I will sometimes say that the police are the ones that are there when no one else wants to be and leave it at that. You can't change ignorance.

Vicky C.

He's got the job, so what now?

Some people are just born to be something and I think you will agree that most police officers were born with some sort of God directed genetic mutation that makes them want to do that job more than anything else in the world. Who would willingly choose to witness death, depravity and the evilest of human actions on a daily basis? It takes a very special, incredibly strong person to not only accept that challenge but to embrace it whole heartedly, often at the expense of those around them that they care about the most. More than likely the LEO you are married to is one of those people. The job is so ingrained in their very being that it's far more than what they do to earn a paycheck- it is who they are right down to their very DNA.

My husband is, without a doubt, one of those people placed on this planet with the sole purpose to protect and serve. He spent ten years of his adult life trying to realize his dream of becoming a police officer. In the state where he grew up, hiring of civil service positions was directed by the state civil service commission. Every two years they would offer a state wide examination to hire police and fire fighters. The score on the exam combined with factors such as active duty military service would then rank each individual on an eligibility list for hiring in the various towns. The catch? You had to live in the town you hoped to work in for at least 365 days prior to taking the state exam and then hope that town would be hiring in the next two years before the next exam. My poor LEO took that test no less than five times before he hit the cut off age of thirty two. He never seemed to live in the right city at the right time. The last time he took the exam he was thirty one. I looked at him and said "If you don't get hired this time, you need to either find a different dream or find a place to go where you can still pursue this dream."

His choice took us seven hundred miles down the east coast.

Within six months of relocation he had gone through the hiring process for five different municipalities and received four job offers.

He probably would have received five if he had finished the hiring process for the fifth one.

The day he received the letter of appointment to the job he still has today, I had discovered that after a long bout with infertility I was expecting our second child. Talk about bad timing.

If you were with your own LEO when he attended the training academy then you know exactly what I am talking about. For us it was twenty two weeks of him commuting 90 minutes each way- leaving the house at 0430 and not returning until sometimes as late as 2300 if they had night training. It meant acting as a practice dummy for handcuff and take down techniques, carrying the list of 10 codes around for impromptu quizzes and making sure every day he had a clean, sharply pressed training uniform. For me it also meant being extremely pregnant, running the house, going to work, taking care of a three year old and telling the neighbor to stuff it when he complained that our grass was way too long.

And I would do it all over again.

Academy, as we refer to it in our house, was miserable, stressful and hard on our personal life. I won't lie- by the time he was half way through we weren't even sleeping in the same bedroom. His hours were so scattered and unpredictable; we just couldn't sleep at the same time. His class was the very first one to graduate from his city's academy instead of attending a regional one and those instructors had something to prove. What they ended up with was an amazing group of men and women highly prepared for work out on the streets. As well as a few exhausted spouses…

It was all worth it the night he stood up on that stage and received his badge. I was so incredibly proud that I had married a man literally chosen to spend his life trying to better the world we live in. My children could grow up full of pride as well, knowing their daddy was making a positive difference in people's lives.

When he graduated the academy, I felt like I had too. It was the beginning of a sometimes very tumultuous life yet one full of honor and integrity. One I wouldn't trade for anything.

If you were married or dating your LEO when he went through the academy, what was the experience like for you? Did you take an active part in his academy experience?

It was stressful and exciting. I washed and ironed his uniforms, made him lunch every day and helped him study. It was a team effort.

Maggie D.

I was happy for him and excited, but also a little scared. He ended up dislocating his shoulder during defensive tactics training. It made me worry more about what could happen when he was out in the real world.

Beth C.

My husband went through two academies. He retired from one police job and moved to another state to start a career again as a police officer. I was married to him for the second academy experience. Our decision to move and change jobs happened all within a month. We had three kids at this time with the oldest in first grade and the youngest was a newborn. We had to sell our current house so I stayed behind with the kids and my husband started the new academy in another state. On some weekends, I would bring the kids to visit in his temporary apartment, with traffic, it was a twelve hour ride. When we finally arrived, my LEO needed to study and being the "new guy" his schedule was never set. One thing in our favor was that because my husband had been in law enforcement in the past, he only had to attend a modified academy. I also met another LEOW in the apartment complex who was in a similar situation so we became friends. The other LEOs in the class were also very nice and their families welcoming.

Those few months of transition and time apart felt like an eternity. When I was in the new apartment, the friends I did know were not available the times my LEO was in class. It was an exhausting and sometimes lonely existence in a new place. My LEO was not in the military but in some regard, it felt like being married to a soldier. You are alone while your soldier is off fighting. You can't count on your LEO for anything while he is in the academy. They are either in class, out on the road training or home studying.

Due to our living in different states during his academy training, I did not take part.

Denise N.

My husband's academy was across town but he was required to stay there during the week and was able to come home on Friday afternoon through Sunday. I suppose I supported his academy experience as any new bride would. He'd practice handcuffing techniques and submission holds and it wasn't in the fun way. He soaked up all of the law enforcement information like a sponge, I knew it was going to be the career for him.

Tanya D.

We were married for about a year when he went through the academy. I was very excited for him. I was very active in his schooling…as we both tested for the job at the same time and he got hired and I didn't. I lived through him. Everything he learned, I did too. It was like I went through it as well. It was a very rewarding experience for us.

Jessica B.

We were not married when he attended the academy but we had been dating four years. It was a huge transformation, not only was he changing as a person into this new role and career but we were in our twenties when we ourselves were changing and finding out who we were. So this was a hard transition for us. We were young and I was in college and he was starting his career. We were in two different places in our lives, we managed but definitely struggled and the key was to be as supportive as I could so he could get through the academy. I took an active role in his academy experience. I was there every step of the way. I was involved in all the spouse activities they did at his academy. From the shooting range day, to the self-defense classes and meeting all his new friends and to the parties. I helped him study and gave him all the time he needed. We didn't live together so I didn't make his lunch or iron his uniforms but I helped when I could.

Kelly F.

It was hard at first, going days without seeing him while he was in the academy. Even though we had only been dating a short time, I missed him dearly. The academy was only forty five minutes away from where we lived so I took quick trips down to see him and his friends that were in his class. We would go to dinner, they would tell me all the interesting things that they were learning and gave me insight into their experiences. It was fun listening to all the stories they had and the likes and dislikes of each subject they learned. My husband's friends even helped him pick out my engagement ring. Five police recruits picked out the beautiful ring my husband gave to me as he proposed on Christmas. I would help him study and ask random questions to help him (and myself) learn all the laws and ins and outs of the police world.

Ashley B.

We were married when he attended the police academy. I hated being away from him. Our daughter was one year old at the time and I kept four other people's children during the week to keep me busy. I only got to talk to him at night for maybe five minutes and saw him on the weekends.

Becky N.

What did you get your husband for his Police academy graduation gift?

Instead of a gift, we went out to dinner with family and friends.

Maggie D.

I didn't know to get him a gift for graduation. He received money from family members that was truly needed. Today, I would recommend something useful they could use at work such as a personal camera or equipment / gear bag.

Tanya D.

For his graduation, I gave my husband a card and a racy picture of me to keep in the trauma plate pocket of his ballistic vest. My recommendation to other wives, is you know your LEO and what he likes, go with your gut.

Jessica B.

When my husband went to school for law enforcement, we were married with two special needs children. He worked full time and went to school full time. When he graduated, the gift I gave him was to be able to lay down and sleep for eight hours straight without being disturbed. It was exactly what he wanted!

Beth C.

I gave my husband a G-shock all black super nice watch. He still has it to this day and uses it. It's been broken two times and almost lost once. He put his buddies to work on the scene to find it. It was in the grass where they took down the suspect. The guys told me he was super worried about losing the watch and HAD to find it! This watch has a lot of meaning to it. It was my first expensive gift that I bought him as a young twenty year old with a part time job. I would recommend a watch, Bible for Police officers, some type of gear that would be used day in and day out like a flashlight, with your initials engraved in it, a handmade friendship bracelet that can be stuffed in their vest every day or laminate your favorite Bible verse for him to put in his vest or hang in his locker.

Kelly F.

I met my husband after he'd been a LEO for a while so I did not get him an academy graduation gift. My friend gave her husband a watch with the State Trooper logo on it. You can buy watches with various Police agency logos on the face of the watch.

Patty R.

I was only with my husband (then boyfriend) for a short time before he graduated so I got him a card and I made him a nice home cooked meal of his choosing. He had to eat academy food for six months so he was beyond grateful for a good meal.

Ashley B.

My husband's department does not provide much equipment for new officers. His department gave him a gun, gun holster, pepper spray and holder so I bought him a black belt that goes underneath, handcuffs with his name engraved on them, handcuff holder, radio holder, baton and baton holder. I got a job babysitting just to be able to buy all these things for him.

Becky N.

I bought mine a St. Michael charm along with a cross that he never takes off. Now that he's a detective he got a customized holster with a Bible verse on it that I love. Luke 10:19 behold, I have given you authority to tread on serpents and scorpions, and over all the power of the enemy, and nothing shall hurt you.

Cathy T.

I threw a surprise graduation party for him.

Chrissy B.

I bought him an off duty gun.

Eve T.

For my husband's graduation gift I called his grandma that lives out west and flew her to our state. We had not seen her in about six years. I drove up to the academy the night before graduation and told my husband that I wanted to go out to dinner because I knew the next day would be crazy with graduation. I got him in the car and drove to the airport and he did not know what was going on. I just said that there is a great place to eat here. The next thing I know, his grandma who was about sixty five at the time, was walking up to him. The look on his face was priceless. This was a great thing because his grandmother had not been to visit us in fifteen years. She had always told us that if you want to see me you have to come to me because I will never get on a plane. She did, for my husband's graduation! A priceless gift!

Dana C.

I got my husband a trauma plate for his vest.

Faith S.

I bought my husband a clipboard to write his tickets on, notebooks, pens, shirts, hand sanitizer, Clorox/Lysol wipes and disposable gloves.

Meagan S.

I bought my husband a thin blue line ring, which he now wears as his wedding ring and a police / military watch that he wears every day.

Pam J.

I was nine months pregnant when he graduated and gave birth two weeks into field training. His baby was his present!

Maggie F.

I got mine a good bag and stuffed it with black socks, notepads, white shirts, black and blue pens, clipboards etc.

Gail V.

I got mine a duty bag filled with snack foods for those days he doesn't have time to stop for food, disinfectant disposable hand towels and laundry spot remover towels. I also put in a little bag that had hot wheel cars and small stuffed animals for the kids he encounters when working.

Debi S.

Being the wife of a LEO is not exactly what you thought it would be.

When your LEO first gets hired, it's exciting but you soon find it's not all that you thought it was. A career in law enforcement is quite different than you see depicted in movies and on television. If you think about it, how often do you even see the officer's family on television or in movies? Many times the officer is depicted as a bachelor or family is only mentioned in passing. Surprise! We do exist! And without any help or role models from movies and television, we are now on our own to figure "the life" out. Until you have lived the life, you probably have no idea about the daily compromises and the issues unique to being married to a LEO.

What most surprised you about the life of a LEOW?

What was hardest to accept?

I was most surprised about how many people would walk away from us as friends. It was also hard to accept that my children do not get invited to birthday parties and get-togethers like the other kids do.

Beth C.

I'd have to say that I am surprised by how tired I am of the constant schedule changes. When we were young and first dating and even for the first fifteen years of marriage, it was not that big of a deal. We worked our life around his schedule. Twenty something years later, I'm tired of never having a regular Monday to Friday work/ Saturday and Sunday off work life schedule. I feel out of sync with family, friends and the rest of the world. On Fridays people rattle off the phrase "have a good weekend!" Ah, no.... it's only Tuesday in my world. I can never plan to go out with friends without first checking to see when my husband is working. We can't stay out too late on a Saturday night if he worked all day and has to be back to work early the next morning. I'd love to take a continuing Ed class with my husband but we can't because he is never home at night for several weeks in a row on the night of the class I want to take. Even planning something as simple as grocery shopping revolves around if he is on nights or days. Am I buying dinner food or lunch food? Is he doing other things before his night tours and am I home by myself or will he be home with me before he goes to work? If he is coming up on nights, I best get some girl TV on DVR and some books from the library. Plan, plan, plan and always in flux. Write the yearly schedule out in pencil, never pen because you know it could change at any time. I'm also surprised by how much of myself has been lost to his job schedule. I used to be very independent and I still am, in some ways even more so but I never thought my life would be so tied to his schedule and job. I would love a little normalcy in my life right about now.

Kathleen D.

I was most surprised by the fact that truthfully nothing has changed. We still go out, we still have fun and enjoy our time off as a couple. I was worried that once he became a police officer, he would become a shut in. One of those guys that protects his family so much, we wouldn't have a life. I think the hardest to accept for me, is the fact that my husband may not come home. I can handle him missing the holidays, the anniversaries, birthdays, etc. but I truly can never cope with the fact that there is a possibility that he may not come home from his shift. It scares me daily.

Ashley B.

I have always been a very independent person but it was not until my husband became a LEO that I realized just how strong I am. I work full time, we have two kids and a crazy night shift schedule for my LEO. I have had to handle a lot of things on my own that I never imagined I would have to. The other thing that shocked me was how willing people were to get in my business. If I had a dollar for the number of times someone has informed me that they hate cops or asked me if I were afraid he would get shot, I would have a tidy nest egg tucked away somewhere.

Maggie F.

The schedule surprised me the most. To be honest, I don't think you ever really get used to shift work. Once you get into the groove of one shift, it changes. It gets even more challenging when you start a family. The added stress of trying to keep your kiddos quiet during the day because daddy worked all night and is now sleeping is crazy! You can go through periods where, even though you are married, you feel single. You can be two ships passing in the night. But, it gets easier and after you've been through several different shifts with your LEO the adjustment time is less and less. It was even harder to accept the changes in his demeanor and attitude. I met and married my LEO before he became a cop. I feel like that person is long gone. It was a very tough transition for the first few years. I felt like he was trying to find his way, to adjust to the life/ work of a LEO and I was trying to adjust to a different man than whom I married.

Maggie D.

Becoming a LEOW has turned me into a strong, independent person. It's amazing what you pick up from your LEO over the years just by listening to their stories. I'd love to be able to brag about my LEO more to friends but they wouldn't understand "the life."

Tanya D.

I wasn't surprised by much of the LEOW life because I was a private investigator before we met so I knew what was "out there." I think just getting married is such a big adjustment already. Adding in his mid-night shifts and holiday/weekend working was just how our marriage started out so I have nothing to compare it to. I was twenty two and he was twenty four when we met. We've just grown into our own normal. Just as our daughter was born into it, she (hopefully) won't think it unusual. For me personally, the hardest thing to accept is the lack of respect and pay the city gives them. Constant pay cuts for people that lay their lives on the line is infuriating.

Cassie S.

There were not too many surprises when I became a LEOW. The one thing I was disappointed in was how the police department really doesn't back its officers or support or promote any camaraderie with police families. The hardest thing for me in the beginning was the constant change in scheduling. Also not celebrating holidays on the holiday. We learned to celebrate them when we could, that it isn't the actual date but being together as a family.

Jessica B.

It surprised me that some of the friends I had before we got married were no longer friends. I also was surprised at having to be more alert to my surroundings and the people that I talk to. The hardest part was the shift changes and the sudden calls to come to work. You can't really set dates because inevitably, the date will be interrupted.

Cathy L.

I wasn't really surprised by the life of a LEOW because my Dad was an officer so the life style was sort of normal for me. I grew up with end of shift barbeques, family get togethers, annual family department picnics and the craziness of some of the guys. So this kind of life style was not new to me. It was different in how the young man I knew and fell in love with was slowly changing and his views on life were shifted due to the stuff he would see on the streets. The fear that I first felt when he was on the streets was definitely a surprise. I knew my Mom did it, and she did it well. She never showed fear or concern for his safety but I'm sure she felt it. When I was faced with it, I somehow knew how to deal with it, I just didn't know how REAL that fear was. The hardest to accept was the fact that I needed to learn to accept the fact that I would be alone a lot and attend functions alone. Holidays were celebrated on a different day and I learned how to be independent and strong due to the long hours of work, overtime and anything else that came along. I had to accept that we wouldn't be able to do all the family things that came along with life such as weddings, birthdays, get togethers, dinners and anniversaries. Missing holidays and birthdays and family functions is still hard and it never gets easy but it has gotten easier to deal with and accept as the years go on. So what if Thanksgiving is on a Friday for us, or if we celebrate our anniversary the weekend before the actual date, and we do our Christmas breakfast two days before the twenty fifth? We still celebrate and still make plans. So I have learned to deal and manage with change and accept the fact that we are not your normal couple nor do we live a normal life and I am okay with that.

Kelly F.

Being a somewhat nervous person (can't be helped... I'm Jewish... it's genetic!) I am surprised I was able to cope as well as I did. I think I learned to just accept this was his career and I couldn't worry constantly. Thank God for cell phones though... if he was late in the early years, before cell phones, I was a frequent caller to headquarters! The hours were the hardest to accept. Going around the clock and not being able to attend family holiday dinners, not being able to have a normal social life, going to my kid's functions alone. It made it much easier when I had a close friend and neighbor whose husband worked shifts. Going out to dinner or the movies with our kids on the weekends made it more bearable. But on the other hand, we never had to wait on a line at the movies on weekdays in the middle of the day, our date day when the kids were young and in school.

Elarie S.

I was most surprised by how well known I've become since marrying my husband. Once I married him and he introduced me to the numerous people he knows (judges, other officers, solicitors, etc.) I became "Officer R.'s wife." I never expected to not be able to go anywhere and not find someone who knows me because of my husband. I think the most interesting thing is since we live in the city where he works, people know me and they know better than to do anything to hurt me or mess with me because they know they'll get the wrath of my husband and the whole department. I also never knew how many kids knew my husband and they are always coming up to him to talk to him. It was hardest to accept the crazy schedule and the concept that no matter what we were doing, my husband was always on call and could always get a call to have to go to work. I could plan a family dinner and have everything ready and he gets caught up dealing with something and not be home and dinner gets cold or overdone. I think another thing that I wrestle with sometimes is that it seemed like my husband was always worrying about the needs of others and not concerned with what was going on with our family. I know that wasn't the case, but I wrestled with those thoughts a lot. I just had to do some soul searching and praying and realize that being a LEO was my husband's job and to do it right, he had to be focused on it. Another hard thing was not being able to call and ask him questions without having his radio go off and interrupt us.

Patty R.

Every day is a surprise. Just when you think you have heard it all, planned for every possible hitch, something new comes along you never expected. The hardest to accept was the lack of control, which is very different than the corporate wife. When you are a LEO or LEOW, you give up control over your daily life.

We have no control over when accidents, disasters and arrests happen. As a result, our LEOs are left with the greater possibility of unscheduled and mandated overtime and cancelled plans including vacations that you seem to never manage to get back. We have no control over how people view the LEO and most might be surprised at the lack of respect our LEOs actually receive. They are rarely seen as the hero. Instead they are often criticized and put under scrutiny, for how they responded and handled calls by someone who doesn't have the facts, or who has never been in the field. Where we currently live, my LEO's car is parked in front of our house. Apparently some believe that makes our house a twenty four hour emergency call center. Yes, if your house is on fire, by all means, knock down the door to use the phone to call for help but my LEO is not here to get you out of a speeding ticket or able to take care of homeowner association issues. The home phone or doorbell will usually ring as we are eating dinner or trying to get the kid's homework done and off to bed. Because my LEO now works in a "right to work" state where there are no unions, he can't say everything he wants about issues at work to his superiors. Unlike the corporate world, when you are given orders from superiors, you are expected to follow them, not question or provide your opinion. There is a chain of command. LEOs just don't walk into the boss's office and complain about work, vacation time or ask for a raise because they are greatly underpaid. LEOs have no control over many of their assignments or pay. There is a chain of command and set pay scale. If cost cutting hits a town or county, LEO departments are the first department on the list to be affected. The fact that we have lost a great deal of control over our lives for a profession in which my LEO is gravely underpaid, underappreciated and could very well make the ultimate sacrifice of losing his life, the hardest thing to accept.

Denise N.

In the public eye... no longer just an anonymous face in the crowd anymore. Just one more surprise of the job!

Your husband is always in the public eye, it is part of the job and what he signed up for. When he asked you to marry him he forgot to mention that you will also be in the public eye, whether you want to be or not. You may not recognize someone but you can bet that if you live in a small town or the area your husband works, everyone knows who you are and watches your every move. Even when you don't live where your husband works more people than you may suspect know who you are and watch your every move. Perhaps you don't want to wear your ratty house sweat pants to make a quick run to the store for the quart of milk for the kids breakfast. Don't slow shuffle through the stop sign. No matter how late you are, never exceed the speed limit. Don't get a tad too cranky with the grocery store bagger when she drops the canned tomatoes on top of the bread. Someone curses you out due to your husband's job? Smile and walk away. Some families move out of the work area just to avoid the pressure to be perfect and "on" all day every day.

Do you feel pressure to act a certain way in public due to your husband's job?

I am constantly careful about my actions and attitudes in public especially since we live in the city he works in. Every action and decision can impact my husband's career and I will not do anything to jeopardize that. There was an officer at his department whose wife accused him of domestic violence and he had a rough time. He was cleared of it but his wife's actions and the way she was living made it hard for him at work. Sometimes I feel like I'm on display and held to a higher standard because of my husband's job but most times I don't mind. Other times I wish I didn't have to worry and focus constantly on how I'm dressed or acting because of his job but I just remember it's for him and I don't have trouble doing it for him.

Patty R.

Of course I do because I have to set an example not only as a citizen of our town but also for my husband. If I give a bad impression then it can reflect on him. This really does not impact me, unless I get angry at another person and then I have to remember that if I respond to my anger, then my actions can reflect on my husband.

Cathy L.

We do not live in the town my husband works in so most people in my town don't know my husband is a LEO. Having said that, I grew up in the small town that we now live in so I am used to always acting properly in public. I learned early as a kid that if I did something out of line, my mother had received a phone call about me before I even got home. Small town life keeps you in line. That is more pressure than the fact that my husband is a LEO!

Terri W.

I think just in general people should act a certain way in public, like with respect for others and such. But with my husband's job, I think it's a little more important to be aware of your surroundings and to try to be a positive person. Whether it's letting the car next to you go in front, or talking to the other city employees, it's important to be positive. Too often where we live, a silly situation can be blown out of proportion and if the news gets a handle on it, then the world is out to get you. You don't want to find yourself in that situation, so that is where I feel the pressure. When I read stories in the news about how cops get persecuted, but rarely praised, that is what affects yet motivates me.

Kelly P.

I would say I don't feel pressured to act a certain way. I do have respect for the nature of my husband's profession and I don't broadcast that we are a LEO family. My neighbors obviously know he's an officer: he leaves in uniform, brings the squad car home on occasion and has all kinds of crazy hours and long stretches where his non-duty car is absent.

Annemarie J.

I follow the law to the letter, try not to speed and carry myself carefully in public. I don't want it to be said, "Oh she thinks she's above the law because of her husband's job."

Colleen R.

I honestly think people hold us to a higher standard because our husbands are LEOs. I don't let it run my life but don't do anything that would make him or the department look bad.

Vicky C.

I don't necessarily feel "pressure", but I do feel the need to be more cautious. I remember a time not long after we were married, as we were getting gas in our car and a man that my husband had arrested a few weeks before walked up and started talking to my husband just as I was walking back to our car with a soda in hand. It made me realize that this man now knows what I look like and what kind of vehicle we have and that he may see me in public someday and in an attempt to retaliate against my husband, do something to me.
Jennifer H.

I don't feel pressure, I feel that it is my duty out of respect to act a certain way. I am not saying that you should change who you are. Once we become married, it is our duty to respect our spouse and to respect their profession. They deal with enough disrespect in their profession they shouldn't have to question or worry about how we will act.

Bjae K.

The Middle Years

Ah yes, that long interlude between the excitement of the academy and someday he'll retire and we can have a "normal" life.

My neighbor Cheryl works from home twice a week and we occasionally get together for some mid-morning tea. She had a smile a mile wide one day and could not wait to tell me about her office mate's pre-wedding gift from her future sister in law. The future sister in law sent a stripper and the best part was (you guessed it) he was dressed as a cop! Wow, imagine! How sexy is that? Unfortunately for Cheryl the gift arrived at the office on one of her work from home days. Cheryl was envisioning all she had missed and wondered out loud how great it would be to see a cop strip. Well... duh! I looked straight at her, dead pan expression and said "I see that every night... you get used to it." While my husband is still very good looking and I never tire of him, honestly the whole uniformed cop stripping thing is a little old hat to me. I much prefer him in (and out of) blue jeans and a t-shirt. . Nowadays, it's more a matter of wondering what that stain on his uniform shirt might be and how the heck am I supposed to remove "it", whatever "it" is. Quite frankly, there are times I think I'd rather not know.

The former excitement of ironing his uniform and watching him polish his brass and badge gets lost in the daily grind of raising the kids (often feeling like a single parent because he is always at work when you need him to be home), cleaning up the house, balancing the ever changing schedule and trying to catch a few minutes with hubby between shifts, overtime and a side job. Then there is the ever present nagging feeling of "will my husband come home or will there be a knock on the door?" Why did I think this life would be easy? It's not remotely easy and being a cop's wife is definitely not for sissies. Oh but there are more than enough rewards to make it all worthwhile. Your LEO is rough, tough, reeks of testosterone and is afraid of nothing at work but your heart melts as you watch him gently and tenderly place the band aid on your five year old's skinned knee as he gives her lots of extra hugs and kisses. You thought you would fall apart as you watched his tears falling like rain when he buried his fourteen year old dog, his "little buddy" and the night he held on to you for dear life as he mourned the passing of his father. The first time your son brags that his daddy is a policeman is a day you will always remember. You smile at the memory of your husband cleaning his gun within view of the front door as your daughter waits for her date to pick her up. He is a loving and over protective dad watching out for "his little girl" but yes he is a tad overboard. Catching a glimpse of your husband at a crime scene on the evening news never gets old and you record the eleven o'clock news so you can watch him again. . He is the really good looking one on the right side of the screen. Seeing him in his dress uniform for his first promotion... Yup, he looks even better than the day he graduated the academy. Your heart fills with pride and you stand a little taller when the Assistant District Attorney pulls you aside at a party to tell you that your husband's detective squad is by far the best in the county. The pride you feel when he casually mentions over dinner that he is getting an important award. If you want to know where your husband is when you are at a "civilian" party, just look for the crowd. He always has the best stories. Your friends and neighbors knowing they can count on your husband to help, no matter the emergency or the time of day or night. Yeah, it usually isn't a convenient time but you wouldn't want it any other way. He always knows the answer and how to help. He is the "go to guy" and he is all yours! Your head nestled in the gap of his shoulder during a slow spin around the dance floor, even if the dance floor is your kitchen floor and the dance is between stirs of the pasta sauce. Your heart always melts when you are in his strong and protective arms and yes, it's probably a gun in his pocket. He is still your knight in shining armor even if the armor is stretched a bit by the little tummy he is getting. It matches your "three kids later" figure.

A little time and perspective gives new insights into the life of a LEOW.

If you knew your husband before he became a LEO, how has the job changed him?

It has changed his perspective and outlook on people in a lot of ways. We see a middle aged man on a bike and he automatically assumes the man has a DUI and lost his license. We also have to get out of the area for him to completely relax.

Theresa K.

We were married for four years before he became a LEO. He's a little more moody, withdrawn and takes a little longer to shed the cop demeanor. Usually by the second day off, he's back to fun, joking and relaxed dad. He's also greatly honed his perception and situational awareness. It's the little things that have rubbed off on the kids as well. It's a fine line some days to reassure the kids that the strange car in the neighbor's driveway isn't suspicious. It's hard to keep them kids.

Annemarie J.

I went to elementary school through high school with my husband. He hasn't allowed the job to change him.

Bjae K.

When I first met my husband he was a very fun loving, happy go lucky guy. He was adventurous. We would just get in the car and drive for the weekend with no plan or anything and now everything has to be planned in advance and he is often too tired either physically or mentally to do much on his days off. When we schedule vacation time, we have to schedule it in 10 day blocks because it takes 3 or 4 days for him to relax. The moods are different now too. He is quicker to get mad, probably because he is tired all the time from long work hours. And everyone is a potential danger. He has a more cynical view of the world in general and lacks some of the empathy he used to have. He works in a very crime ridden, dangerous area of a not so great city and I know it has taken its toll. I love him though and I know he loves me and because his job is so much a part of him I have adapted to the changes and we are still as good together now as we were in the early days.

Olivia B.

The hardest to accept is that he never turns off from cop mode.

Donna Y.

My husband used to be an open book and now prying has become second nature to me as he no longer shares his fears openly. I guess you could say that after years on the job he has learned to mask his emotions. I know deep inside he is still the man I married but the free spirited person he was is a far cry from the quiet reserved man who sits at the other end of our dinner table. Not every change has been negative though, as being an officer has inspired him to delve deeper into the career, he spends more time making it count with our children and he holds me tighter at the end of the day. I wouldn't give up what we have learned from his experiences as an officer as it has given us a deeper appreciation for each other.

Angela L.

Before my husband became a LEO he was a "geek" with very little common sense. He has loads of common sense now. I really don't see how it has changed him in a negative way.

Jessica B.

Being a LEO has changed him, and it's all for the better. He has always been a very driven individual whether it be in work or personal goals, but the structure he's found in law enforcement is perfect for him.

Tanya D.

The job has changed him in a lot of ways. We don't travel anymore. I believe that is mostly due to the fact the he looks at people differently. His attitude has changed, his glass seems more half empty than half full. So, I guess you could say he has a more negative outlook on life. He has dealt with major sexual assault cases, child abuse and child porn cases and therefore he worries for our children. I could go on and on.

Maggie D.

How has being the wife of a LEO changed you?

To be perfectly honest, I didn't even know the "word" LEOW existed and that what we do/go through every day is anything considered special until a few months ago. I always thought this was just life, and it still is. Now I just realize that there are a lot of families out there like mine and there are women who probably have the same issues/ annoyances and joys as me. I can vent with them, seek advice from them and laugh with them.

Maggie D.

Being a LEOW has not changed me.

Bjae K.

I think I have become more conservative in my views, especially regarding crime, and the punishment for the crimes. It has also made me become more independent especially since we do not have the same days off. I now feel comfortable going places and doing things like hiking and seeing a movie on my own. Before, these were things I would rather do with someone else.

Theresa K.

Since becoming the wife of a LEO, I look at the world differently and in the opinion of many people, I'm callous and uncaring. I've learned to toughen up when it comes to hearing different things my husband experiences. I look around constantly and always keep my son within arm's reach of me. When my family is distraught over a death or something like that, I'm not one to show emotion and that comes from having to be strong for my husband when he deals with things. I am not as sympathetic as I should be for family and friends. I think the worst thing I had to do was fill out the death/serious injury in the line of duty paperwork while I was pregnant and coming to grips with the fact that I could become a single parent. I have to be tough and not think about it or dwell on it. I am a better person in some ways. I live every day to the fullest and appreciate every special moment that I have with my husband.

Patty R.

Oh, I would for sure say that I have changed for the better. I wouldn't trade it for the world. And I honestly believe that God calls on special people to become a spouse of an officer. It takes a very patient (which I wasn't), very strong and non-clingy person to be married to an officer. I can handle just about any curve ball life throws at me. You learn to compromise and to live in the moment. You learn to cherish every moment you spend with your husband.

Ashley B.

I no longer apologize or think my way of doing things is "different." I've stopped explaining to family members long ago that we won't associate with criminals or enable other extended family members. I don't keep unsafe secrets and I know who the child predators are in my neighborhood. I am used to my husband sitting facing the door and not having his full attention when we are out in public. I also know when to take the kids and go another way if he sees a "known" to law enforcement. I am reassured by the sound of Velcro at the end of a night shift, and the electronic beeping of the safe, alerting me that he is home.

Annemarie J.

I am a proud LEOW. With that being said, I'm exhausted from playing single mom while he works non-stop between his regular shift and secondary to makes ends meet, from the panic that sets in at 11:05 PM when he was supposed to call at 11 PM, to making holidays work without him. In the same respect, I've learned that I'm a stronger person than I ever knew I was, that squeezing five minutes of snuggling in between shifts feels better than eight hours of sleep. I learned that you never let the front door close as they leave for work with things unsettled because no matter what the disagreement was about, within five minutes of him leaving you will wish things weren't left that way because it will cross your mind...what if? Lastly I learned when they are having a hard time coping with things they've seen at work to just let it be and in due time they will share.

Angela L.

I think I am much more jaded sometimes. I don't trust people as much as I used to but, I am also a stronger woman for having to play single parent so often.

Susan M.

I think I am more aware of my surroundings and perhaps a bit more distrustful of people. I think it makes me a great wife, parent and friend, as I have a lot of knowledge about things and they tease me about being the 911 info lady.

Jessica B.

Whereever we are, my husband is always the first person to go help a person in need. This is one of the many reasons that I love him. So I guess he has made me think of others when they are in need. He has also increased my consumption of beer! In college I used to drink it and after I realized I like wine and mixed drinks better. However, when in a "social police function" I find the beer tastes darn good!

Elarie S.

Being a LEOW has changed me for the better. I believe law enforcement is not a job, but who they are. For some, it's in their blood. I believe my husband was sent by God to join the force. It's brought us closer as a couple and strengthened our faith. I have learned to be a strong support for him, adapt to the schedule changes and to be a stronger person for myself.

Tanya D.

I know my husband has changed me for the better. There is a sense of proud that overwhelms you to do good when you know you are married to a local LEO and people know who you are. You try to live up to their expectations. I love it and wouldn't change it for anything.

Becky N.

Not sure how to answer since I am probably not the typical LEOW and the answer could have so many layers in different aspects of my life. While I believe there is a percentage, most wives are not emergency responders themselves. My volunteer career turned into my full time paid career. We can vent to each other and we know exactly what the other is going through. In some ways my life has been changed for the worse because life changing or ending at any moment is more real than if I wasn't married to a LEO. That fear is real and there all the time. My life is better for being married to my LEO because we are not naïve to the fact that what we have is good and to be cherished. My life is also better because I got rid of a lot of stuck up and shallow people in my life.

Denise. N.

Fear: One of the changes in you that comes from being married to a LEO.

The fear of being home alone at night.

The phone call:

LEO: Hi hon, what are you up to?

LEOW: Just watching girl TV.

LEO: Oh, OK, I don't want to keep you too long on the phone.

LEOW: It's fine, I just paused the show. What's up?

LEO: Did you have dinner?

LEOW: Yeah, I had the leftover pasta from last night.

LEO: I'm so jealous! That was excellent! I am still waiting to find time to get dinner. Um, I just wanted to give you a head's up. I just left a woman we are investigating and she said that she was going to pay my wife a visit. She gave me your full name and our home address. I don't think she is actually going to come to our house or do anything but I wanted you to be aware. She is a heavy set woman, rich and does not drive so she goes everywhere in a limo.

LEOW: OK, so I need to keep an eye out for a heavy set woman in a limo… can't be too many of them coming down our quiet street.

LEO: Like I said, I don't think she will show up but just keep an eye out.

LEOW: OK, I love you. See you in the morning.

LEO: Love you too.

So I kept my gun and phone by my side and went about my night. I figured I'd call the local cops first and then my LEO and had the gun nearby in case the local PD did not arrive in time.

As it turned out, the heavy set, rich woman being driven in a limo did not come by. Whew!

Be it the upset and angry suspect or arrestee or the family member or friend of such, LEOWs live with the niggling fear of someone "paying us a visit." We live in high crime areas in cities, in quiet "low crime" suburbs, rural areas and every kind of place there is. We live in the jurisdiction our husband works in and we also live far from where he works. Whereever we live, we all live with the knowledge that we could be a target, the fear of such and we find ways to deal with it or we would go crazy.

We also have the added cynicism of being married to a LEO and know far too much about the amount of crime that occurs. We might have a skewed vision of our safety or lack thereof but most LEOWs live with fear.

LEOWs seem to have a natural instinct to protect themselves and family but that instinct operates on fear. Fear can be a good thing in some circumstances because it alerts you to danger. LEOWs are prepared for any threats to themselves or their family. They need to be the protector of the family when their husband is at work and they take that job very seriously.

Loneliness: Another change that you must adjust to when becoming a LEOW.

Add to the sense of fear a lot of loneliness while he is working and you are home alone, yet again. Wasn't marriage supposed to mean you would have someone to come home to after work and talk about your day with?   Too often an empty home is waiting for you after work. Once you have kids, it is kid talk, kid dinner, helping with homework and the long list of chores all by yourself. Oh what you wouldn't give for five minutes of adult talk and a hug and a cuddle before bed.   Maybe you can get a few minutes to catch up with your husband sometime next week or the week after.   He's on days next week and doesn't have a side job or overtime scheduled (yet) on Thursday.   Until then, it's all on you.

Was it hard to adjust to being home alone when he worked nights or sleeping alone on some nights?   Any suggestions to deal with the loneliness and fear that worked for you?

In the beginning when my LEO worked the overnight shift it was very hard for me being alone.   I spent a lot of nights at friend's homes. Luckily for me my best friend lived two blocks away and was understanding enough to let me sleep at her house many nights, which wasn't too strange since I had lived there with her for many years before my LEO and I were married.   It was kind of like going home to "mom."   When I did stay home I used to lock myself in the bedroom at night with the dog and my gun.   Now after twenty years we are back on the overnight shift and it's so much easier this time around.   I actually like it.   I get lots of housework done now and I have two dogs and many guns along with a fifteen year old teen.

Jessica B

The night shift wasn't so bad for me before we had kids.   The swing shift was the worst when we were newly married because during the evenings he would be gone.   I worked a full time day job, so it was pretty lonely for a while.   The best advice I could give is get used to enjoying your own company.   Don't hold yourself back from anything because you are alone for most of the time. I got to the point to where if I wanted to go out to eat and nobody was available to go with me, I still went! Yes, it is awkward for the first few time you do it, but it is liberating! Go, enjoy, people watch, and bring a book or magazine… whatever! Don't miss out on something because you don't have anyone to go with you. Go out to eat, see a movie, go to a concert, etc.! There is still life to enjoy while you are waiting for the next shift change. As for fear: I have never feared sleeping alone.

Maggie D.

Yes, it is always difficult if my LEO is not home overnight. It has gotten easier over the years and I have found ways to cope. The worst was when I was expecting our first child and my LEO was on a special assignment working a case with the detectives. This was unusual for him and it wasn't like he was going to be able to get up and leave in the middle of this operation. Of course, I went in to labor while he was out working the case. It all worked out, he made it back, but I don't think you ever really get used to it. Early on before children, we had dogs. That definitely helped. My LEO used to be a K-9 handler at another police job. When we met, he no longer was a K-9 officer but we were training our bloodhound pup. When my LEO would work midnights, our bloodhound would come in to the bedroom, push the door shut and use his body to keep the door closed. Our German Shepard was on guard at the front door. No one was coming in, I mean no one! Perhaps from my own first responder days and screwed up sleep patterns or perhaps just being a mother, you never really sleep when you know all the responsibility falls on you to get up if there is an emergency in the house. I just make sure the regular schedule is kept with the kids, the phone and cell phone are close by and I am always comforted to know that the "Blue Family" aka the police, will always come to my aid. The best example I could give is when one night a teenager we didn't know and not from our neighborhood, ran into some trouble and knocked on our front door at 11 PM looking for help because he saw my husband's police cruiser parked outside. When my husband called dispatch on the non-emergency number and the call went out, for some reason the guys out on the road thought I was home alone in the house. Just minutes later, with lots of flashing lights, a screeching tire or two, four police cruisers were in front of my house. If I had any fear of being alone, this pretty much took care of that. If any LEOW has any fear of being home alone, I can tell them, that fear is only beat by what is felt by a LEO themselves when they hear the address of a fellow LEO coming over the radio. Trust me, help will be on the way! For those wondering, the teenager was fine and in this case, I couldn't be upset with the intrusion. He was a good kid who did the right thing. People have no idea how often this happens. How often you will be called upon for help or guidance.

Denise N.

My husband has been a LEO for a few years now and I am just now adjusting to him working night shift. Now I am so used to him not being there at night that it's hard for me to sleep with him in the bed with me.

Becky N.

The 4-12s were harder than the 12-8s. I had to come home from work and had no one to talk to and share my day's events with. Then I would be sleeping and I would hear him come home so I needed to talk to him to see how his day was. But what was worse was when he didn't come home on time and I would try to "be a big girl" and not let my mind go wild on me. I shudder thinking about those nights. I think I got through those nights by mind control, not allowing myself to think those sick thoughts! My problem was always the feeling of being alone, fortunately I had children early in our marriage and we had lots of dinners out and five o'clock Saturday night G rated movie nights! I also found a friend whose husband worked evenings. I always had a dog so that helped any fears of hearing any noises in the house.

Elarie S.

I was a single mom prior to marrying my LEO so I didn't really have to adjust to being home alone while he worked nights. I always double checked all doors to make sure they were locked, made sure a gun and phone were within reach if needed. I usually fall asleep to the TV every night he works. I also use those nights to snuggle with the kids.

Vicky C.

It was very hard and it still is, when he is gone overnight. I have a night light that I turn on, and I turn on my music low. This helps me to fall asleep. I also make sure that I know exactly where the phone and gun are because you never know. The hardest thing though is that I turn into the lightest sleeper when he is not at home. If his patrol car stays at home and it is parked in front of the house, I don't have as big of a fear because then I feel that anybody wanting to try to get into the house will think that he is still home. We live in such a small town that everybody knows where all the police officers live, and they are able to tell if they are home by the vehicles that are gone. I check and double check all of the locks on windows and doors before going to bed. A queen sized pillow is good to snuggle up with when he is gone.

Cathy L.

For me it was an adjustment. I had a hard time sleeping without my LEO and I still don't have a perfect time sleeping without my LEO. I used to have a body pillow that I would put along my back for that comfort of at least something being there. It helped to call him and talk a few minutes right before I laid down to go to bed. Since we live in the city he works for, sometimes he can come home and kiss me goodnight and that really helps me. This is going to sound weird but the one thing that helps is the pillow but also one of his shirts lying beside me for that comfort. I also wrote in a journal that I never let anyone see because I wrote things about how I felt that I never wanted my husband to read because he would have felt so badly for putting me in that situation. I love him so much that I don't want that to happen at all.

Patty R.

I am not often afraid at night. The loneliness was difficult when I first got married. We have two dogs and I have found they are good company when my husband is away. We also keep a weapon near the bed, which helps with any fears that come up when I am home alone.

Theresa K.

I have never minded being home alone. It does not bother me. It allows me my me time and to do things that I want to do. I don't have any fear and my advice would be to put your trust and not your fear in charge. Remember that God is in control.

Rachel H

I miss my husband when he works nights but it gives me time to watch girl TV, work on crafts and read an entire book uninterrupted. I have gotten to where I look forward to "my 4-12s."

Terri W.

I put my husband's shirt on his pillow while he is working nights. It really helps.

Ann H.

Even before he was a LEO, my husband worked nights so it was all we ever knew as a couple. Somehow though, when the nights switched to police work, I suddenly couldn't sleep alone anymore. I heard every sound in the house, had nightmares about officers coming to the door and even with the alarm set, I was afraid of the house burning down or someone trying to get inside and hurt the kids and I. It took about six months but I finally worked out a system of alarm, dogs, loaded weapon, television on and laptop or kindle nearby to read something on if my mind starts to wander to the what ifs. Distraction is key for me. I also say a prayer every night as he leaves to protect him and that seems to help me have more peace as well.

Maggie F.

When we first started dating and while he was in training he was on day shift. As soon as he was out of training, he went to nights. Boy that was something new. Of course I had the academy to prepare me for the lonely nights but it was still a whole new feeling. I would have trouble sleeping and do nothing but worry. It took some time, but it finally just became a routine. I did things to keep myself busy or I used the nights he worked as "me time." The gym became my best friend, and so did awful prime time TV. I was able to keep my mind off of the worry and the lonesome feelings. I always double and triple check all the door and window locks, and closed the blinds and curtains. The little things to make you feel safe and secure.

Ashely B.

The Ultimate Fear

Worrying for our LEO's safety is as much a part of our lives as making dinner and folding laundry. Like all wives we worry about our husband's health. Like our civilian counterparts, we know too many people who have died too young from cancer, heart attacks and car accidents. LEOW's however, have the added very real fear of their husbands being killed on the job. We can control their health to a point. We can help them to eat right, exercise and get annual physicals. We can buy a safety rated car and nag them to drive safely. We have no control over their job. No matter how good their training and how careful a LEO is, some dangers at work are beyond our and their control.

When we hear about the death of a LEO anywhere in the country, we feel sick to our stomach and we fight back the tears. In our mind's eye we see the family we never met and grieve for them and we might call our own husband if he is at work just to hear his voice and to know that he is okay. Many of us may say an extra prayer for God to bring our LEO home safe and sound.

> While my husband was finishing up a training school, he got the call that his mentor and friend who was also his Sergeant had passed away. He suffered an aneurysm while on duty in the Station House. He had immediate help and was rushed to a nearby trauma center but unfortunately, he passed away.
>
> My husband was a member of the Honor Guard and had to "work" his friend's funeral. I had to make sure he had all the things he needed prepared for the burial of his fellow officer and friend. He finished his training early and returned home for the funeral.
>
> If you have never been to a LEO's funeral, consider yourself lucky. It tends to be quite a production to give honor to the fallen. Thankfully, this kind of thing does not happen often in our rural area. I watched all the officers work diligently in the days prior to the funeral searching for things like a horse drawn caisson, a bagpipe player and many other things that we don't have readily available. In one day the entire office had worked together and prepared a beautiful funeral. The visitation and funeral were held in a local college auditorium due to the large amount of people that were expected. The next day was the day that I dreaded the most, the funeral. The service was beautiful and the "last call" and taps were haunting.

Claire D.

A LEO shares her thoughts:

When I first started this job I have to say I was a bit selfish. I didn't really think of what would happen should I be killed. I was willing to sacrifice my life for someone else. It's a question all should ask before becoming a police officer. I knew the dangers that lurked in this job and I've lost friends in the line of duty. I'm not scared to die as I've made peace with God. But I do fear what my family and friends will endure should something happen to me, now more than ever. I hate to think of the sadness they will feel. How would my husband move on without me? It's not just about me anymore. I sometimes question whether I should continue this path even after fifteen years. But I think whether I wear the badge or not, I would fight for someone who needed my help. It's just in me as it's in all good officers. They refuse to just stand by and not get involved. It speaks volumes of the men and women that wear the badge. So for now I continue the journey and pray that God will be with me and bring me home every day.

Lori T.

We all fear that knock on the door. How do you deal with the daily fear of your LEO getting hurt or dying on the job? Does it ever get better? How do you deal with the increased fear if you know he is on a dangerous call or preplanned SWAT raid etc.?

Looking back, I don't know if I climbed into a cocoon or just wouldn't allow myself to think about it. There were the times when I would call him and he would tell me that he couldn't talk because he was hiding under a car being shot at. (I think he learned from that mistake... NEVER tell me what is going on UNTIL he was safe in my arms!)
I think it was total denial that I was in. He was a member of SWAT and it flips me out today to think of the danger he was in. He used to tell me he was in the safest position as he was the guy that broke down the door. (Yea, that sounds real darn safe!!)

Elarie S.

I realized long ago that I don't have control of much. This is especially true as the spouse of a first responder. Early in my marriage, as my new husband was out fighting fires, I listened to the scanner and worried until he came home. Now as a seasoned wife of a LEO and mother to four, I try to stay balanced by enjoying the time we spend together as a family, trusting in God that He has a plan for my life, my kids and family. I do allow myself at times to go to that "what if" place only to help me figure out if I am being true to myself. It might be morbid but I sometimes compare things to assure myself of their value. For example, if this happened, would I regret making this decision or would I be satisfied that I did the best I could under the circumstances and resources I had at the time. Our journey has been difficult at times but for all the joys, I wouldn't change those times of painful growth. I reassure myself and my children that dad protects himself as best as he can, wears his vest always and is armed appropriately. The kids also pray for his safety while on his shift as well.

Annemarie J.

Several years ago when I was still a rookie LEOW, I accidentally set off our alarm system in our house. At the time we were having some work done on our phone lines and that particular evening the phone wasn't working so when the alarm company couldn't reach me, they sent the police to our house. In all my naiveté' I answered the knock on my door expecting one of my neighbors. Imagine if you will, the immediate plummet of my heart into my stomach when two local LEO's were standing on my porch. My LEO has always worked the graveyard shift in a tough area of a rough city so this incident drove home for me the danger of his job. After that I couldn't sleep for months and I obsessed over his death during every waking moment. Until one day I realized there was absolutely nothing I could do if the good Lord chose to take him on any given night. So, every night as he leaves I kiss him, tell him I love him and to be safe. I say a prayer that God protects him and then I don't talk to him again until the morning. We don't have a scanner and I don't watch the news. I guess you could call it the ignorance is bliss method of handling it. I trust him, his instincts and his training. I trust the guys and gals he works with and I choose to trust God to take care of him.

Maggie F.

For my daily fear: I tell him I love him before he leaves for work and say a prayer as he is driving up the street on his way to work. I also ask that he call me if he is going to be more than thirty minutes late so I don't worry. For the times he calls and tells me he might be late because he is going to look for the shooter in a drive by shooting or other such type of call, I pray and ask him to call me when he is back in the station, safe and sound. While waiting for that "all is safe" call I read, watch TV or anything else I can find to keep busy. If it's late at night, I try to go back to sleep but if I manage to doze off, it's a very light sleep and I jump on the phone the second it rings to let me know he is okay. It gets a little easier as I get older and he has been on the job a long time but the underlying fear is always there. I never gave it much thought until recently when a friend retired. I thought of how happy his wife must be to not have that constant companion of fear anymore and that was when I realized how much it is always with me.

I think my Christian faith in God is a great comfort at all times, knowing that God has a plan for all of our lives. I have to trust that whatever God brings me, I will be okay.

Having said that, my husband and I have up to date wills, I know what he wants for a funeral, we have life insurance and our beneficiaries are as we wish and I know all about our finances. I also have had him show me a few things around the house that are his area of knowledge so that I will know how to take care of the house if need be. In a strange way, it also gives me comfort to know I have done all that I can to prepare for the worst case scenario. It puts the fear of the unknown aside as best as possible. I know I can never be fully prepared for the worst.

Terri W.

For the daily fear, I choose not to focus on it. If I did all the time, it would make me insane. I trust him and his training. Does it ever get better? Yes! For the dangerous calls, I pray and distract myself and wait for his call that everything is clear.

Susan M.

Get up, go to work every day and hope that everything will be good. I could get hurt at work. My sons could get hurt doing what they do every day. Anyone could get hurt. You have to think about what you have the day before, and how lucky you are every day to have what you have.

Melissa S.

When I was pregnant I had to fill out the paperwork for the department for "Death and Serious Injury" in the line of duty and I was a mess. I hated even thinking that something may happen to him at all, leaving me alone to raise our daughter. As time went on I resigned myself to the fact that his job deals with crazy people and dangerous calls and though I still definitely worry about him, I can't focus on that thought and worry myself to death. If I am constantly worried, I am not being a help to him or to our daughter. When I'm talking to him and he goes to fights in progress, domestic violence calls or weapons calls my heart sinks and I just send up prayers constantly. I have learned to trust my husband's training and the other officer's he works with to keep him safe and bring him home. He always tells me that he is coming home after his shift and he'll do whatever it takes to make sure that happens.

Patty R.

For dealing with the fear, I have faith that he's well trained, vigilant and has amazing brothers and sisters that are on his shift so the worry isn't much. I have my days where not hearing from him much causes worry. I don't think it will ever get "easier" but I'm used to it so the worry is part of my "normal" day. If I know he is going on a bad call, I keep my phone with me all the time, I don't listen to the news and I hope everything will be as peaceful as possible.

Colleen R.

We are strong in our faith so I pray daily for my husband's safety. I do worry about him but I can't let it consume me because we have children to stay strong for. I make sure I kiss him and tell him I love him each time he goes out the door because we never know if it will be the last time. When he has SWAT call outs he usually tells me he is going out and tells me he loves me. Then he always lets me know when it's over and everyone is safe. During the call out, I try to occupy myself with either the children, cleaning or a good book.

Vicky C.

The Daunting Prospect of Adjusting to His Ever Changing Shifts

Your husband may work a rotating shift or maybe a steady night shift but more than likely you don't work the same schedule. You will spend countless hours by yourself while he is at work. You might be ships passing in the night or missing each other entirely as he leaves for work before you get home and you are long gone in the morning before he wakes up. You can be miserable and lonely or you can find a way to make the best of the situation.

I ran next door from my work for a soda. On my way back a car was driving alongside me really slowly. I'm thinking creepy guy! He rolls down his window and says "Hi" and I give him dirty look and a "hi" back, with attitude and enter my work as he pulls into a parking spot. I tell my coworker a guy is following me and I think he's coming into the store too!! In walks the guy.... and my coworker says "you do know that's your husband, don't you?" He was wearing glasses, which I hadn't seen him wear in years because he normally wears his contacts and I haven't seen him out of uniform in weeks.

Lauren T.

Do you have any suggestions for a new wife to help her adjust to his shift changes, odd hours etc.?

What helped me in the beginning was that I didn't work and we had no children, so we just lived "backwards." I followed his schedule. If you can do it, it helps.

Jessica B.

Remember that they need their sleep too, even though you may not have seen them or spoken to them in a few days. They still need their sleep. Just take advantage of every minute you can.

Becky N.

If you don't already have a hobby, I strongly advise it. There will be many hours spent without your spouse and if you sit and worry about him the entire shift, it will drive you crazy. If he works nights and isn't a heavy sleeper you may have to adjust your way of doing things by doing housework at night while he is working instead of during the day. You really just have to figure out what works best for you and your LEO.

Vicky C.

I know it sounds cliché, but be flexible. Flexibility is the key to living with a LEO and not getting so upset you end up divorcing him/her. I found that if I plan to have dinner ready right when my husband should be getting home, it never works and when I don't plan to have dinner ready, he turns up on time. I've learned that I just roll with the punches and plan my larger meals on days he is scheduled to be off. It's not a glamorous life but it is so fulfilling and in some strange way, worth it. It also helps to talk to your husband about how you are feeling while trying to adjust to the changes and loneliness because chances are, he's going through some of the same feelings that you're experiencing. Talking may end up helping both of you. Please, please, please, don't clam up and bury your feelings because that's a recipe for disaster. I used to hide my feelings and hold things in until one day I almost exploded and it all came out. I felt so good after getting it all out and I realized that if I talked about it to someone it would make things easier to endure.

Patty R.

The best advice I could give to a LEOW or someone about to become a new LEOW is that you will need to respect their need to sleep. Don't try to schedule social gatherings or make plans on weeks you know might be difficult to adjust or when he/she is going to be tired. Use that time to go out with your friends, go to the gym and do things that you like to do that your LEO doesn't necessarily like to do. Give your LEO a quiet house. A LEO with a rotating shift is really taxing their body. If you are in the dating or engagement stage and having serious trouble with this, then you really need to consider if this is a lifestyle you can live with. You can talk about options with your LEO but I don't think it would be fair, as in my LEO's case, to ever give ultimatums or blame them for a career they chose if it was their dream. If you and your LEO partner can't come to an understanding or work out a realistic lifestyle that works for both of you, then the reality is, the relationship, long term probably will not work.

Denise N.

Find things that you like to do that your husband may not enjoy that you can do when he is working. My husband works most of my weekends, but I have turned it into me time. I watch girly shows that he hates, go to farmer's markets, shopping, go for hikes or do other hobbies.

Theresa K.

I do not change my household schedule because my LEO has to work. I keep my family on the same schedule no matter what.

Rachel H.

I do not work so I can adjust to his schedule. Now that my daughter is getting older and will soon be in school, his schedule might affect ours. He is currently off mid-week so he will be able to take her to school, help her with homework and take her on fieldtrips. Which, in my opinion, is a blessing. Most jobs don't allow for that.

Cassie S.

My boys were born into the LEO life so all they know is Daddy's night shift schedule (he has worked night shift his entire career). When it comes to school activities, Mommy goes and if Daddy can't go, Mommy records it for him. If something goes on during the day, Daddy is usually the one to attend because I work so it sort of works itself out so that we each get time with the boys that way. Athletics are hit or miss. I generally attend all baseball practices and ball games, with my LEO getting there when he can. Many a Saturday he has met me at the ball field after an all-night shift and made it through a double header before going home to sleep. He is as involved as he can be and we make it work.

Maggie F.

If you work opposite schedules like my husband and I do, I believe in sleeping together when you can. It sounds silly, but it makes a very big difference in a marriage. It was very hard for us at first to do this but my husband now comes to bed with me when he is off. He just sleeps when he is tired. Some days he is only awake for six or seven hours before crawling right back into bed with me. If you are capable of adjusting your life to his schedule, do it. It makes it easier on everyone, especially his internal clock. Date nights on Tuesday at four in the afternoon, or anniversary celebrations at six in the morning, nights out with friends or a few drinks on Thursdays instead of weekends. You just have to go with the flow. No reason to plan in advance, everyone knows a LEO's schedule is subject to change any minute. And yes, sometimes they even change for the better.

Ashley B.

Take a bad situation and make it positive… if he had off Tuesday, we made Tuesday night our date night! If he had to work four to twelve on Saturday we would do something earlier in the day. We had to make it flexible to make it work for us.

Elarie S

There are times I hate the schedule but I must admit, it can be beneficial at times. We go out to dinner during his weeknights off and we always get a good table, never have to wait and are never rushed. We go out to lunch or take long walks together on his four to twelve tours. It helps to have understanding friends who work our nights out together around his schedule.

Terri W.

Happy Holidays….or Are They?

Your mom wants Thanksgiving dinner at her house at exactly noon.

Your in-laws expect the whole family to show up on Christmas Eve for cookies and cocoa as Grandpa reads **The Night Before Christmas.** Your LEO is on duty Thanksgiving, Christmas Eve *and* Christmas this year. Sound familiar?

As you may already know, trying to manage normal holiday activities with a LEO schedule is often about as easy as giving a cat a bath. If you are lucky, your family will understand his absence and not harass you too much about it. At the very least you might get a few well-meaning single mom jokes. At the most, the wrath of angry family members who can't understand why he can't just take the day off like everyone else does.

Those very same people would be mighty upset if they dialed 9-1-1 and were told their domestic dispute…stolen car…missing Christmas gifts…. would have to wait until the officers were done with their ham and Eggnog.

As you will see, every LEO family has its own way of dealing with the trials and tribulations of the holidays and eventually you will find what works best for yours. There will always be the well-meaning friend or family member who thinks it is easy to just take the day off or skip sleeping (night shift officers) just one day. After all it's Thanksgiving… Christmas…great grandma's 100th birthday, right? But when it comes down to brass tacks, holidays are just dates on a calendar until you add traditions and loved ones. Who needs a little box on a piece of paper to tell you when to give thanks or honor your higher power?

Turkey tastes just as good at seven in the evening as it does at two in the afternoon. Santa Claus may only come one night a year but he doesn't leave an "open at six in the morning only" directive. If you have children and they were born into the LEO life, they will surprise you with how adaptive they are. If LEO living is new to you, as a family you just have to find your groove. But it can be done, as long as you remember that dates on a calendar do not dictate your life as a family nearly as much as your love for one another does.

How has shift work affected your family life? How do you handle the holidays?
If it is needed, my husband is able to take a day off for an event or even doctor's appointments. Try your best to plan on his off days to have special events with the holidays. We always plan holidays around his work schedule. Our daughter is young enough that she won't be upset if Christmas isn't until the twenty sixth. She wouldn't know any different.
Becky N.

Holidays, we just go with the flow and our family is very supportive and understanding that we may have to schedule our holiday times different than the actual holiday. I have a big pet peeve about going ahead with the holiday while my LEO is working or unable to join in, so we make sure that we make it so that we can all be together. This year we are inviting all the officers and families that have to work on Thanksgiving to our home for dinner.
Cathy L.

I wish I could say that my husband's family is understanding about his schedule when planning family activities but they are not. They live one hour away and they usually plan family parties for weekends at two or three in the afternoon so no matter what time he is working, he can't attend. They have gotten a little more flexible on time lately but still do not ask about when his days off are. We rarely attend his family's parties. My own family has said they would never have a family get together without my husband and they work around his schedule. A birthday might have to be celebrated several weeks late, but my husband is always there. My husband has enough seniority that he can get holidays off with the understanding that if something major happens he will have to go in. As for day to day events, I pretty much know that any plans we make are always tentative.

Terri W.

It's hard to explain to your child why her daddy isn't home because he is out working and has to provide for us. I try to go along with normal routines so that she isn't thrown off by Daddy not being there. When he has to work nights my daughter doesn't sleep well at all. We've missed family get togethers due to scheduling but we do our best to try to be there. Just be flexible and do your best to arrange activities when your husband is supposed to be off.

Patty R.

We have different days off so when we have a day off together we always try to do something fun and different from our ordinary. Family events can be difficult. My husband is the only LEO in the family so they are still adjusting to the fact that he doesn't always have control over his schedule. I have gotten better at going to events by myself. It was hard at first as I was self-conscious going to events alone and fielding questions about where my husband was, but it gets easier. You realize most people think it's strange for a second but they quickly get over it. The hardest part of the job is planning events that are at set times. When we were first married I bought us tickets to a hockey game for Christmas. He had to work during the day of the game, but was planning on being home on time. I got all dressed and ready to go and then got a call that he was running late. Then about twenty minutes later, I got a call from him that they had been in a wreck but that he is okay. Due to the wreck, he told me he would be home late so we would miss the game. A few hours went by and there was a knock on the door, which totally freaked me out. Turned out his boss dropped him off and he wanted to show him the work we had been doing to fix up the house and didn't want to surprise me when he came in. It took a while after that for me to be willing to buy tickets to an event again, as I was afraid of the outcome if I did.

Theresa K.

There is no way to sugar coat it. Sometimes it just stinks. The police department doesn't close on Thanksgiving, Christmas or New Year's Day. There are no federal holidays off and there are kids everywhere waking up without their LEO parent to see them open Christmas presents, blow out birthday candles and missing school plays and activities. To help our kids cope on holidays their LEO Dad could not be there, we talk about how important their Dad's job is, that not everyone can do it and how he is out there keeping all the other little boys and girls safe. We would try to do something special alone with them, open a present, and have a special cake. Make that moment just about them and their Dad.

How to make it work? We made some really important decisions early on in our relationship and in our marriage. Our family was to come first whenever possible and to spend as much time together as possible. We knew those early years and that time with our children was going to be precious, you can't get that back. It didn't matter how much more money my LEO could make by working a different shift, working overtime so we could have a bigger house, a more glamorous vacation or the bigger or better car. Rather than buy a bigger house further away resulting in what would be a long commute time for my LEO, we stayed closer to his work and did without some other things. We determined which holidays and events were most important. Maybe right now you have no kids so your wedding anniversary is important. Take that time off and let your LEO give Christmas to a LEO that has kids. How are you going to work school activities? Is it better for your LEO to work nights, sleep while the kids are in school and be there when they get off the bus? The decisions you make are the ones that have to fit into what means the most to you as a couple and a family. It really is what works best for you and what is going on in your life. You can be sure of one thing, life is going to change, so make sure your core mission, as a family is solid. Things changed for us through the years. We never forgot everyday as my LEO kisses me and walks out the door that could be the last goodbye. I don't mean to sound morbid, that just the reality of it all and we were never so sure of the decisions we had made as when 9/11 happened. After 9/11, family time was not only important; it also became clear my LEO needed to be home in the evening. My oldest, then age 3 would kneel on his bed, pull up the shade and lean against the window and cry asking, "Will Daddy be coming home tonight?" Holding back the tears myself, because I knew I could not promise him that, I knew it was time to readjust to meet our core values. We realized we could work a little with holidays and weekends but for our son's sake and eventually other circumstances, my LEO would need a steady daytime schedule so he could be there in the evening hours for my son. Eventually, we relocated to another state where my LEO could work a steady schedule, be close to home and I could be with the kids. We now have three children and that son is now fifteen and amazing. We do everything we can to keep my LEO's schedule as steady as possible and our son does well. The occasional schedule change is all right but if it starts getting changed too much, especially during the holiday months, you can see the anxiety return. It's a work in progress. As a LEOW you can be sure that a LEO's schedule will always be a challenge but then so is life. You can do it!

Denise N.

Holidays, birthdays etc. we handle like most LEO families. We just schedule around his shifts as much as possible. My family is very understanding and accommodating but his family actually struggles with it. They don't understand the police department way and think he is lying when he says he can't get the time off for something.

Maggie F.

My husband's schedule has drastically affected our family life. We do holidays whenever we get to them. Our first Christmas we exchanged gifts at four in the morning. When it comes to family events or holidays with the family, he has gone in uniform, says hi, grabs a plate and goes into work just about every single holiday since we have been together. I spend more time with his family than he does. And sometimes he never even makes it to my family's holiday celebration.

Ashley B.

This was our way of life... we didn't know from anything else. In the early days my husband would flip out when he couldn't make my son's little league games. So I figured a way around it. We did not have cell phones back then so I would call the dispatcher at headquarters and I would give him my son's stats every time he came up to bat. It made my husband's day a little brighter knowing how his boy was doing!

Elarie S.

A LEO shares her thoughts:

Shift work has been hardest on my family. It's tough working nights and not being able to tuck my little one in bed. I see him for a short time in the morning but then not again until the following morning. I'm so thankful to have a supportive husband who is capable of "taking the reins" when I'm not there. Without him, I'm sure I would be more worried about my son. My husband and I have had arguments over my job. Mainly the hours and how inconsistent they can be. But since I've been in the detective bureau, I have a little more flexibility and make adjustments to accommodate his schedule if needed.

Lori T.

Finding a Way to Connect With Other LEOWs and LEO Families.

Your co-workers and friends tell you to "Have a great weekend!" on Friday. Maybe for them but it's only Tuesday in your world. They might invite you and your family to a barbeque or out to dinner for Saturday night. Nope, hubby's working. Maybe they invite your family to go away with them to the mountains or the shore for the long holiday weekend. It's not a three day weekend in your world. In fact, hubby's working the entire weekend but he is off on Wednesday and Thursday, just in time for you and your friends to be back at work. If you are lucky enough to find a babysitter on a week night, it's out to dinner by yourselves again. It's nice to have a night out for just the two of you but it'd be nice to do things with friends from time to time.

Hopefully, your family and friends are somewhat understanding about your LEO's work schedule but it doesn't mean they can always work around it. You soon find yourself losing friends or maybe you are not as close as you once were. You might even drift a bit from family when schedules don't align. Hence, LEOs often socialize with other LEOs. They tend to be off when you are and they understand when your schedules conflict. Add into the mix that they understand the unique stresses you and your family are under and hopefully, friendships blossom.

If your husband works in a large department, it might be easy to find another family that you click with but on the flip side, it might be too large a department and a bit impersonal. Small job? It might be hard to find other families in the same life stage as you and with similar interests. Finding a way to connect with other Leo families is not always easy. It also might be nice to have some LEOWs alone/girl time. Talk, laugh and enjoy time with women who truly understand all the challenges you face being married to a LEO.

The crazy schedule, working holidays etc. can make for lonely times for a LEOW. Are the LEOWs on your husband's job close? What do you do to get closer to the other wives?

> We live in a small county so we all know each other and hang around each other if we are all at an event but we do not do a lot with just LEOWs.
>
> Vicky C.

> On his first police job, some of the wives were close but I was working and traveling a lot so I wasn't close to too many wives. This second job, I am friendly with some of the wives but the dynamic is very different this time. This time, for me, medical issues have kept me more house bound at times and not as out and about as I usually had been and then I'm with my kids the rest of the time.
>
> Denise N.

> We have set up a supper club once a month for the LEOWs. We plan it on a weekend when our officers are working and then someone hosts and we do potluck dinner. We drink a lot of wine and eat a lot of food and do a lot of girl talk and gossip. It's the best!
>
> Meredith K.

> My husband's job has a lot of people so the wives are not close. I am part of a few local and national support groups and I enjoy that.
>
> Susan M.

I am friends with one of the wives and that's because we have kids that are really close in age. I'd love to be close with wives there but most of them aren't interested in their husband's job or interacting with other wives. We do interact some at the Christmas party but that's about it.

Patty R.

Some wives are close. With nearly one thousand officers on the department, it's not feasible for all to be close. One of my closest friends is a wife of one of the guys from my husband's academy.

Cassie S.

In the early years it seemed like the wives were close but we didn't live near everyone else so I never had a relationship with the women. In my husband's later years we spent more time with some of the couples.

Elarie S.

We have a LEOW's group and we love it! We had a first meeting where we gave everyone a survey to find out what they were interested in the group doing, i.e. social, Bible study, meals in case of emergency, playgroup etc.. For us there are a number of women who were interested in Bible study which has begun. A bunch more wanted some social activities so that we could know each other better. We do those about once a month. As we have gotten to know each other we found that a number of the wives are interested in making a difference in our community. We have passed out popsicles wearing custom shirts at the local Safetyfest Day, are doing shoeboxes full of goodies for Christmas and shop with a cop as well as a craft day I do for a homeless shelter. All of these activities started because of us talking. We made it very clear up front that we were not a group who was going to sit around and bash the department or members of the department. That behavior was not going to be tolerated. Our purpose was to have a safe environment to share our burdens and the things that only we can understand. We wanted to know each other. The group is meant to be positive and if we ever feel that it is becoming negative we will take a break from it… all of us!

Beverly S.

We have a group called Sisters-in-Law. It's held in a local non-denominational church whose pastor has always been very supportive of law enforcement. The church offers child care so wives will be more inclined to come. We meet the second Monday of every month that school is in session from 6:30 PM to 8 PM. The wives bring snacks and drinks to share. Every month we do something different. Sometimes it's a social month so we play Bunco, UNO or poker. Some months we have a topic or guest speaker who volunteers their time and expertise such as a marriage counselor or parenting coach.

My husband's department has over two hundred and fifty officers but we don't limit the group to just his department. Our county is inter twined and our SWAT team is composed of five departments so we say that if you are a LEOW and are within driving distance, we WANT you!

To keep things low drama (as low as can be with so many women), we have a panel of sorts, with one to two wives from all departments in attendance so everyone has a voice. Also, that way one department doesn't overwhelm all the decisions. We do not have monthly dues.

Francis J.

We have a Facebook group for the wives which has the security status of "secret" so others can't find us on Facebook and harm us. We can connect, blow off steam etc.

Stephanie H.

Is there a lot of general socializing within your husband's Department?

We are lucky that my husband got his start on a squad that promotes socializing outside of work. On the "Friday" of their shift, they have something called Choir Practice. It was the code word they would use when setting up drinks after work. They couldn't say "let's go get drinks" so they called it Choir Practice. I attend many of them as do many of the other wives.

Meredith K.

There is little socializing of the LEO's and families outside of work.

Susan M.

Patty R.

My husband does not socialize with his coworkers outside of work. Twice a year or so the Sergeant will throw them a "team party" which consists of the five to seven guys he is working with at the time. Sometimes it's just the team, sometimes families.

Cassie S.

Since we all know each other from being in a small county we socialize some but not really as work socializing. The department has a Christmas party for the families to get together.

Vicky C.

In general, I don't see a lot of general socializing within the departments anymore. My LEO's first department, there would be department holiday parties and picnics where you would see the whole family come out and that was nice. During the summer, one of the local camps that was closed on weekends, would let the police department use their grounds for the day for the department picnic. There were swimming pools for the kids to swim, barbecues going all day and all kinds of games for the kids. It was fun and it went all day so the shifts rotating through all had a chance to enjoy it. During the holidays, there was the annual Christmas party with Santa Claus, of course. Santa would bring presents for all the kids of the department and the parents would socialize and there was more than plenty of food. Then during the course of the year, there would be the occasional retirement party or the individual department party to attend. I don't see that here at the second job. Occasionally, I will hear my LEO talking about going to a section gathering but that is with a very small number of people. Nothing like the big parties and gatherings we used to have. I don't know if it's geographical or just the sign of the times.

Denise N.

My husband's job has some PBA events such as a Christmas dinner dance. The PBA also does some charity functions and social events such as ballgames, picnics, trips to casinos etc. that officers and families can attend. The retirees have a party twice a year in which active, retired members and spouses are invited to attend. Several different Christmas parties including the Detective Division and many individual squads have their own parties in December. There are usually a few retirement parties a year too. Many officers are friends outside of work and socialize. There are always weddings to attend. The officers and their wives are very supportive at funerals. My husband's squad also tries to organize a yearly dinner with the wives. My husband's job has about one hundred and twenty employees plus civilian employees so there are a wide range of people to become friends with. I enjoy the friendships we have made and also the "we just see each other at functions" friendships.

Terri W.

Those "Not So Great Days" When Your LEO Earns His Pay and Then Some

As the saying goes, it's not all fun and games and our LEOs deal with a lot of "not fun" things in their jobs. They need the socializing with the guys to blow off steam but they also need to be able to come home and vent, complain, sulk or whatever works best for them to process their day.

LEOW: Hi honey, is this a bad time?

LEO: No, I'm just here at the train tracks with a DOA... he jumped in front of the train.

LEOW: Oh, OK, sorry, I'll talk to you later. It's not important.

LEO: No tell me now, this guy isn't going anywhere.

And so the conversation goes.

When he gets home, I pour him a beer and he asks about my day. My hair cut looks nice, dinner smells good and what else did you do today after your haircut? That conversation lasts about ten minutes and then it's his turn to talk about his day.

LEO: So we had a follow up call today that we thought might be the burglars from a few weeks ago. Do you remember me telling you about the call where the older couple had two people distract them at the front door while the third went in the back door and stole the old man's military medals? The three people we had today seemed like a good fit but when we brought the older couple in they said no. The one woman we had was wanted on three warrants.

The call at the train station was a mess, with brain matter and the guy's skull all over the surrounding cars the commuters left this morning. We had to call the fire department to hose off the cars so the commuters wouldn't find brain matter on their cars tonight. I ran into an old friend from the Medical Examiner's office at the scene. It was good to see him and we spent some time catching up.

I don't know why that guy jumped in front of the train. We think he might have had drug issues.

A ten minute "scenic detour" to discuss the other responding officer's personalities, work strengths and weaknesses etc. Doug is a great cop, a lot like his brother Jake.

Thankfully, the guy was thrown away from the train when he jumped in front of it and not dragged underneath. What a mess that is to investigate and clean up. They finally opened the rail line next to the suicide. Some commuters were glued to the window, others just read the newspaper, oblivious to the drama outside the safety of their train car.

And so we go tip toeing around the details as he re-lives the day. I listen, ask questions, laugh when appropriate, because yes, he will sprinkle laughs into the story. The gorier the police call, the more they need to find a way to laugh. We seem to be finished with this conversation for now but we may revisit this part of his day during dinner or maybe in a few days.

Does your husband share with you the details of his day? How do you get him to open up and trust you with the details of the uglier parts of his job? Do you encourage him to share or would you rather not hear?

My husband has always shared all details of his day. I used to be a police officer so he knows I understand the uglier parts of his job. I really care about what he does all day and look forward to hearing about it... the good, bad and the ugly. I am just as interested in what he does on his days off so conversation has never been an issue with us. I listen, ask questions and give feedback. I am not always as patient about waiting for the long story to get to the point and my husband will be the first to tell me that. He's right and I am trying to do better. I would suggest that wives get in the habit of setting time aside each day to listen to their husband's stories. Listen to stories about all of his days, at work and days off. If need be, let him start with the funny and work his way around to whatever it is that he has trouble telling you. Listen and let him know that not only do you want to hear it all but that you are capable of hearing it all. Let him know that you don't need to be protected from the seedier aspects of his job. He needs to be able to talk with you.

Terri W.

My husband does tell me a lot about his day but he doesn't tell me everything. He knows that he can trust me to keep what he says between us and not go any further. His belief is that if he didn't have someone to share stuff with he would go absolutely insane and be a basket case. I encourage my husband to talk to me (if he feels like he can share) because I want to be involved in his life and career and show him that I support him completely and I care deeply about him.

Patty R.

My husband is retired now but he used to share the serious cases and the funny ones. I never really had to encourage him to tell me of his day's events because my man loves to talk!
Just the other day he brought up an accident from over fifteen years ago. The child had died and he spoke about it like it was yesterday.
Elarie S.

I encourage him to tell me about his day, including all of the good and bad things that may have happened.

Cathy L

I ask every day about his day. I'm very interested in what he does and I love to hear how much he enjoys his job (even the crazy stuff). Usually he will tell me about the funny/interesting/frustrating calls.

Colleen R.

My husband shares his day with me but not every detail or every call but when I ask how his day was, he will talk about it. I encourage him to talk about his day because if he sees a lot and if he keeps it all in it will wear on him.

Vicky C.

How do you help your husband if he had a particularly upsetting incident at work? Does he tell you about it or does he have classic signs that something is wrong?

I listen closely to what my husband is telling me. My husband's department has had several fatality collisions that were terrible and several other incidents recently that can be bothersome. He's been in law enforcement for twenty three years and he's become "hardened" I guess is the way to put it. He tries not to let things bother him but they do. I can read him well enough to know something is bothering him and I'll ask him if he is okay and if he needs to talk but it has to be in his time and in his own way.

Patty R.

My husband has classic signs when he has had a bad day at work. I can generally pick up on it the minute he walks in the door. When he is in a really bad mood, I generally will just leave him alone. The only time that I may step in is if his bad mood is being directed towards me or the kids. Then I will tell him that we are not his work, we have nothing to do with his work so if he cannot treat us as a family then do not talk to us at all.

Cathy L.

I think the best thing to do is listen, and be patient before giving advice or talking. If it's something that's really upsetting him he usually tells me in person when he's off. It's part of our weekly time to connect and for me to ask him about work and that is how I look for signs if something is wrong. A conflict of ours is that I often interrupt him, so I have had to work on staying quiet and patient. He tends to talk slowly when telling his stories, where as I like to have an interactive conversation. So recognizing those differences in communication and trying to be supportive is what I do.

Kelly P.

He usually mentions something about it, and I follow up with questions as needed, out of kid's earshot or after the kids are in bed. Being married for almost seventeen years, but in LEO for almost twelve years, you know when something isn't right. Thankfully, my husband will talk to me if needed. Most of the time, he can compartmentalize but talk to our parish priest if needed as well.

Annemarie J.

I listen, offer advice and make sure he knows that I support him and whatever he did or didn't do was the right decision. He's very open to discussing any incidents that happen.

Jennifer H.

If my husband has had a bad day at work, he calls on his way home and says, "I had a rough call, in case I'm a little snippy tonight" so I know to expect more distance and frustration. When the kids go to bed he will talk to me.

Colleen R.

I can tell by the way he talks or acts if he's had something bad happen. When I notice I ask if he wants to talk and if he does great we talk; if not I understand and leave it at "I'm here for you". There are times that talking about something makes it worse because they are reliving it.

Vicky C.

A LEO's thoughts:

Prior to meeting my wife, I lived with my parents for the first ten years of my law enforcement career. My father was a LEO and being able to come home from a difficult day at work and talk with my father and my mother was a great help. My wife came from a family of LEOs and firefighters so she too was always willing to listen to my stories and let me vent. Being able to talk after work was a big help in my life and our marriage.

To help my wife understand my daily stories, I explained to her in great detail what each unit in the police department did, what the unit was responsible for and how they worked with the other units.

I want to share an aspect of the LEO life that many civilians may not understand. The morning that my wife passed away from a long terminal illness brought back a feeling that I had forgotten. On the way home from hospice, after my wife passed, myself and my kids stopped along the banks of a local lake and watched the sun come up. There was no crying or showing of emotion because in our situation, our emotions were already spent a long time ago. However, I did feel another emotion that I hadn't experienced since retiring from the law enforcement. It is a feeling/emotion that you have after work on a day when you experience a horrific event such as the serious injury or death of a child or a close call with your own death or an injury. You need to unwind and talk. I knew that my kids were experiencing this emotion and that is why we went down to the lake to watch the sun rise and talked about what was on our minds. Unfortunately, the inability to deal with this emotion causes many cops to turn to alcohol or results in other family problems. I was always grateful that I could talk about my life as a LEO with my wife and share my thoughts and feelings.

Nick F.

If you have had a tough day, what do you wish she would do? Talk with you, leave you alone? Any suggestions to help us know how to best help you?

Sometimes I like to talk about my day and sometimes I don't. I can't come out and tell her that I don't want to talk, it's something that she can read by knowing me and understands. For the most part, I want to discuss my day with her. Be understanding and extremely supportive but don't be afraid to tell your LEO if they do something you don't like. Get to know your LEO's vibes to be able to read if they want to talk about their day or not.

Doug S.

Sometimes a Little Change in the Work Routine is Good For The Soul

Stress and law enforcement go hand in hand and there is no avoiding it. There might be ways to mitigate the stress including having someone at home you can talk with. Some officers find that a break from their routine or a change is all they need to get a new perspective, a renewed enthusiasm for their job and a relief from some of the stress. Becoming a K-9 handler is often a much sought after position and can bring much happiness to the officer and his family. The officer has a partner he can talk to, a "buddy" to ride with all day and another "officer" to always be there to watch his back.

My husband Mike had wanted to be a K-9 officer for a very long time. At the time, the Sheriff's Office only had one K-9 so it wasn't a sure bet that my husband would be able to expand the unit to two K-9s. I encouraged my husband to share his interest with "the powers that be." Soon after, his dream of becoming a K-9 handler was coming true when the Sheriff's Office received funding for two more K-9s. We were beyond happy and excited.

Mike and his Lieutenant were sent to a nearby state to pick out his dog. As it turned out, he didn't have much to say about which dog he was going to get, as his dog picked him. There was a beautiful Belgium Malinois named Patriot. As Mike was discussing options with the breeder, Patriot walked up to Mike and nosed his way underneath his hand and made Mike pet him. Patriot remained there with him the entire time. The Lieutenant said "I don't know if he can work but he's going home with us!" Patriot didn't get to come with them that day but it wasn't long before he became a member of our department and our family. Patriot needed proper training in drugs, search and apprehension before becoming a full patrol dog. After all was said and done, Patriot cost the department twelve thousand dollars but he was well worth it!

Within a few weeks, my husband went to the kennel for an intense eight week training course. He was there Monday thru Friday and came home on weekends. After three weeks he was allowed to bring Patriot home for the weekend. He instantly became a part of our family. He was so well behaved and well mannered.

One weekend I went to visit my husband and as I drove into the driveway of the kennel, I could hear Patriot barking his very distinctive bark. He heard my car and remembered it from his visit to our home. These dogs amaze me by how smart they are. Mike took me directly to Patriot to see him and I don't know who was more excited, me or Patriot but we were both very happy to see each other again.

That weekend, my husband and I decided to spend some alone time at the beach. Patriot however, had other plans. The owner of the kennel called us soon after we had left for the beach with the news that Patriot was not happy. He knew this was supposed to be our time with him and he let everyone know it. My LEO was given a lecture about not spoiling the dog because "he is a tool, not a pet." I totally ignored this. I feel dogs need love and deserve to be spoiled, even K-9s!

Patriot became an integral member of the department and our family since he came home to stay. We loved him so very much. He also helped my husband enjoy his job that much more and my husband has never regretted becoming a K-9 officer. Unfortunately, Patriot passed away a year ago and we still miss him. We got a new K-9 three months after Patriot passed away. Rex is a great Lab but I still miss Patriot, who will always have a big part of my heart that belongs to only him.

Claire D.

To Take a Promotion... Or Not?

Certain positions/ units/details in law enforcement can bring about more stress than other positions. Maybe one too many upsetting calls has your LEO thinking a little change in his work routine might be nice but there are times that the available position is not what your LEO has in mind. The schedule may work better for the family but the actual job may not be so attractive. Knowing when to make a change and when not to, is not always an easy decision.

Some jobs take a test for a promotion in rank, some jobs are the "good old boy network" promotions. "You gotta go along to get along" and not all want to play the game. Some guys have no desire for or intention of ever becoming a boss. Some guys love patrol work, some hate it. Some live for the detective division promotion, some would rather drink bleach than do that job. juvenile unit... great if you love kids but not so great if you prefer to only spend time with your own kids and not so much time with someone else's kids. traffic division... if it's steady days the hours are great but ticket writing day in and day out is not for everyone. Bigger departments may have Monday to Friday nine to five jobs that keep an o fficer inside headquarters, sometimes referred to as house mouse

86

or Palace guard jobs that some find a welcome change after years on the street. SWAT team... he'd love it but over my dead body! The list goes on for possible assignments and each square peg works best in a square hole. Perhaps your LEO is happy exactly where he is and he is not interested in a change of routine, even if an opening is offered to him.

Has your husband ever struggled to decide if he should turn down or accept a promotion or lateral move within the department? Do either of you regret his decision?

My husband stepped down from a Sergeant's position and honestly it was the best decision he ever made. He was so stressed out from his position and once he stepped down his stress level dropped and he enjoyed going to work again. Once he stepped down, within a year the School Resource Officer (SRO) position came available at the local high school and he went into the position and he has never been happier. His days are definitely busy and crazy but he loves going to work and helping the kids and people in the community because he does still work patrol. I have never regretted him stepping down from the Sergeant's position or taking the SRO position because it really was the best thing for our family.

Patty R.

He has never turned down a promotion. The only problem he has now is that he has been a Sergeant Detective for over ten years, and he is getting passed over for a Lieutenant position, which makes him very angry. His next promotion will either be a Lieutenant or he will apply for Chief once he has finished his college degree. My husband sometimes feels like he is getting burned out and sometimes wishes that he would have gone into another line of work. These feelings usually pass within a couple of days.

Cathy L.

My husband has been a Sergeant in the detective division for more years than I can count. He has not taken the Lieutenant's test and does not plan to because that would mean leaving his current unit and going into patrol as a road boss. He loves detective work but is not crazy about patrol work. He has thought about other assignments within the framework of the detective division but he likes the crazy schedule he has now. It gives him lots of time to get things done around the house

86

and enjoy his hobbies. We don't regret his decision because he is happy about his job most days. As long as he is happy, I am happy.

Terri W.

My husband did lateral with another department in the city next door! He had been with his city for maybe three years, and there was so much turmoil amongst officers, he wasn't liking what he was seeing. To add to that, the Sheriff was in talks to take over, which wasn't necessarily a bad thing, but it would be a major change. We did not regret his decision because he ended up at another good department and this city seems to be more stable. He is, however, struggling with the thought of whether or not to go to the Sheriff's department because there would be more job opportunities than just being a patrol officer as he is now. So that is something that he and I go back and forth with, however for now, with him being the only one working, we decided to hold off on a major change.

Kelly P.

A few years ago, my husband tested for another local department and was next on the hiring list. Shortly thereafter, there was a hiring freeze and he stayed in his initial department. This was the biggest blessing as that lateral move would have cost him a job. That second department laid off the last hires. My husband would have been one of the ones to go. As far as a promotion, we are currently in the midst of starting a K-9 program. My husband has been after this for years, and a new police chief has agreed to give it a go. Funds have been raised for the purchase of a dog and this spring, hubby goes to North Carolina to train with the K-9. Our family is very excited to meet the dog too.

Annemarie J.

Marriage: The Good, The Bad and All The In Between

Our fourteenth wedding anniversary is just around the corner. If anyone had told me twenty years ago that I would not only be married for almost a decade and a half but also raising two amazing sons and that my husband would be a veteran police officer with a distinguished career I wouldn't have believed them. Yet, here we are fourteen years in and counting. Some days are a struggle with his long hours and the other effects of the job while others are absolutely amazing. Just like any married couple we may disagree over parenting ideas, how to spend the tax refund or what show to watch. On the flip side, I get to sleep with my hero three nights a week (nine years on the graveyard shift means we only get a few nights home together) and I am absolutely secure in the fact that he would do anything, even lay down his life, to protect me and our children. Not to mention, the stories at the dinner table are *always* entertaining.

Cops often get a bad rap when it comes to marriage but the truth of the matter is LEO marriages can be just as strong and healthy as any other marriage. Maybe even more so. Police officers handle terrible things, deal with the dregs of society and sleep with horrific images in their minds that I wouldn't wish on my worst enemy. It is bound to take an emotional toll on them. It doesn't excuse poor behavior by any means but as a LEO wife, it has helped me to understand the occasional grouchiness or short temper sometimes surfaces inexplicably. It took me a long time to realize it wasn't directed at me specifically, just a knee-jerk response to whatever may have happened at two in the morning when he was at work the previous night. Over the years, I have grown wiser and developed crafty ways of getting to the heart of the matter. Now, when he is in a particularly sour mood, I simply ask him what happened at work. Usually that is all he needs to start talking.

Marriage isn't an easy prospect for any couple. As we get older we grow and change- morphing into two individuals very different from the young couple that once stood at the altar pledging our lives to each other. That doesn't mean the changes are bad by any means, just that they happen.

What little things do you do to let your husband know that you love him and support him?

I put love notes in his cooler he takes to work. They always say something along the lines of I love you and I am proud of you or I find a cute quote. I also text him once a day with something positive I like about him.

Gail C.

I let him use our bedroom for his radio/computer programming office. I put up with his silly antics...

Bjae K.

I go to local law enforcement officer appreciation at a local church. I go each time no matter where, what religion, culture or whatever, to show my support for him. I attend any function he asks and participate in an online LEOW group. There are lots of things the online LEOW group does to support officers that my husband knows nothing about.

Rita A.

I plan ahead to prepare his favorite meals when he's home to enjoy them. The kids and I try to plan something fun and make sure we tell him we are excited to do this with him so we wait etc. I try to take the kids out if he's trying to sleep off nights so they can be wild and loud outside the house. I try to do stuff that I know he would appreciate taken off his mind while making sure to tell him when I've handled it so he doesn't have to keep a mental list.

Annemarie J.

We keep a "love note" journal. We write special notes to each other. I make his lunch/dinner for him every day so he can have home cooked food. I also do my best to cook for him when he is not working nights. I text him throughout the day just to let him know I love him and appreciate all he does for our family. I attend his work functions. I make time to listen to him.

Jody M.

I make "fancy" dinners for him when he is not working nights. He likes something new all the time so I try to make a new main course every week at least once but often more. I leave him "I love you" notes. I encourage him to stay on the job for as many years as he wants and never pressure him to retire. I encourage him to only take promotions or new assignments that he wants and not do things at work that might work better for us, but he would not like doing. I often thank him for working so hard for us. I also attend all work functions and often bake for his crew. I also try not to call him at work unless it is truly important and time sensitive, knowing he is usually busy. He calls me when he has time so I leave the calling up to him.

Terri W.

I talk things through with him and not put in my opinion until he is done and/or asks for it.

Faith M.

I write notes on the mirror or leave notes in his car. I also bake him lots of goodies. I tell him every day how much I love him and I appreciate everything that he does.

Reese H.

I leave him notes in his lunch box, patrol car, on the mirror, etc., just to let him know how much I appreciate him and all that he does. I also send supportive and loving texts while he is on duty. I also always pack him a good dinner and a thermos full of hot coffee. A day never goes by without me telling him how much I love him and how proud of him I am.

Daniella K.

I leave him notes in different places telling him I love him. He has one that has hung on his bathroom mirror since we got married saying I love him so that he can see it every morning. I will send him a text when he's not expecting it just to say I love him and appreciate him.

Vicky C.

I send him pictures of our daughter because he misses out on a lot of little things. I always make sure to thank him when he takes paid jobs.

Cassie S.

I write lots of notes and we make his favorite treats for him to enjoy when he gets home. Kids and I often hide messages for him in his duffle or around the house. When he stays the weekend at work, I am always sure to answer when he calls and the he gets a couple of minutes of Facetime with the kids.
Bev J.

I'll leave a note in his lunch box, pack a sweet snack, send a random text and every now and then I'll take him something to work. I love meeting him when he's on duty.

Sybil C.

A word from the LEOs:

What things does your wife do that you find supportive?

My wife brings our boys by the office to see me or meets me for lunch when we are able to, which I enjoy and find supportive. My wife is very supportive of me and my career.

Doug. S.

My wife bakes for my crew from time to time. She is very understanding when I have to work late or my schedule gets changed at the last minute. She also lets me vent and talk about my day, which is very helpful. If you are not sure what your LEO likes or feels like at any given time, just ask him. Most guys don't like to play guessing games and just want honest discussion.

Ed W.

What does she do to help you when you are missing your family when working?

She sends me texts with pictures of the boys or lets them call me if I am available to talk.

Doug S.

Any advice or thoughts that you would like to share with other wives to help them better support their husbands?

Be supportive of their career choice because it is not just a job to most it is a calling and what is in our hearts. Be understanding that there will be dinners, holiday, birthdays, school functions, etc. missed because of his career but we hate missing it as much as you hate us not being there. Remember that we can't just turn off being an officer when we are off duty, it's something that is with us 24/7.

Doug S.

Don't pressure them to take an assignment or promotion just because it might have a better schedule. Support them in the decisions they make for what is best for their career and what they want to do each day.

Ed W.

What little things does your husband do to make you know he loves you?

He constantly tells me which feels great!

Elarie S.

He buys me flowers, gifts and takes me on dates. We don't celebrate Valentine's Day because we show our love throughout the year and don't need one day to show it. He sends me texts throughout the day to tell me he loves me and can't wait to come home to me.

Patty. R.

I like to try new recipes. No matter how bad they turn out, he always eats it and never says a word. He will go outside in the cold and fill my windshield washer fluid or start my car to warm it. For me it's not about flowers or candy or gifts but the little things.

Maggie F.

Things that he knows are important to me. Surprising me with my favorite Dunkin Donuts Iced Coffee. Cleaning up the kitchen on a Sunday night when I just want to snuggle and read a book before I start the week over again. Saving the last chocolate donut, even though I know he wants it. Cueing into my down days or the days I just need extra hugs and surprising me with a real good strong bear hug. Letting me cry and not getting ticked off because he wants to move past to solve it.

Annemarie J.

He sends me texts to just say he loves me and is thankful to have me as his wife and mom to our boys. He will get up with the children on his off days and let me sleep in if I am tired or feeling bad or just need a break. If he sees something that he knows I like and we have some extra money he will get it for me. For example, he was working Thanksgiving sales at one of the stores in our county and he saw fuzzy socks, which I love, on sale so he bought some for me along with some chocolate which is my addiction. It's the little things that mean the most.

Melanie S.

He talks about me all the time to friends and coworkers. Randomly buys me something he knows I'll love.

Cassie S.

He listens, he is extremely supportive and VERY patient.
Bjae K.
He tells me several times a day that he loves me, kisses me good night every night and buys me special foods that I love from time to time. He does not buy me flowers because I had to ask him to stop when they bothered my allergies. One thing he does that means a lot to me is that he willingly volunteers to clean up any serious cat litter box messes that are too gross to think about. I'll take that over a dozen roses any day!

Terri W.

How do you find time for the two of you to be alone and connect?

We go on "lunch dates" while the kids are in school if he has a day off. Every night we send the kids to bed at eight and stay up until at least ten to have adult conversation.

Colleen R.

Sadly this is one area in which we could do more. We are pretty good about finding a sitter and having a monthly dinner date. Sometimes, it's in conjunction with an obligation but we make time for ourselves afterwards. I am looking forward to grabbing some time next school year when all four kids are in school. We also have mutual interests that make the dates fun. We love country, antique décor so going "picking" is fun too.

Annemarie J.

We try to do a date night once a month but that is hard at times with four boys and him being on call most of the time. We try to always go to bed together so that we have that time to talk and connect without interruptions from the children.

Vicky C.

We don't! Once you throw kids into the mix, it's really hard. We don't have grandparents to watch our kids and so we rarely have date nights. For now, we go out as a family maybe once a month for our "date night." Last month we watched a movie and had dinner out.

Kelly P.

With my husband's hours, it honestly isn't that difficult. He works twelve hour shifts, on two, off two, on three, etc. so we are able to spend time alone on his off days.

Bjae K.

With five kids, it's hard to find alone time. We try to spend a few hours together at least once a month. In the summer, usually on a Thursday evening, we go hang out with the other cops and wives.

Susan M.

We have such different shifts that we rarely get to spend time alone together. Often, our only method of conversation is via text messages.

Jennifer H.

We always made time for each other… if it meant me waking up in the middle of the night when he came home or him staying up after a midnight tour. Once the kids got older, we had date night and we still continue that tradition.

Elarie S.

We have a hard time because of his schedule but we manage to have date nights. We're blessed to have family and plenty of friends who are willing to watch our daughter so we can go on dates and have "us" time. We also strive to set time each night after our daughter goes to bed to sit and talk with no TV and no phone on to talk over what happened during our day, whether we're having problems that need to be addressed, or just sit and cuddle on the couch and enjoy each other's company. It can definitely be difficult to make time and so tempting to go to bed at night because we're so tired from our days but we have to make sure we come first as a couple.

Patty R.

Every night after we both get off of work, we go into our bedroom and shut the door. We are able to express our feelings towards our day and most of the time get our aggression out by talking to each other before we allow our feelings to carry over to our kids.

Cathy L.

Intimacy: Are You On The Same Page?

If you are married for any period of time, you will find you both have your ups and downs with intimacy. Sometimes you are on the same page, sometimes not. Life and the addition of kids may change what once seemed like a perfect marriage.

An old joke, but always a good one. An elderly couple had been seeing each other for a while. Finally they decided to get married. Before the wedding, they had a long conversation regarding how their marriage might work. They discussed finances, living arrangements and so on. Finally, the old gentleman decided it was time to broach the subject of their physical relationship.

"How do you feel about sex?" He asked, rather tentatively.

"I would like it infrequently" she replied.

The old gentleman sat quietly for a moment, adjusted his glasses, leaned over towards her and whispered, "Is that one word or two?"

How do you spice up a lagging sex drive in you or your husband?

I do little things like make his favorite meal or his favorite dessert, give him a sensual massage and buy a new sexy nightgown. Sometimes I slip personal things into his pockets so he'll find them later on in the day (fortunately it hasn't' led to awkward situations yet ha, ha). I also send him flirty texts or leave him suggestive voice mails.

Patty R.

We don't have a lagging sex life (yet).

Cassie S.

We introduce the "quickie" concept and sometimes that's all that is needed to jump start things. If the other isn't expecting full on romance, and a quickie will do, it's putting it out there that the desire to reconnect is there but the energy level is not. I think honesty is important here because the last thing you want is to feel like your spouse isn't "into" you. Fatigue is a big factor, more than we think. I know if my husband wants to reconnect, but falls asleep on the chair at nine after a long twelve hour day shift, I know that sex is not happening. I might let him know later, that he lost out so that he doesn't think I don't care. But only in a joking kind of way.

Annemarie J.
Like anything, you have to make it work for you. It's really important for a successful union. When we were younger and the kids were in school, the 4-12s made having sex easier. Sometimes you just have to grab the moment.

Elarie S.

Ha! What's that? With our opposite schedules, it's almost impossible. Especially while being super pregnant and having a toddler with me twenty-four/seven. We sometimes really have to plan for sex, with one of us waking up early or staying up late at night. I think with any marriage, it should be important because it's time for you two to connect on an intimate level and so if it feels like it's been a while, then it should become a priority.

Kelly P.

4-12s are great date days for us. Lunch and some alone time before he has to go to work.
It's not all about the physical aspect and you need to connect as a couple for the physical aspect to be desirable for both of you. Make

time to focus on just the two of you and forget about the rest of the world for a few hours.

Terri W.

When It's Not An Easy Fix, It May Be a Medical Issue

There are many medical conditions that can cause a low sex drive including depression, diabetes, high blood pressure, obesity, medication side effects and low testosterone in both men and women. An honest discussion between partners and a medical evaluation with a doctor may be helpful.

Low testosterone:

For men, testosterone naturally declines after age thirty. For some men, the decline is due to other medical issues and a medical evaluation is necessary to determine if testosterone is indeed below normal levels for his age and if so, the cause. For some men low levels of testosterone may cause symptoms that include low libido, erectile dysfunction, fatigue, depression, loss of body hair and decrease in strength. If you suspect low testosterone, consult with your family physician to determine if further medical tests are needed. While medically prescribed testosterone replacement is a remedy for some men, as with all medications, fully discuss with your doctor the risks and benefits of any prescriptions you may consider.

For women, the birth control pill or hormone replacement therapy in older women may sometimes negatively impact a woman's sex drive due to the artificial hormones and unnatural hormone levels in the medication. Peri-menopause and menopause in women causes a drop or imbalance in the body's natural production of estrogen, progesterone and testosterone. Yes, women have and need testosterone but in much smaller levels than men. Pharmaceutical and bio-identical estrogen and/or progesterone and/or testosterone replacement in women may help a lagging sex drive but it requires a prescription and needs to be taken in consultation with a doctor who is well versed in both pharmaceutical and bio- identical hormone replacement.   Prior to visiting your doctor, you may choose to read up on the subject and then find a doctor who understands hormone issues in women.   Bio-identical hormone replacement is not popular with all doctors and you may want to research and understand the issue so that you can make an informed decision with your doctor as to what, if any hormone replacement is right for you. **As with all medication, there are side effects and should not be taken outside of consultation with a doctor to determine if the risks are worth the benefits for you.**

If your husband has become less affectionate, what do you do to make him be more affectionate?

This is going to sound crazy but I just talk to him. My husband is a very direct person and he doesn't like me to beat around the bush and drop hints that something's wrong. He wants me to sit him down and talk to him about any issues or concerns that I have about our marriage. I actually had to sit him down earlier this week to talk to him about how I was feeling, like he had lost interest in me and such. We had a long, good conversation and he makes every effort to make up for the lack of affection and interest.

Patty R.

He and I are outwardly affectionate. Both don't like public displays of affection, but we show our love in other ways often.

Cassie S.

My husband is very affectionate in ways that work for us. He comes up behind me and hugs me and kisses my neck when I'm cooking, he gives me lots of hugs throughout the day and always kisses me goodnight. If I have an issue, I know he is always willing to listen and talk.

Terri W.

I'll point it out to him! I think with my man he is just the type of person that isn't incredibly affectionate, and I learned this about him over the years so I have to give him hints. He is not good about romantic stuff, so I give him suggestions.

Kelly P.

My husband is actually very affectionate most of the time. The only exceptions are when he is very tired or aggravated over something – usually work related.

The little things like leaving a note, sending a text, a phone message. Let him know he's loved and missed when he's working.
Elarie S.

Communication is key. We've talked about deposits and withdrawals in the love account. Non sexual touching is key for me with BIG deposits. If I refuse him sex due to fatigue or whatever, I usually promise to cuddle and rub his hair instead. I think it's important to figure out how each of you receives and communicates love so you aren't wasting your time depositing, and your spouse doesn't receive it as a deposit. For example, if I communicate my love by acts of service, and his laundry is clean and folded in his drawers, but he receives love with time and attention, he's not feeling my deposit.

Annemarie J.

Have you ever had a rough patch in your marriage and if so, what helped you through it?

We have never had a rough patch in our marriage. I have had some cranky hormone induced times and my husband patiently waited it out. I think the fact that we always talk helps keep things from getting rough. If we have an issue we talk about it openly. I don't expect him to guess what is wrong and he does not expect me to guess either. We also let any past discussions stay in the past. We talk respectfully and openly. We both always put the needs of the other first. Neither of us is selfish.

Terri W.

We've had moments where we've argued and fought in our marriage over things but we never stopped communicating through it all. We kept talking and went to separate rooms and thought about what had happened, came back together, and talked through the issue. No matter what rough patches you hit, you have to keep the lines of communication open or things won't get better. You have to be honest with each other.

Patty R.

Nothing serious but our faith in God is what our marriage is founded on.

Cassie S.

A few years ago we reached a point where I often felt like we were nothing more than two people living in the same house. We actually ended up having a huge fight followed by a long heart to heart. Also lots of prayer.

Maggie F.

We haven't had a rough patch but my advice to anyone that does would be to stay committed to your marriage and talk to each other or even a counselor or minister if needed. Spend time just the two of you so that you can reconnect. Do things for each other that will remind them of why they fell in love with you.

Melanie L.

I know it's not helping the book but we really never went through a rough patch. We can't stay mad at each other and it helps make a healthy and happy marriage.

Elarie S.

Helping Out Around the House and Other Chore Duty: A Cause For Marital Discord In Many a Home

Does your LEO help out around the house? I'm guessing some but you each probably have your areas of expertise. Even with lots of spare time due to the shifts they work, not all LEOs do daily laundry, cooking or other such chores but LEOs often tackle a lot of house projects before going to work 4-12 shifts, saving us money. Just a few money saving LEO projects might include installing a new bathroom or kitchen, installing a hot water tank, building a deck, refurbishing a found at the curb piece of furniture into a beautiful sideboard, installing windows (preferably not during a snow storm, been there, done that) or painting the inside and outside of the house. I am great at helping my husband paint. He does all the work and I stand at the ready to run to the store for more paint, drop cloths etc. He helps install computer software and hook up a new computer by leaving the house and calling later in the day to see if it is safe to come home. He lives longer this way.

Our new neighbors, Ed and Peggy asked me to cat sit for the 4th of July weekend. No problem! Cat sitting for neighbors is my area of expertise. Oh wait, one little twist, the added duty of taking care of their chickens. We live in the suburbs and I don't know a darn thing about chickens but how hard can it be? I get the added bonus of all the eggs they lay for my morning breakfast. There really is a difference between store bought and fresh from the hen eggs and I was looking forward to an easy weekend with delicious eggs. Fed the cat and then stopped to check on the chickens and remove my eggs for the first two days. Day three meant changing the chicken's water and letting them out of their coop to stretch their legs in the fenced area by their coop. No problem! Piece of cake! My husband decided to take a walk over with me to take care of the chickens that afternoon. Chickens out, eggs collected and now to change the water. Drop the water bottle on the ground, spill water everywhere but what the heck, no harm no foul/fowl. Ouch! Couldn't resist the pun! Get it all sorted out as I slap at the fleas nipping my legs. Ok maybe it's not all glamour but it's not too bad. Time to put the chickens back in the coop and go home and have a cold drink to reward my hard work. Scatter the peanuts in a nice little line to lure the chickens back into the coop just as Ed showed me how to do. They aren't as dumb as they look! They steal the peanuts but refuse to get close to the coop. I ask hubby to give me a hand getting all five chickens back into the coop. I ask him to walk behind a chicken and get it to come close to me so that I can grab it and throw it into the coop. The darn birds fly! Not far and not high but enough to escape my grasping empty arms. A wild chase ensues around the pen as we both try to grab a chicken. A slip on the ground from the water I spilled. Being careful not to hurt my bad back, but I manage to get mud and chicken poop all over my shorts and legs. I'm not a happy chicken catcher now! Finally manage to grab four chickens and get them into the coop. One to go! The chase is on as we swing at air as the last chicken gives us a run for our money. Finally grab the last dirty smelly chicken and gently toss her into the coop. What the heck? The other four are now back out in the fenced yard. My dear sweet husband left the back door to the coop open! Grrr! Honey! I can't believe you did that and other words are exchanged. Grab them! The chase is on again! Swinging arms, chasing chickens into each other's arms and peanuts tossed to no avail. We give thought to getting my husband's gun and having chicken for dinner, but we figure that Ed and Peggy wouldn't be too thrilled with that idea. Twenty minutes later we have managed to round up the four escaped chickens but of course the fifth chicken sneaks out while we are tossing the last of the four into the coop. She hides behind the coop and the fence. Now what? My husband tries to chase her to my end of the area and I toss my peanuts to lure her. For such a small brain, she is not that stupid. Lots of coaxing, peanut tossing and a broom handle later we finally get the fifth chicken into the coop. In all the commotion, the eggs are smashed, my shorts, legs and shoes are coated with mud, fleas and chicken poop. I thank my husband for the help as we swear off chicken sitting for the rest of our lives and we walk home arm in arm, laughing and ribbing each other over our chicken catching antics. If we survived this escapade, we can survive any Laurel and Hardy moment we can come up with.

Does your husband help out around the house? Do you have any advice to help other wives to get their husbands to help out around the house more?

My husband is very helpful around the house and always has been. When he cleans the bathroom, I tell him how nice it looks and how much I appreciate his hard work. I try to make a point of admiring his leaf raking and other outside work and let him know how much I appreciate that part of his house responsibilities. When I do the laundry, he always thanks me for his clean clothes and thanks me for making him dinner every night. He gushes a bit about how good his meal is and I appreciate that. We truly appreciate what the other does. If someone has a problem getting her husband to help, I'd suggest she tell him exactly what she needs him to do and then be happy for his help. Don't criticize his work and show lots of appreciation, thanking him often. I think it also helps to talk openly about what each person needs to do around the house and start your marriage off with this in mind. If circumstances change such as the birth of a child, talk about what chore duties need to be rearranged.

Terri W.

My husband has always been helpful. I usually have to ask him to bring the laundry down or up (even though it's right in front of the steps.) But if I ask him to vacuum or clean up the kitchen, he is usually fine with it.
Elarie S.

If I want things done I have to write a list. My LEO works very well from a list. He always gets things done like oil changes on the cars, cutting the grass etc. but he wouldn't usually just think to do the dishes or something like that. Especially if it is during the course of his duty days. Off days are different. I might come home and find a new cabinet built in the kitchen or the refrigerator cleaned out. As far as advice? Do not nag. They have an instant instinct to tune out nagging.

Maggie F.

I think that husbands tend to have the same problem with some wives and we tend to forget that. I am not sure I can answer with advice. I have an awesome husband that tries to have something cleaned up for me on his days off. It isn't everyday he is off but I don't clean every day I am off either. When he fixes some things, it can be pretty funny. He helped me in his creative way when I lost my mixer but still had the attachment. He took the attachment, put it on a battery powered drill and made it into a mixer for me. It actually worked!

Bjae K.

My husband hardly helps around the house, mainly because I'm a stay-at-home mom right now, and will be for a couple more years. But when I was working full time, he would occasionally help with the dishes and laundry (but of course doesn't put the laundry away), and would always wash his uniforms since that had to get done every week. It can get frustrating because I like to have a clean house, and when chores pile up, I get stressed out. The thing I have had to do, and still do, is communicate my need for him to help. After eleven years of living with him, he still doesn't do things that I naturally see needs to get done. I can't expect him to read my mind, and I can't instill that sense of urgency into him of cleaning the floors. He would probably never vacuum if it were up to him even though we have pets! Getting on a schedule seems to help. Like every Monday is vacuum. And I do it later in the day after he's woken up and can help. If I ask him to help clean up right when he wakes up at noon, he's going to be grumpy and useless about it. So pick your schedule to what works for both of you.

Kelly P.

I'm a stay at home mom and you would think I completely run the home but he actually helps out quite a bit. He has three days off per week and will always help clean. Deep clean the carpets, wash the cars, pool maintenance etc. I'm very grateful.

Cassie S.

My husband is amazing helping around the house. He cooks, cleans, does laundry, takes care of our daughter etc. I work part time in the evenings during the week after he gets home and on weekends and what I can't get done, he does. On nights I work he has dinner ready when I get home and has things straightened up. He feels like it's our house and I take care of our daughter all day and shouldn't have to do all the housework by myself. Talk to your husband about how you're feeling.

Patty R.

This is a definite point of contention in my house – housework. He helps out more than he used to, but still not enough to make a real dent in the overall chore that is housework.

Jennifer H.

My husband helps out a lot around the house and with our four boys. He says that we are in this together and need to work together to get things done so that we have that much more time together. A funny story that just happened this weekend is that we worked together cleaning our master bathroom and later he told me that he knew it sounded crazy but he enjoyed us spending time together cleaning because it gave us time together to talk and enjoy each other's company. I would tell other LEOWs to express their wants and expectations with their spouse. For most of us, we feel it is our jobs as the wife to do the housework and care for the children but if you will let your husband help you, you will find that he actually wants to help and enjoys it. If you have a spouse that feels you should do everything at home, talk to him and let him know that you need help. Even if you stay at home you still need a break so get him involved so you aren't doing everything by yourself. Also, tell him if he pitches in and helps that will make the housework get done faster which means the two of you will have more time together. A great way to spend time together is preparing meals together. My husband and I enjoy cooking together and it gives us time to talk about the day and just enjoy each other's company.

Melanie L.

My husband would say he helps out around the house. We have certain responsibilities and we handle them as needed. For example, my husband does car maintenance. He schedules both cars for oil changes, inspections, tires, etc. He handles all lawn care, shoveling, yard maintenance, flower beds, landscaping and all inside repair jobs. I handle everything else due to the nature of being a full time employee inside the home. When I was working as an RN the workload was shared a bit more, as we both juggled watching the kids and being the parent "on" for different days but I prefer our system now. I would encourage the wives to give their husband a few jobs that would make their life easier and write them down somewhere if needed as well as a timeline for completion. Then leave them to it. I find my husband works more efficiently if I stress what a big help it would be, with a little wink. Early in our marriage, I spelled it out, if you help, I am not so tired at the end of the day, get it?

Annemarie J.

Do you have any marriage advice to help other LEOWs? Simple, profound, humorous, what worked for you or any thoughts you would like to share?

As a wife of 26 years, who has "survived" infidelity and came out on the other side with a stronger marriage, I have learned a lot about it and wanted to offer a little advice. Marriage is not 50/50...you both have to give 100%. You both have to build hedges to protect your marriage. Just like women need affection, affirmation, to be listened to and understood, so do men. And, of course, they need sex, but they also have a deep need to be respected, especially by the person they chose to stand by their side. Nagging, jealousy, disinterest, whining, busy-ness with other things, complaining...all of these things push a husband away. Even good men who "would never cheat" have fallen and done the very thing that disgusts them because another woman built them up and filled a need that wasn't being met at home. I'm not saying there is any good excuse for adultery, simply stating a sad fact. Of course, there are some men (and women) who have warped morals or character flaws and will cheat no matter what, but don't automatically assume that's the case. Take a close look at your marriage and start making changes to yourself. Become the spouse that you want your husband to be. Either he will be forced to change and your marriage will start healing or he won't and you will know that you gave it everything you had.

Make an investment in protecting and caring for your marriage like you would anything that is precious to you. Read books on marriage (I highly recommend the owner's manual - the Bible). Schedule time with your hubby and don't let the busy-ness of life steal it away. Don't be afraid to seek counseling, even if you have to go on your own. Put your marriage above everything else because it's meant to last a lifetime.

Angee K.

I think some of the best advice I have heard, I believe came from Ann Landers. She said each night to ask yourself "what is it like to be married to me?" Would you want to come home to you every night? Are you cranky? Dressed like a slob? Etc. If you woke up next to you, would you pull the covers over your head or sneak out of bed each morning? Be the person you wish to be married to.
I also think you need to put your marriage first. Sometimes your own needs will need to take a back seat. If you put one hundred percent into your marriage you will reap far more in return. I also think you need to treat your marriage as if divorce is not an option. Live each day with your spouse as if you were not able to ever leave. You will find yourself working that much harder to make it work. If it won't matter in one year or five years, don't fight about it. Pick and choose your battles.
Finally, when you are wrong, and even sometimes when you are not, say I'm sorry. Admit your error or your part in a fight and apologize with sincerity. It will go a long way!

Terri W.

Keep the lines of communication open through everything that happens. Be there for your LEO. He goes through a lot on the job and he deals with people every day who are not very receptive to the police's help and he needs to know that he can come home and feel loved and supported and not attacked. Show your husband that you appreciate him throughout the year.

Patty R.

Don't demand anything of them. Neither one of us responds well to that. For his sanity, we take a small trip every few months. Disneyland, Lake Tahoe, etc. We always like something on the calendar.

Cassie S.

Communication is key, sometimes you just have to communicate in different ways. No man I know will pay any attention at all if you just stand in front of them and rattle off all their flaws. Try honey do lists, taking them out to breakfast, making a "date" once a week for major discussions or something like that to set the stage for the conversation.

Maggie F.

I think the most important quality in a LEOW is flexibility. Don't be afraid to make plans for fun family events when it fits your officer's schedule. We've had breakfast dates to reconnect when the kids are in school. We've taken the kids to a museum in the middle of the week, because my officer is off. We go out to dinner, in the middle of the week, because it's cheaper and quieter than weekends. I plan fun things for the kids and me to do on night shift nights at home when I can snuggle with them and be safe inside my house.

Annemarie J.

Never leave the house without a kiss. Tell him you love him every day. Let him know he's your best friend.

Elarie S.

Be understanding because LEO life is totally different than most others. There will be times he comes in and feels great and wants to spend time with everyone or go somewhere and there will be times he just wants to rest because he had a tough day. Always let him know you love him and don't take him for granted because as much as we don't want to think about it, that may be the last time you get to say this to them. Enjoy every minute you have together. Don't let the little things cause problems or arguments because it's not worth it because again, we never know when they walk out the door if they will be walking back through it at the end of the day. Leave love notes or send texts letting him know you are thinking of him and love him. The most important thing for any marriage, but a huge thing in ours, is to pray for your spouse. We all know we are not guaranteed another day but our spouses have a dangerous job and need all of the prayers they can get, especially from their wife. If you are having a hard time with anything that he is doing or that pertains to his job, talk about it with him or if it's something you feel you can't talk to him about talk to another LEOW. Trust your husband because they deal with all kinds of people and work crazy long hours.

Melanie L.

I have found that by supporting my husband's career and becoming more involved I am more comfortable in what he does for a living. I will bake cookies for the officers and take them to the station just before roll call, make sandwiches and drop them off during a holiday, offer them bottled water when it is extremely hot, etc. I attend community meetings whenever the police are there and I am sure to introduce myself to them. I go on ride alongs frequently to see what goes on and that has made me more comfortable when he is working. In turn, that has strengthened our marriage because he sees that I support him, his brothers and sisters in blue and his career. Another piece of advice is to listen, listen and listen some more. His job is stressful and he often sees the worst point in one's life, so he may or may not want to get it off of his chest.

Jennifer H.

You have to be happy with who you are and with yourself before you can make a marriage work. You should be submissive to your husband; some people cringe at that word submissive but those people that cringe don't take time to understand it. It simply means to respect one another; you don't need your spouse's permission to do anything or spend money but you should respect your spouse enough to discuss what you want to do or buy instead of just going out and acting as though you are still single.

Bjae K.

Do you recommend any books or videos about marriage?

A great movie that has such a good message is "Fireproof." It teaches couples to not give up even when you think the other one has and to try to win them back and make things right.

Patty R.

Books: The Five Love Languages by Gary Chapman, The Power of Prayer to Change Your Marriage by Stormie Omartian, The Love Dare, The Power of Praying Wife by Stormie Omartian, Draw Close a Devotional for Couples by Willard and Joyce Harley.
Movies: Fireproof and the movie Courageous.

Melanie L.

My Minister recommended The Love Dare for people who have a difficult marriage but also for people who are very happily married. It is Bible based and good for Christians to read.

Terri W.

To Wear or Not To Wear The Wedding Ring?

Most married people make a decision prior to the wedding ceremony about wearing wedding rings. More often than not, both husband and wife wear the wedding ring. A lot of meaning goes into that ring! It's not just a simple piece of jewelry, it's something you will wear every day for the rest of your life to remind you of your love and commitment to your spouse and his love and commitment to you. After twenty five years it might show some wear and tear. After fifty years of daily wearing an intricately carved ring may have a little less detail but will still evoke those same thoughts of love and commitment within a couple's hearts.

For a LEO, to wear a ring or not is not always such an easy decision with added weights on the wedding ring decision scale to consider. Will it impede their ability to do their job by getting caught on something or will it give their "customers" knowledge about a LEO's family life that a LEO would prefer to keep private. A wife might prefer he wear a ring so that women a little too attracted to her husband and the uniform be made aware that he is indeed already "taken."

Does your LEO wear a wedding ring to work? If he does not, why does he choose not to and how do you feel about it?

My husband stopped wearing his ring to work after someone he had arrested threatened to hurt his wife. The criminal, of course, had no knowledge of his actual family situation, but that was enough for him to take it off. The less the bad guy knows, the better. It really bothered me at first, but I understand why he did it so I support his decision. He would do anything to keep us safe. I am ok with that.

Hillary. A.

Mine wore his until he went to the academy. He's left handed and he had an incident that almost ripped his ring finger off. He used to wear it when he was off duty but now he keeps it on a chain with his St. Christopher medal.

Tanya D.

Never takes it off! Well once for surgery. He has the kids trained. He points to it and my oldest (4) says, "Yeah that means God gave Daddy Mommy."

Brianna J.

Mine has taken his off when doing something around the house and accidentally left for work without it. Within five minutes he noticed and called me to meet him at the end of the drive with it because he doesn't go anywhere without it. We live in an area where everyone knows everyone so they know he's married anyway. He has pictures of us all over his office as well.

Vicky C.

Mine doesn't and doesn't carry pictures of me or our children in his car. He would rather the people he arrests/deals with not know who we are. I am one hundred percent comfortable with his decision, I like that our safety is a priority.

Connie D.

No. My husband does narcotics and interdiction. He does not wear it because he doesn't want to risk the thugs he deals with knowing too much.

Hillary M.

Mine does unless he is called out for SWAT. Then he puts it on his key ring. My request, as his ring is Titanium and if something happens to his fingers/hand they can't cut the ring off.

Nicolle H.

Mine always wears his. Funny story to go with this. He pulled over a car filled with mid-twenties women. When asked where they were going, the driver responded that they were headed out for her bachelorette party. "I see you are married (pointing to his ring). Any advice for my husband to be?" And being who he is, he responds "Yeah…. A happy wife is a happy life. Have a nice day Ma'am."

Emily T.

"Badge bunnies": A wedding ring is no obstacle!

What's a "Badge Bunny" you ask? Why it's the same as a "Holster Sniffer, Light Bar Licker, Donut Slut, 5-0 Hoe, Belt Keeper Creeper, Badge Fly, Cruiser Critter, Holster Hoochie, Handcuff Heifer, Cruddy Cruiser Kitty, Copper Hopper, Donut Dolly, Buckle Rider, Badge Fly, Shield Slut, Baton Polisher, Holster Whore and Badge Buzzard." In short, a cop Groupie who will do anything and everything to make her next conquest a cop, and the next and the next after that one too. No, they are not looking for love or a life partner but just want to sleep with a cop. She usually makes no secret of her goal and is pretty brazen and at times pathetic in her single minded mission. Is the cop married or single? Makes no difference. Some women are proud "Badge bunnies", some are in self-denial and some are wrongly accused when their only intention is to flirt. Some guys love to use them, some are repelled by them. Some guys dabble on the wild side and then regret it. As LEOWs, we all know about "Badge bunnies" and we might laugh at them, ignore their existence or we might secretly fear them. One more thing to add to the long list of new experiences that your hubby forgot to mention to you prior to marrying him. Oh Joy!

A "Badge bunny" encounter:

I was twenty seven years old, about a year out of Rookie school and one of the few women in my department. I had been riding patrol in a poorer sector of town for a few days and each day that I passed an older man of about seventy, he would smile and wave from the front stoop of his building. I'd give him a smile and a big wave, building good will in the community. One day he waved me down and stumbled over to the patrol car in a haze of alcohol fumes. With a big toothless grin he said "I wanna ax you somethin. Do you have kids?" I told him that no, I wasn't married. He replied "I didn't ax if you was married, I just axed if you had kids." "No", I replied, "no kids." He shuffled ever closer to the car and while swaying and barely standing upright, he told me what was on his extremely foggy mind: "Do you wanna go bowling with me tonight?" Now I know you are thinking, but of course she said yes! What woman could turn down that invitation? Alas, I forced myself to say that I could not go bowling with him but, I let him know that I appreciated the offer. He took the rejection well and shuffled on back to his stoop. I give him credit for still having the gumption to give it a try. Apparently, "Badge bunnies" can be male or female, young or old and come in all shapes and sizes.

The uniform has the power to attract! Yes, it's true and there is no doubt about it in my mind. Men who would never give me the time of day while I was in civilian clothes would often flirt, ask for my number or a date when I was in uniform. I found it funny, ironic, strange, at times annoying and at times a bit of an ego boost. Of course, my ego quickly realized that their attraction had nothing to do with me but the uniform I was wearing. I was never as sought after when in civilian clothes as when in uniform.

Officers in uniform are out in the public eye all day every day, coming into contact with people they would never have the opportunity to speak with in their civilian life. The uniform and the situation can lead both the civilian and the LEO to act in ways they might not normally, flirting with and sometimes approaching a person they would normally not even think of approaching.

Does that mean all LEOs take advantage of the opportunities? By no means. Some LEOs love the attention, love to flirt and that's as far as it goes and some are clueless that they are even being flirted with. Some LEOs cheat on girlfriends and spouses. Is it more frequently than the unfaithful rate of the general population? I don't know the statistics but I tend to doubt it. If a person is going to be unfaithful, they will find a way. Be it meeting someone while taking a police report, an executive with his secretary, a doctor at a conference, a construction worker who stops for a beer at the bar on the way home from work or someone who uses the internet to find a willing partner. Accidents don't happen, it takes work to make an affair happen. In my experience, most LEOs, like the general population, love their spouse and would never be unfaithful. Having said all of that, some LEOWs worry.

A LEO shares her thoughts:

When working you always get the "you can put me in handcuffs anytime" or I didn't do it" as they throw their hand in the air, "You can frisk me if you need to" etc. I usually laugh and sarcastically say "I haven't heard that one before." But on a more positive note, I have had men compliment me on my appearance in uniform, in a nice way. We are a representation of our police department and should take pride in the uniform.

Lori T.

What would you say to a LEOW whose husband told her about a "Badge bunny" and this LEOW is concerned?

This is going to sound really harsh, and I apologize in advance. Your worrying about this is an insecurity of yours and is not something that you should project on to your husband since he has been honest and upfront about her. The only thing you can do is to continue to have open and honest communication with your spouse. Sure tell him about your feelings and fears, but in such a way that doesn't accuse him of any wrong doing. You want him to continue to tell you about things and if you pitch a fit about things he will stop talking.

Jessica B.

I would ask her if she has specific concerns or is she speculating? If her husband told her about it, I would continue to watch and listen for things he's NOT saying. But, in my experience, the fact that he mentioned it is either a big deal or not a big deal. It could go either way. Also, I would tell her to trust her gut. Our womanly intuition is usually one hundred percent accurate.

Annemarie J.

I had an experience with a "needy" woman friend... my husband was oblivious and in denial that she wanted more than friendship, until I finally made it clear that he needs to explain to her that he can only be her friend. Thankfully, it worked out. I did make it clear that work it out or end the friendship.

Elarie S.

I've never been in that situation, and to me it really sound like a teenage-ish situation, but I would tell her to do what she feels would be right and that would make her feel in control of the relationship. If she is worried her husband will step out of the marriage, there may be insecurities and lack of trust, and that maybe they should work on their relationship. It's not necessarily to blame the LEOW, but she and he need to figure out why she is concerned, if she should be concerned and do they have any issues to work out.

Kelly P.

Have confidence in your husband, your marriage and yourself. If a man or woman is going to stray, he or she would stray regardless of what your partner does for a living. If your marriage is strong there is no reason to be concerned. If there is an issue with your marriage, resolve it; if the issue lies with your confidence, fix it.

Jennifer H.

If you trust your husband and he has never given you a reason not to, I wouldn't give the "Badge bunny" a second thought. Most of them are pretty pathetic and are more entertaining than anything else. If your

LEO is strong and loves you, nothing she does can sway him. If he does fall into her trap, you are going to have to work on your relationship. As of now, I have no experience with this so I cannot offer much more advice.

Maggie F.

When we were first dating my husband told me that some civilian PD women voted him "best butt" in the office. I agreed with their assessment and did not give it another thought or worry. I knew where his heart and loyalties were (and still are.)

Terri W.

It would depend on the context of what was said but again, regardless of the context I am not a jealous person; there is no place for jealousy in a marriage. I would ask the LEOW why she is concerned; lack of self- esteem?

Bjae K.

As long as your husband has not given you a reason to not trust him, I would not worry about her. If you feel confident in your marriage and that your LEO loves you then don't second guess your marriage or him. If you show that you are jealous or start questioning him, he will start feeling like you don't trust him. Trust is a big thing in the foundation of a marriage. If he is being honest with you and telling you about her then he probably is not interested in her. Take his telling you about her as a sign of honesty on his part and as long as he is being honest with you don't worry about her. It doesn't matter that she is a "Badge bunny" if your husband loves you and is committed to you then she can't be with him no matter how hard she tries.

Melanie L.

A fellow LEOW is worried about the new female LEO that her husband is training. She is pretty and single. This LEOW thinks her LEO should ask for the trainee to be given to someone else to train and she is thinking of contacting his boss and speaking to him. What do you say to this concerned LEOW?

I would suggest that she calmly and nicely express her concerns to her husband and listen to what he has to say. I would also tell her to understand that this female LEO is probably not remotely interested in your husband and that she is aware that he is married. As long as the female LEO does not over step her bounds, don't worry about it. She wants to be a LEO as much as men and that is her primary focus when at work. Even if she has your husband in her sights, he still has the power to say no. If the female LEO acts inappropriately, he could explain the situation to his boss and ask for the female LEO to be transferred to another training officer. As long as the female acts professionally, you have nothing to fear and your husband should train her like any male LEO he would train. If you have an opportunity, get to know her. You might find that you like her and also find out you have nothing to fear. My husband works with a female and I like her a lot.

Terri W.

I would say no way, don't contact his boss! Wives should not interfere with their LEO's jobs, under all "normal" circumstances. Who cares if the new female is pretty and single? It is also not fair to the female officer to single her out because of her status, because it is likely she has hurdled so many bars to get to where she is. And even more so, as a woman in law enforcement, she is likely to have additional challenges in this job. There is a beautiful new officer at my husband's department who is also married and my husband has told me that some of the guys were worried. They were worried that she wouldn't be taken seriously as a cop, and that it would be hard to train her and be around her. As the months went on and she completed training, she is a hungry cop that is doing great! I met her once and she was professional and awesome.

Kelly P.

It is his job, stay out of it. He doesn't need anyone calling and being "his mommy." Again express your concerns but trust him enough to have some integrity.

Jessica B.

I would tell her respectfully as I could, that the decision is her LEO''s to make. She can discuss and give her advice all she wants to her LEO but at the end of the day, she needs to have trust and respect for her officer.

Annemarie J.

As far as I know, the only cheating my husband has done is on his diet. I worry more about finding fast food wrappers in his car than I do about a female trainee. I trust him until I am given a reason not to and so far I have had no reason to worry. When he was a Field Training Officer (FTO), it never occurred to me to be concerned about his trainees, female or otherwise. I would never interfere in his job.

Maggie F.

She has no right to contact his boss and she needs to get over being jealous. I personally would ask my husband if she is blonde and would she do in a "pinch." (Just joking)

Bjae K.

If he has not cheated on you and you trust him then don't worry about it. I would not ask him to ask for a different trainee because that will make him feel that you don't trust him and his boss will possibly look at his asking in a negative way. If you are worried about it you need to express your concerns to him so that you don't end up becoming jealous, which can do harm to your marriage.

Melanie L.

Of course I would be concerned. Be aware, get involved, but I definitely would not go to his boss. Marriage is based on trust. If he is a good guy and is committed to your marriage you should have nothing to worry about. But I would turn up the flirty, sexy side of you when he comes home. Let him know why he married you!

Elarie S.

A LEO shares her thoughts:

Being a woman in a predominately male position is quite interesting. I will tell you what I tell all of the women coming aboard this whirlwind career. You have to have pride in yourself. Make smart decisions because we are NOT men and don't always have the strength of a man so be smart and do not put yourself in dangerous positions if you can help it. Those who have worked with me know I will be there when things go bad. I stay in shape because this work demands it. I want to be prepared for the worst and the worst could happen at any moment. It's okay to joke with the guys but have respect for yourself. Of all the years I've been on this department of over three hundred officers, not one has made an advance on me or spoken to me in a derogatory way. Why? It's all about how you carry yourself. I don't try to be someone I'm not. If you sleep around, you will get a reputation and it will follow you till the end whether it's true or not. I get along with everyone, I'm fair and I think I carry myself in a way that men respect me. I speak highly of my husband and my successful marriage. If you constantly talk bad about your relationship, it's an invitation for some men and they think they have a chance. A good friend told me recently that he's never heard anyone say anything bad about me, rumors etc. Not that men haven't commented about me behind my back, which I guess is expected. I consider this an accomplishment in itself and it was nice to hear.

Lori T.

Your LEOW friend is concerned because her husband has been getting text messages from a woman at work. They don't really have a reason to communicate outside of work and every time he is asked about the texts, he mumbles and deletes them. In your opinion, might he be cheating and what should your LEOW friend do?

If you are concerned that he is communicating with someone more than he should be and that he is keeping stuff from you, then yes, you need to confront him about it but choose your words wisely. Don't go to him and accuse him of anything because that could make him feel that you don't trust him and could cause harm to your marriage. I would make sure he didn't have a bad day at work when I talked to him so that he doesn't come into the conversation in a bad mood. I would tell him that you are not accusing him of anything but you feel uncomfortable with him talking to her so much and deleting messages from her makes you feel he is trying to hide something. I would definitely not just hope it stops if it is something that you are seriously worried about because the worry and doubt will get to you. If he has or does cross the line, then I would pray about it and see what you feel you really need to do for your marriage and yourself. If he has never cheated before and you really love him and want to try to work it out and feel that you would be able to trust him again after some work, then I would suggest counseling as a couple and for yourself to be able to deal with the emotions and to be able to move forward. I would also get some books on marriage that deal with trust and cheating.

Melanie L.

I would suggest that she express her concerns in a neutral environment. Timing is important. You don't want to start an argument while he's getting ready for work, or even as he is just coming home after shift. Maybe have her suggest going to dinner, in a low profile place, and just express her concerns. Remind her to listen to him and not be accusatory and also explain why she is concerned. They should leave the dinner with the goal of a common understanding, some sort of guideline, like not texting with females because it makes me feel like _____.

Kelly P.

You have something to worry about. If he is not hiding something he would not be deleting messages. I would be in his face before you can say "Cheater!"

Elarie S.

I would say that at a minimum he is crossing a line that could lead to cheating if he is not cheating already. My LEOW friend needs to sit down with her husband and calmly discuss why she is concerned and why this kind of behavior can be a threat to their marriage. She can ask him point blank if something inappropriate is going on and if he denies it, my friend needs to help him understand why this behavior needs to change. If he fails to see the problem with his behavior, counseling may be needed. If he refuses to attend counseling, my LEOW friend should go alone so that she can better understand her own feelings and what she ultimately needs to do for her marriage, herself and her children.

Terri W.

The issue lies with the husband and it needs to be addressed with the husband. People only do to you what you allow them to, so let him know that this is unacceptable and needs to be discussed and a conclusion found that makes both of you comfortable. That does NOT mean that you should approach the subject with this woman.

Jennifer H.

Ask him why he finds it necessary to hide her and the texts, why he deletes them when brought up and if he isn't happy in the marriage then maybe consider separation or get a divorce.

Bjae K.

This is a tough one. There is probably is cheating of some kind. You need to confront him and directly ask what is going on.

Jessica B.

Ask the LEO about the nature of this relationship point blank. See what his response is. Then, I would do some investigating either before or after she pulls phone records from her cell phone carrier. With whatever information I gathered, I would point blank ask what was going on with her and ask him to set some boundaries with her. Or he would have some problems with his wife. If his wife is uncomfortable, he already has marital problems whether he realizes the extent or not.

Annmarie J.

In this age of technology, I believe the line between appropriate and inappropriate has blurred greatly. It may be true that the communication is innocent but I would definitely confront my LEO. Who cares if he knows you checked the bill? If he isn't doing anything wrong, he won't care. I am not the "keep quiet" type so I would never be able to just sit back and wait it out.

Maggie F.

Your LEOW friend comes to you and tells you that she knows that her LEO is cheating on her and she wants to kill him but at the same time she wants to crawl into a ball and die. What do you say to her?

You have to decide if what you have is worth holding on to. Will he stop seeing her? And most important, you probably are going to need professional help either way.

Elarie S.

You can only control your behavior, no one else's. Only you can decide what and how much you are willing to take.

Jessica B.

I once told my husband that if he ever felt compelled to cheat on me, she better be richer than me and prettier than me because I would see to it that he would be left looking at her while paying me everything he had for the rest of his life. That being said, I have never been in this position so I am not at all sure how I would handle it. My heart goes out to anyone who has.

Maggie F.

I would first ask her how she knew. I would help her rationally determine if she's thinking or just jumping to conclusions, if she actually has proof or she's assuming based on facts or feelings. Then, I would ask her what this means for her? How she feels about it? Does this mean she is through with the marriage or does she want to work on the issues in her marriage? Whether she wants to confront her spouse and what boundaries she feels she needs to maintain with him. What does finding out that he is cheating make her want to do? Then I would support her in whatever she decided and be there to commiserate if she needed to talk. Mostly, I would encourage her to maintain some class even if she wanted to let her "ghetto" hang out.

Annemarie J.

Kill him literally or figuratively? She needs to confront him and go from there. Some people decide to work through it and some find no other way but divorce.

Bjae K.

You cannot stop him from cheating if it is something that he wants to do. I would definitely let him know that you are aware of his cheating and that you need to discuss it so that you can figure out what to do as far as your marriage. I have been cheated on in a previous relationship (we were engaged) so I know from experience that you will go through every emotion there is from being mad to crying. With some people it is a one-time mistake and you can save your marriage if you both are committed to it. If he has never cheated before and you want to save your marriage then talk to him about it and see what you need to do for both of you to be able to save your marriage. It will take time to trust again but don't let it control your marriage forever because that can do as much harm as cheating. Be open and honest with him about your feelings as well.

Melanie L.

While trying to keep her marriage together is my main suggestion, if my friend does not want the marriage to continue or she fears her husband might leave her I would suggest that prior to confronting her husband, my friend first seek a consultation with a divorce attorney to know exactly what her rights are and what if any steps she may need to take to protect herself. I would hate to find that her husband had cleaned out bank accounts or made other preparations for a divorce to be with his "girlfriend," leaving my friend in shock and in a very bad financial situation. She needs to be prepared for the worst. I would then suggest that she speak with a counselor if needed to understand her own feelings so that she can have a rational discussion with her husband. They may, as a couple, decide to work out the marriage and get therapy or they may decide that it is not fixable and that they need to divorce. In either case, she has prepared herself for any decision they may make without having to worry about her husband taking advantage of her fragile state. No one can walk all over you unless you lay down and let them.

Terri W.

Unfortunately, these things happen, in LEO marriages and of course all marriages/relationships. I would be as supportive of a friend as possible, and assure her that she is going to go through many feelings of hurt, anger, etc. She needs to also be reminded that her worth is not determined by any man or any person, and that she should always take care of herself and children if she has any. And especially if there are children involved, spare them the details to protect them from the added pain.

Kelly P.

Have you ever been divorced and if so, are you happy with your decision or do you regret it?

Yes, I have been divorced. Yes I am happy with the decision, but I am sad that we were not able to work out our differences. We were young. We were married for seven years. I am married again… this time to a LEO and we have been together for eighteen years. I attribute our success to the fact that we were both married before, and have very drastically different views on marriage than mainstream. We talk about everything. Even things that are uncomfortable.

Jessica B.

Yes I have been divorced and do not regret it. I did everything that I could to try to save my marriage. I gave more than one hundred percent but unfortunately, it was an unhealthy marriage. I also do not regret it because I wouldn't be with my LEO who treats me better than I have ever been treated. I honestly couldn't ask for a better husband and father to my children.

Melanie L.

Is Divorce More Common among LEOs?

We all "know" that law enforcement officers have a much higher divorce rate than the general public. We all know the statistic that seventy five percent of LEOs are divorced and it's repeated in every article and many conversations about LEO marriage. Unfortunately, the seventy five percent number is never sourced to a research study. Look around and ask yourself, are seventy five percent of the LEOs who you know divorced? Does their divorce rate seem that much higher than your civilian friends of the same age, education and financial background? Wait one second! Perhaps it's possible that what we all know may not be true. Sigh, breath deep, relax. According to a 2009 study by Shawn P. McCoy and Michael G. Aamodt, the 2000 US census shows fewer LEOs are divorced than their civilian counterparts. Yes, statistics show that it's possible that "common knowledge" may not be so knowledgeable. The Study gives the following statistics: The divorce and separation rate for all LEOs was 14.47% vs the national average of 16.96% and when demographics and income are added, the expected rate would be 16.35%. The five broad occupations with the highest divorce rates are dancers and choreographers (43.05%), bartenders (38.43%), massage therapists (38.22%), gaming cage workers (34.66%), and extruding machine operators (32.74%). The five occupations with the lowest divorce rates were media and communications equipment workers (0.00%), agricultural engineers (1.78%), optometrists (4.01%), transit and railroad police (5.26%), and clergy (5.61%).*

The authors give the caveat that these numbers reflect divorced or separated officers and civilians at any given time and not those who have remarried because the 2000 United States Census gives a snapshot at the moment the census was taken. Comparing LEOs and civilians in this situation, gives the marriage edge to LEOs. In any case, throw conventional wisdom out the window, be glad that you did not marry a dancer or choreographer and enjoy your marriage to a LEO. Statistics are on your side!

Throw into the mix that the only marriage that is in the control of you and your LEO is your own. If every LEO in the world was divorced, you and your LEO still have the power to decide if you will stay married or divorce.

*A comparison of Law Enforcement Divorce Rates with Those of Other Occupations. Shawn P. McCoy   Michael G. Aamodt   Published online 20 October 2009 Springer Science + Business Media LLC 2009

Kids

Kids, children, rug rats, crumb snatchers and whatever other terms of endearment you may call them, most of all they are our everything and our universe! LEO families are just like other families with a few added zigs to our zags.

> Sitting outside, enjoying the sun and watching my hubby train a new detection dog. He says to our 7 year old daughter, "Put the heroin in the black box and the cocaine in the brown." Only in a LEO home...
> Heather C.

Once you and your LEO have been together for a while, adding a child into the mix might seem the natural course of things. After all, that is what a lot of married couples do- they start a family. While all new parents worry about money, keeping their children safe, college and million other things, LEO families have a very different set of concerns.

Once the decision is made to start a family there are many things soon to be parents must consider. Will mom stay at home or will daycare be utilized, is probably one of the first things to come up. LEO salaries are tight. Being a one income family can be tough in this day and age under the best of circumstances, however, as you will soon see it can be done. If mom must or chooses to work, then day care will be a consideration. When our first son was born, we were fortunate to work a schedule that kept my son home and out of daycare for the first two years of his life. However, when my LEO was accepted to the police academy, we needed to find care for him. Shopping for a daycare is stressful; shopping for day care with a LEO is on a whole other plane. While I was inquiring about curriculum and discipline policies, he was checking emergency exits, door locks, window access, playground safety, security codes and a hundred other little details. On one of our visits to a well-known chain daycare center, we walked out onto the playground and instantly saw a little girl who had flipped her tricycle up against the fence and was calling for help. Not a single worker noticed, let alone went to her rescue. After my LEO righted her and her bike, he turned around and walked out leaving me to apologize to the director and follow him.

Eventually there is grade school to consider. Do you live in the same town where your LEO works? Is it safe for your children to attend the local public school or are you considering private school or homeschooling? The definition of "safe" changes dramatically when your spouse is a cop. They see more evil, hear more evil and know more evil. They see that big brick building as a potential crime scene for school shootings, hunting grounds for pedophiles and a potential pool of members for gang bangers and drug dealers.

Forget about play dates. I have had parents actually tell me they are not comfortable with their children playing at our house because my husband has a gun. I'm sorry, but I can assure you that he does not leave loaded firearms lying around the house like décor. If anything they are safer at my house because my children know that guns are NOT toys and they wouldn't even think to expose their friends to a weapon. On the other hand, we do not generally allow our children to go to homes of their friends whose parents we do not know personally. My LEO constantly questions every single potential interaction. What if someone in the house hates cops? Will they harm our child? Has he arrested someone in the family? Will they take it out on one of our boys? Is someone in the house "dirty"? The list goes on and on. In our case, it works out fine. The boys enjoy each other's company, they are very involved in sports and they love to hang out with their cousins.

Then there is that LEO schedule. It is almost a given that every LEO spouse is a single parent about 90% of the time. My LEO does as much as he can, he works the night shift so he sleeps while we are at work and school and meets the boys off their respective school buses in the afternoon however, and I can count on one hand the number of practices or games he makes it to during baseball season. I don't mind, I know it's part of the life but it definitely took some getting used to. Independence is a must!

As unique as it is raising LEO kids, it's just as exciting, challenging and rewarding as it is for any parent. All the regular stuff is there, you just have a few extra things to adjust to. Your little ones may worry excessively for the parent's safety, act out in an extended absence or have a better sense of situational awareness and good and evil.

Do you think children are necessary for a marriage to work? Do you or others you know not have children and do those marriages work?

We know a few childless couples who have been very happy for many years.

Elarie S.

We do not have children by choice and have been happily married for over twenty years. We have many family members and friends who do not have children and they are all happily married for many years. I think it depends partly on if you are childless by choice and if not by choice, do the two people in the marriage turn to each other for support if they wanted children but could not have them. It could be an issue that tears a couple apart or brings them closer. It depends on how the couple handles it. We love our nieces and nephews beyond words and are happy being their Aunt and Uncle.

Terri W.

Children become a part of any marriage but having children should not be the only reason for a marriage. I also do not believe that children should be the only focus of a marriage or the reason for staying together in any relationship.

Maggie F.

Absolutely not. I think way too many people feel as though having kids will fix a marriage or bring a troubled couple back together when it actually tears them further apart. Marriage takes a ton of work and when you add kids in the mix, it only adds more work.

Bjae K.

No, I don't feel like you have to have children to have a wonderful marriage. God puts two people together for a reason. I know couples who can't have children and they are devoted to each other, charities, church, etc.

Krissy A.

Have you struggled with infertility and if so, do you have any words of wisdom for other women?

I had a miscarriage before my oldest was born. If I didn't have my husband to lean on I don't know what I would have done.

Elarie S.

I have two kids from a previous marriage so when my present husband and I got married we did try for a year and nothing happened. We agreed to try for a year and if nothing happened we chose that we would enjoy the kids that we do have and enjoy having each other and the time we have on earth. I know that I personally have two kids but I went through a period of time where I was depressed because I couldn't give my husband a child of his own. He is extremely supportive and is okay with not having any kids of his own. We live life to the fullest and enjoy each other.

Bjae K.

I have been pregnant eight times and had six miscarriages and one near loss. I consider my two boys miracles and am grateful every day for them. Still, I feel the loss of my other babies acutely on a regular basis and it has taken many years to get over the anger and sadness. As hard as all the loss was, I would do it all over again. If we had not been fortunate enough to have two, we would have adopted and still might one day. There are many children out there who need someone to love them and we have a lot of love to give.

Maggie F.

Do your kids wear police clothing in public? Do you? Why or why not?

Once in a while they would wear a PBA t-shirt. They were always proud that dad was a policeman. In the early years, my husband was always one of the favorite Dads to go to school and talk about their jobs.

Elarie S.

We do not. My kids wear Firefighter clothing. My husband is also a volunteer fireman in a local township. My husband thinks it is too much of a target for our small community surrounding his patrol area.

Annemarie J.

Our daughter and I will occasionally wear a police sweatshirt or t-shirt, but not any more often than we wear anything else.

Jennifer H.

So far we have a "police dress" for our three year old, that is pink with a badge and she wears it in public. I actually don't find much for little girls to wear, but I wouldn't mind her wearing it at her age. Now, when she gets older we may have to hold back on some clothing. If she wants to wear a "police shirt", I would choose where it gets worn. This is simply because there are SO many people who dislike police, and someday our girls will have to learn that although our Daddy is police, they will have to deal with teasing from some children and even adults. I want them to always be proud of who their Daddy is, and teach them to not let the teasing affect them.

Kelly P.

No we do not wear police clothing in public. My husband and I feel that it's putting a target on our family. We also see people he has arrested or questioned in public and don't want to draw attention.

Krissy A

My kids don't wear police clothing in public but I do. I like to show support.

Bjae K.

Yes, occasionally my daughter will wear a police shirt but it is usually when we are around other officers. I will sometimes wear a shirt to the gym.

Cassie S.

My children do not wear police clothing in public. There are plenty of people out there that do not like the police and we just figured it was easier to avoid making them any more of a target than they might already be as the kids of a cop.

Maggie F.

Yes, my kids do wear police related clothing. If you look in our children's closets, the majority of their clothes are DARE, police and department shirts. My husband and I also wear clothing that is police related in public. We do not live in a police hate area so we feel safe wearing them. We live in a small county where everyone knows each other and my LEO has been with our county Sheriff's department for twenty plus years so everyone knows he is a LEO.

Vicky C.

Our daughter does not wear police clothing in public. She has a big enough mouth about her father, she doesn't need to be any more of a target. I do wear police clothing in public and I'm not afraid of being a target. I carry a gun.

Jessica B.

My daughter does not wear anything police wise in public. I have two shirts I got from Wives Behind the Badge and I wear those out and about, especially if I'm going to be in an area that's not where my husband works. I try not to advertise he's a cop but I do love my shirts.

Patty R.

How do you keep them quiet when daddy is asleep?

With much difficulty! My husband used to say he didn't hear the kids but me yelling to "be quiet, Dad is sleeping!" He tried ear plugs for a while with not great results.

Elarie S.

Most of the time the boys are at school while daddy sleeps but when we are home, they are well trained on the expectations. Daddy sleeps with a box fan turned on high to help drown out the sounds as well.

Maggie F.

My husband is really good about getting up between 10 and 11 so that isn't an issue.

Bjae K.

We use a noise maker in the bedroom. We have pre-teen and teenagers so I ask them to play video games or watch television in their bedrooms or be super quiet in the living room. When they were smaller we would spend a lot of time outside in the yard or on field trips.

Krissy A.

How do you handle gun safety with your kids?

When my daughter was four days old, he stood in front of her while she was in her swing and held his weapon up, and explained that she was never to touch his weapon and that when she was old enough he would teach her how to shoot. I was laughing because she was only four days old and already getting her first lesson in gun safety. We make his gun belt and anything he uses on-duty off- limits to her.

Patty R.

We keep her familiar with his weapon and tell her it can "hurt the baby." We always keep it locked whenever my husband removes it from his side.

Jennifer H.

The kids know not to touch but my husband is really good about locking up weapons in the safe. I know the kids have asked questions and hubby always answers. He does not like them to get anywhere near him when he's got his weapon on his duty belt.

Annemarie J.

We haven't gotten there yet because my daughter is so young but when I was a teen, my dad would teach us gun safety when we went camping every year and do target practice in the mountains. It was a thing of respect for the gun, and us kids learned to respect its power and the ways to be safe.

Kelly P.

We teach our kids how to properly handle fire arms.

Bjae K.

My oldest child was two when Daddy took a full time police job. His preschool teacher at the time happened to be a LEOW so I asked her this very same question. Her husband's lieutenant told him to take his duty weapon home, sit his kids down and take the whole thing apart in front of them. He let them hold the parts, handle the unloaded weapon and essentially take all the mystery away. We did exactly what she said and to this day whenever my LEO cleans his weapon, he has the kids sit and he gives them safety lessons. Also, when they were old enough he bought a couple of BB guns to teach them to shoot and properly handle a firearm.

Maggie F.

Our kids have had play guns since they were babies. They have had it drilled in their heads about gun safety. They know not to touch our guns. If they are curious, they know they can ask to see them with adult supervision and unloaded. Some are secured safely away.

Krissy A.

Our daughter has grown up around guns and she was taught early on that she was not to touch them. She was never shielded from how one works or the devastation that it can cause, so there is not "curiosity" for her to handle one. She has been to the range and is not a fan of guns for herself. They are okay for others but her words are "she is not a gun girl" but maybe she will be when she is older.

Jessica B.

Our two oldest boys, thirteen and eleven have been taught how to use a gun by my husband. They both are Boy Scouts so they have learned gun safety through that as well. Our children, even our four year old, know that there are guns in our home and that they are not to mess with the guns. We are always reminding them of gun safety.

Vicky C.

My husband plans to teach our daughter about guns in a year or so when she is a little older. She is only three now.

Cassie S.

My husband has offered to take our kids shooting so they know how to handle a gun safely. My now grown son has shown some interest, but thankfully has never taken his father up on the offer.

Elarie S.

Do you have issues with other families not wanting their kids to play at your house due to there being fire arms in your house? If so, how do you deal with it?

We do not have this issue because we live in a rural area where most people hunt and have guns in their own homes.

Vicky S.

No, the friends we have over to the house, know what Dad does and know he has guns. We secure them when friends come over.

Krissy A.

We haven't had this come up yet. We do a lot of playing outside. I have no problem if asked that we have a large safe where all is stored. Duty weapon as well as personal.

Annemarie J.

We have not had an issue with that. Anyone who knows us knows that we are probably more vigilant about gun safety than most other folks.

Jessica B.

Most people are okay with my husband being a cop and they know that he's super responsible about putting his weapons up so they are not accessible to anyone but him or myself.

Patty R.

No, everyone in our town knows who we are so that isn't an issue and everybody in our town has fire arms in their homes.

Bjae K.

We haven't run in to this yet, simply because our child is so young. But, I have found myself in a conversation about safety with another non-LEO mom. I blurted out how my toddler is getting into everything and we will soon have to find a safer place for his off-duty weapon. It was so natural of an issue for me, but the other mom's jaw dropped. So, I think I'll keep those conversations to myself in the future! My husband is very responsible with his gun and I think when the kids get older, it is going to be something we both have to be conscious of.

Kelly P.

I have been told once or twice that people were not comfortable having their kids at my house. I always say I understand their feelings and then politely remind them that my husband is a trained professional and that it's not like he leaves guns laying around the house. I also use that as my opportunity to explain that their child is far safer at my house than somewhere else because MY children have been taught gun safety and they understand guns are not toys. Then I let it drop.

Maggie F.

While I do not have kids, not long ago I had a discussion with a woman who knew I had guns in my home because she knows my husband is a LEO. She wanted to discuss what was a national news story at the time, about a New York newspaper listing all pistol permit holder's names and addresses. She said she thought all newspapers around the country should do this so parents would know which homes they should keep their children away from. She said she would never let her children play in such a home but she also felt too embarrassed to quiz the people her children are visiting about gun ownership. She felt the newspaper article was a great public service for people to know where "the gun houses were." I explained to her that she was giving herself a false sense of safety with this small snapshot of gun ownership. The newspapers only printed the names and addresses of law abiding citizens who registered their pistols and they were more likely than not, conscientious about keeping their guns locked up as required by law because they followed the law of registering their handguns and getting a permit. This news story would give her no knowledge of the homes with unregistered/illegal guns or shotguns and rifles which are not required to be registered and therefore, she might inadvertently send her children to play at such a home and have a false sense that there were no guns in the home. This woman had a tough time letting go of thinking she could know all about where to send her kids to play by the pistol permit map. I let it drop and just shook my head as I walked away. Some people are afraid of guns and no amount of common sense, logic or discussion will change their minds.

Terri W.

This issue never came up. The gun was always hidden in a place that the kids could not reach. My children are now thirty one and twenty eight and to this day they do not know where the gun was hidden. Today it is in a vault because my husband has retired.

Elarie S.

As wives, we worry about our husband being injured or killed in the line of duty. We see the news stories of other officers being shot or killed in car accidents and we fear that it could be our husband next. It's a legitimate fear and one we learn to handle as best we can while finding a way to live our lives every day and not be paralyzed by this fear. Doesn't it stand to reason that our kids worry too?

Are your children afraid that "Daddy" might get hurt and how do you calm their fears?

> For the most part, our children do not dwell on this but they know Daddy's job is dangerous. We have a strong faith and always pray for his safety.
> Vicky C.

> No, our daughter isn't afraid. That fear is learned behavior and she doesn't see me act that way so it is all "matter of fact" for her. She doesn't know life without her father doing what he does. She is fourteen and he has been doing this for eighteen years.
>
> Jessica B.

> My daughter is afraid. She is fifteen years old. She has watched a lot of the cop/investigative type shows with us. We have sat her down and explained that Daddy has trained for years to protect himself and not to put himself in certain situations. He has learned to handle things differently than the average person.
>
> Krissy A.

> They have never been worried that their father would get hurt at work.
>
> Melissa S.

> Our daughter is only two so she has known nothing other than her Daddy is a "PoPo." To keep her comfortable as she grows, he will come home while working and we will have her sit in the cruiser, listen

to the police radio and familiarize her with Daddy's badge and weapon; the weapon by sight only and it is kept locked when not on his side.

Jennifer H.

A few of them have verbalized their fears of his death. I reassure him that Dad is in good shape, always wears his vest, (we took it out and showed them how strong it was) and has safety as his priority. I've also told them that we have no control over how Daddy's day goes so all we can do is enjoy our time with him, pray for him during his shifts and be happy to see him when he comes home.

Annemarie J.

I can honestly say I don't think it has ever come up. Both of my boys have grown up with Daddy as a police officer so I am not sure they realize that it is a "dangerous job." We try to minimize our discussions in front of the kids about things that happen when he is at work but there have been times we have talked to them about bad people. When my oldest was in kindergarten he struggled to understand what his father's job was. One day he told me that "Daddy puts bad boys and girls in timeout" and I thought that was a good way to sum it up. Of course now that they are older they know more about being arrested and going to jail but they really don't talk about it much. As I said, this is all they know.

Maggie F.

My kids never verbalized their fears but they were comfortable going to see Dad at headquarters and seeing the other guys at work. I once had to drop my son off with my husband who was finishing his tour at a crime scene. My fourteen year old was eating fried rice and walking about. The Captain told my husband to "get your kid away as he is contaminating the crime scene!"

Elarie S.

We have a strong faith in The Lord. We pray every day that The Lord will keep our LEO safe, but we also know that we are okay with whatever The Lord's wishes are.

Rochelle H.

Our kids are thirteen and fourteen and live in their own world so they don't worry about their father getting hurt.

Bjae K.

We have a strong faith in The Lord. After my husband's shooting, my daughter had a hard time falling asleep until Dad was home. She is special needs/cares and doesn't comprehend much due to her disorder but knows when Dad gets home. I would lay in her bed with her and we would watch TV or read books.

Shelly T.

We try not to dwell on the fact that he could be hurt. As a family we know he wants to come home as much as we want him to come home and that he takes every precaution available to make that happen every night.

Heather J.

We have a strong faith. Our kids worry, but know that he is well trained and good at what he does. He has been in multiple shootings in two different police jobs. Both kids handle it differently and in their own ways. Our son sticks to him like glue and our daughter secludes herself and then when ready, she talks to him and me.

Cortney S.

How has their attitude toward their father being a police officer changed as they got older and into their teen years?

Their attitude hasn't changed.

Bjae K.

When our kids were younger, they were excited and thought it was cool that dad was a cop. Now that they are teens, they are embarrassed. Some of their friends don't want to hang out because Dad is a cop. They aren't invited to some parties because the kids may tell Dad, which is okay by me. If it's something that Dad can't know, the kids don't need to be there. The kids don't want to ride in the patrol car.

They say when they are dropped off at school, kids joke about what trouble they are in. It makes them feel uncomfortable.

Krissy A.

Their father's job never affected their attitude as to what they thought of their father.

Melissa S.

The drinking situation was always a little difficult. It was very difficult for my kids to talk to my husband about alcohol or drugs because he's not a big drinker and never did drugs. However, they always were proud of him and to this day they call upon him about any legal matter (parking tickets etc.).

Elarie S.

Did you or would you encourage your children in becoming a law enforcement officer:

We do not encourage or discourage a certain career choice. We teach our children that they can be whatever their hearts desire. We will support whatever career choice they make.

Vicky C.

I think being a LEO, military or any kind of service is awesome. I most definitely encourage my children to be whomever and wherever they are called to serve.

Annemarie J.

I would encourage her in any profession she would want to pursue. At this time, she has a desire to go into Forensic Science for crime scene investigation. She has great mentors since her father is great at his job and I am pursuing a career in Funeral Services in addition to being a Private Investigator.

Jessica B.

We encourage our children but I don't sugar coat how life as a LEO is going to be.

Krissy A.

We encourage our kids to become what they want to become; if it is a LEO then we would most definitely encourage it. We are extremely open with our kids and talk to them about the dangers but all jobs have different levels of dangers.

Bjae K.

Our daughter can be whatever she wants. My husband is fifth generation LEO in the family, so we expect she'll follow in the family footsteps. But, if she chooses not to that is fine as well.

Jennifer H.

I would do neither, we want them to become whomever they want to be. There is no pressure of entering the military or law enforcement in our family. If there is interest, then we would be open and candid about his career, but also realistic. It takes a special someone to do this job and I would want our children to really understand that. I think when I was seventeen, I wanted to become a LEO, so I looked into it and it wasn't long before I figured out that physically, mentally and emotionally, I could not do it!

Kelly P.

I will always encourage my sons to do whatever it is they want to be in life. How can I discourage them from following in their father's footsteps should they choose to do so? I would be teaching them that what he is, is not good enough. Law enforcement is a valiant calling in life and I would want them to follow their hearts. That being said, I would pray every day for their safety and for a woman who has been called to be a LEOW to support them and love them through this challenging yet rewarding life.

Maggie F.

I wouldn't encourage my daughter. I don't think it's a good job for women.

Cassie S.

We would encourage her if she wanted to be a LEO but would encourage her to go Federal because the way most cities are, pay isn't enough to live comfortably on without stressing over money and how bills are going to be paid. My parents had the "no daughter of mine is going to be a cop" mentality and when I began studying Criminal Justice it was very rough. They banned police related shows and such and it made me miserable. I would never want my daughter to go through the same thing if she really wanted to be a LEO. I want to support her in all that she endeavors to do.

Patty R.

I totally discouraged my children from being a LEO. My husband "nagged" my son from the time he was twelve to take the test. He did take the test just as a back-up plan. He fortunately found a job in the business world and is very happy. You have to know your children. Neither of them showed any signs of wanting the job, unlike their father who desired to wear the uniform from the time he could speak!

Elarie S.

Children of LEOs Sometimes Grow Up to Become LEOs Themselves

Children of LEOs sometimes grow up to become LEOs themselves. They have "been there, done that" from both sides of the coin and have an insight into raising children of LEOs that many do not have.

Thoughts on being the child of a LEO and a LEO with kids

By Nick F.

As a third generation and now retired LEO and father of two, I would like to share my thoughts on being the son of a LEO, and a LEO raising two kids.

My father was a LEO after the Lindbergh baby kidnapping in the 1930s. The kidnapping of a wealthy man's son influenced other wealthy people to change their lifestyles to protect their families. Many wealthy people moved out of New York City to the suburbs and made room on their estates for LEOs and their families to live, as a way of protection for the wealthy estate owner. The arrangement worked well for all involved as the LEO was given an opportunity to live in an area he would not normally be able to afford and his children could attend schools normally not within reach of those on a LEO salary in the wealthy school districts of the suburbs. We lived on a wealthy family's estate until I was about five years old. Some of my early childhood memories include my father working on the estate during his off duty time caring for the livestock and mowing lawns. All wonderful memories of a life I would not have gotten to enjoy had my father not been a LEO providing added security on the estate.

When I was about five, my family moved off the estate and to an apartment house in the late 1950s and I started kindergarten. This was the era of the hula hoops, Davie Crockett shirts and a Ford Edsel was parked at the curb in front of our building. It was during this time that I observed my father get involved in two off duty incidents. The first occurred as we were driving to a nearby town in our 1950 Chrysler. We noticed a road construction dump truck that had made contact with some overhead electric wires while raising the bed of the dump truck. The wires were on fire and the driver could not exit the vehicle. My father responded to a nearby call box and reported the incident and then returned to the scene and waited for responding police units to arrive and for the electric company to turn off the power. We left and went on our way. It was at this time I realized that my father was different than other people.

The second incident occurred when I was in kindergarten. We lived close enough to the school that my fifth grade sister and I were able to walk to and from school together. As I said, it was a different era, a more innocent time (or so we thought) and children walked freely to and from school. One day my sister and I had just left our building after coming home for lunch and were on our way back to school. My mother looked out our first floor kitchen window and observed a man in his late 20s who was exposing himself and committing a lewd act while sitting in his car that was parked at the curb in front of our building. This person then exited his vehicle in order to approach my sister and me. My mother started to scream out the window at us and called for my father. My father ran out of the building, as my sister and I started to run into the building. My mother also called the local police. While waiting for the local police to arrive, my father came to the window and said to my mother "Mary, get my gun." As my father was being handed his gun two local detectives, who my father knew, arrived at the scene. The suspect had fled into an underground parking lot under our building. My father and the two local detectives apprehended the suspect and placed him under arrest. There was an article in the local paper the following day. It turned out that the suspect was the son of some high ranking official and had a history of sex offenses. Needless to say, I never learned all of the details of the incident until I was much older. However, I knew that my father was able to protect me in a way that other fathers couldn't.

As a young child growing up in the 1950s and 1960s, most of the television shows of the era were either police or cowboy shows. I can remember watching the original Dragnet, Code 3, Highway Patrol, M Squad etc. Other kids I was in school with would talk about these shows the next day on the playground or at lunch. I had the satisfaction of knowing that my father did the same things in real life. When I talked about police issues, my friends knew that I was some kind of insider. I had a different view of the police life than they had. As a very young person, I was envied by some of my friends. However, as I got older and especially in high school, the attitude of my friends began to change. The social unrest of the late 1960, the rise of the drug culture and the Viet Nam War protest movement caused a very strong dislike for the police within our country's culture. Something like we never saw before or since. It was during this time that the term PIG originated. The Chicago Democratic Party Convention riots occurred at this time which made the Chicago PD look bad. Being related to a police officer during this time was difficult. I remember one incident when I was in eleventh grade and one student who was very far on the political left said to me "Is your father a PIG?" I said to him "You're damn right he is one and he has been one for over thirty six years and I am damn proud of it." We almost came to blows. My fellow classmates who had fathers who were cops experienced incidents like this. I think this experience caused many of us to bond closer to the profession that our fathers had chosen. As we were growing into adulthood, some of our peers were starting to make bad choices and getting arrested or getting tickets and this did not elevate their opinion of the police.

One aspect that helps some kids walk the straight and narrow is that when you are the child of a LEO, you know that if you get into trouble, the television news will lead with and the press will sell their newspapers with headlines screaming: "Child of police officer arrested!" Your friends might be arrested too but not a peep from the press about their parent's occupations. You will never see the headline "Child of landscaper arrested!" The privilege of appearing in a press headline for teenage escapades falls on the children of LEOs, ministers, politicians, judges and famous people.

Now we fast forward to my own years a LEO and raising my own family. My wife and I were showing them some sights in the New York City where I was working on a special assignment for my suburban police department and where my wife was a teacher. While driving down the Grand Concourse, a NY Fire Department (NYFD) engine truck passed us in the next lane. The men on board were all typical FDNY firemen at the time; mostly Irish and some Italian and big enough to be NFL players. Several of them were looking at us as they drove past because I definitely looked like someone who was retired off the job. My wife said "I bet they think you are taking the family to show them where you worked." Little did they realize that I was showing my kids where my wife worked. Watching the FDNY pass us by had a positive impact on our kids.

As our kids were growing up, the typical role models for young children were sports stars like you see in the NFL or NBA. I considered myself lucky having grown up in the 1950s and 1960s. We admired Mickey Mantle because he was a sports hero. In fact, I actually saw him hit a home run and win the game for the Yankees in the ninth inning with a count of 3-2. No experience could beat that, as it was a young boy's dream come true! However, in those years, as we had other heroes that included people like Dwight Eisenhower, Douglas MacArthur, Chester Nimitz and so many of the other great leaders of World War Two who were still alive. We also had astronauts like Alan Shephard, Gus Grissom and John Glenn. These men were the present day heroes who were leading our nation into space. My children's generation was not given examples of any other heroes outside of sports. I wasn't going to let that happen to my children. I made it a point to explain how many people had sacrificed for our nation.

One day, I had the perfect opportunity to show my kids some real heroes, New York Firemen. We were visiting family in New York City and I observed a FDNY Rescue 3 truck driving down Broadway. The truck was grimy and dirty because "real" firemen don't have time to polish their trucks! The truck had a large black bull snorting smoke out of its nose painted on the side of the truck. The nickname of Rescue 3 is Big Blue. I pointed to the truck and told my kids that those men are among the best firemen in New York City. I went on to explain that there are only five rescue companies in the entire city and only the best men are able to get on rescue. I explained to them what the men assigned to a rescue company could do in saving lives. A few months later we made another trip to the city, which ties us into a 9/11 story.

It was the year 2000 and my wife and I brought our kids with us into New York City. When we finished our personal business, we decided to show the kids a real firehouse with real firemen. We went to the quarters of Engine 95, Ladder

36 and the 13 Battalion. When I mentioned that I was retired off the PD job, the firemen were very friendly and allowed my kids to climb on to the ladder truck and turn on the emergency lights. They had a good time! We then left and proceeded to do a few more personal errands. After our errands, we stopped to visit the quarters of ESU Truck 1, a New York police unit. When I told the Sergeant who I was, he was friendly and allowed my kids to see the photos they had on the wall of the garage bay located next to where Truck 1 was parked. These were photos of bridge rescues, train rescues, pin jobs etc. As it turned out the Sergeant knew about my old PD's ESU program and we found we had mutual friends. I explained to my kids that these police officers were not just a SWAT team, but these police officers were far more experienced than any SWAT team in the world. Over ninety percent of their calls involved rescue work that was only performed by fire departments in other cities. My kids heard several good war stories about rescue incidents including what an ESU cop calls train jobs, water jobs and building collapses. A NY Post newspaper photographer arrived and gave the Sergeant a photo of a female EDP (Emotionally Disturbed Person) that the unit had just saved a few hours before. The woman was positioned on a railing of a fire escape with a knife to her throat. ESU did a grab on her and saved her life. We were told that the photo would be in the Post the next day and my kids got a kick out of seeing the photo in the newspaper the next day. We thanked the ESU guys and continued on our visit to the city.

We decided to take the Staten Island Ferry over and back again, just to enjoy a boat ride. On the way back we were on the front of the boat looking at Manhattan and the World Trade Center. At this time a Swiss family asked us to take their picture with Manhattan in the background. We took their picture and then asked them to take our family picture for us. Little did any of us realize what would happen in the months ahead. Fast forward to 9/11. My children arrived home from school and they were upset about the fall of the Twin Towers. They asked if the firemen and ESU cops we had met were alright. I said that we had no way of knowing at this time. As it turned out, two members of ESU 1 died on 9/11 and a member of the firehouse assigned to the 13 Battalion was also killed. My kids had a connection to 9/11 that was very different than their peers. My children know of the connection that our family heritage has to the NYPD and the FDNY and my police department. They also had a relative who was killed at Normandy in World War Two and a cousin who was wounded during the Blackhawk down incident.

Guns seem to be in the news lately and I definitely have an opinion on that issue. News commentators often refer to old time gun owners as hunters or target shooters. My father and his brother had guns because they were LEOs and never used a gun to target shoot or hunt. For them a gun was a tool of their trade like a carpenter has a hammer or a mechanic has a wrench. However the use of a gun in the most extreme situation for a police officer was much different than hammering nails or turning bolts. The gun was not for recreation such as hunting or sports shooting. Every time my father put on his gun to go to work we were reminded of the possible danger that he faced when he went to work. A generation later my wife and children would feel the same way every time they observed me do the same thing when I would go to work. All of us in the LEO community train to defend our life from a criminal assailant if necessary. However, we hoped and prayed that it would never be necessary.

I also took my wife to the range and showed her how to shoot. When getting ready to retire, I obtained a full carry permit for myself and my wife.

Another aspect of gun ownership during the past twenty years was a series of articles written in many parenting magazines about the danger of your child visiting the home of a family that had a gun in the home. Some parents would ask if I owned a gun before they would let their child visit my children in our home. Needless to say, I was greatly offended by this action. Yes, they lacked common sense when they did not want their children to play in a LEO's home because he owned a gun. Where would they be safer than in a LEO's home?

LEO Children share their thoughts

As with all of us, as you become an adult you have an appreciation for and perspective on all that your parents did for you as a child. What might have once been annoying, embarrassing or seemed like you parents didn't care, now becomes a cherished memory of how much your parents really did care. They managed to do so much with so little and loved us more than we could ever know. The adult children of LEOs can give special insight into what helped them most growing up. What can we as parents learn from their childhoods that will help us raise our own children?

Lessons Learned as the Child of a Police Officer

By Laura Watson

As a child of a police officer who later became the wife of a police officer, I do not claim to know it all. I am not sitting at the kitchen table of every law enforcement officer's family so cannot understand all of the idiosyncrasies of your family. However, based on my own kitchen table experience, I have come to understand the delicate balance of being a child, spouse, and parent in this lifestyle. My father is an old-school beat cop who rose in the ranks to later become chief. He came up in the mid-80s and has seen a lot in his nearly 30 years of police work. However, I was not a police officer. I was the only child, the only daughter, of two exceptional parents. I could brag on my mom and dad for hours and will if given the opportunity. I could tell you many stories of growing up, growing older (though not wiser), finding my own hero, and raising a child. But that is another story for another book. Instead, maybe we have a conversation about how children adapt to this life from my own experience.

Maybe we dispel some rumors while holding others true. Pull up a chair at my table and join me for coffee?

Patrolmen work the worst hours of anyone in law enforcement. The shift between days and nights are brutal on their bodies, minds, and attitudes. But if you are reading this, then you already know that. As a law enforcement spouse, you can feel the mood shifts coming and adequately prepare. But how do you prepare a child? As a young girl, my mom worked double duty as Mom and Dad and threw in cheerleader, disciplinarian, and entertainer as needed. We lived in a very small house where the two bedroom doors and bathroom door were all at the end of one very small hallway that had a remarkable ability to echo. When it was noon and the bedroom door was shut, my Mom knew it was quiet time. Dad had just come off a night shift that turned into a morning shift as he finished paperwork. But as a young child? That door meant nothing! It was noon! Time to play! As a parent, I realize now that play time is never quiet. I remember my Mom hushing me, desperation in her eyes, as she tried to get me outside. Now, on the other side of it, I probably have that same look in my eyes as I try, unsuccessfully, to hush my two year old. On the not so good days, that door would swing open and a very tall, very tired man would be standing on the other side of it.

"Please, I'm begging you, just a few hours of quiet!"

As an adult, I feel guilty for those times. But as a child, I felt shut out. Why didn't my Dad want to play? Why was my Dad so upset? Why was he so *tired* all the time? It wasn't until I was a bit older that my Mom's conversations with me about schedules and shift work made sense. My Dad wasn't upset with me, wasn't forgetting about me, wasn't uninterested in me. He was doing everything he could to provide for me, for us. Soon it was realized that the outside swing set was the best place to be on a sunny day and that reading was an important passion to have during the months of night shift. My mother helped show me the greatness of worlds within books when I was young. We would read together, we would read separately, we would take hour long trips to the library. Quiet time became a fun, enjoyable time instead of a constant battle. Don't be fooled however. It took many conversations and many promises of a cookie after dinner for me to understand that, but I did with time. I learned and I grew and I began to realize that my Dad was a lot more fun when he was rested so I needed to do my part to help with that. They say placing responsibility on a child is a good thing and, whoever they are, they tend to be right. I soon became a part of helping my Dad get rest and ensuring that he was the best Dad he could be when he woke up. I went from feeling pushed aside to feeling important. And there is no greater feeling for a small child than feeling like they are important. Foster that within your own child. Make them a part of the shift change process instead of a nuisance to it. They will thank you one day and your police officer will be eternally grateful for a peaceful slumber. On the other side of that is waking up, which to a child is the best part. I got to see my Dad! I got to tell him all about my day and show him my newest project from school. Often these stories were told on his bed while he was gearing up for work. I spent years watching him put on his duty belt and boots before walking out the door. But those hours before were precious. They were mine! It is important to ensure that the police parent remembers that. Let the child sit on the bed. Let them grab boots from the other room to help get ready. Let them babble the entire time because soon, work will call and your child won't see their parent until the next day, if not longer.

When I was really young, I didn't always understand where he was going as the door shut. I knew my Dad fought bad guys to keep my Mom and me safe. I knew he'd be gone for a long while. I knew every knock on the door made my Mom pause. But I didn't get it. It was just before I hit my awkward teenage years that I truly understood. I still have an old photo somewhere of my Dad standing in our living room in his dress blues with a band tightly around his badge. Many years later I can't remember who it was that passed but I do remember that was the day it clicked: my Dad may leave for work and not come home. Those bad guys weren't just monsters under the bed but real people who could hurt my family. I don't know that I ever told my Mom that I understood but I started holding my breath the same as she did if there was a knock at the door. I can't say I was always scared. I was taught that scared was not a way to go through life. But I was always cautious. Vigilant even. Your child will have that turning point as well. As my Mom realized my change in awareness, her attitude towards Dad leaving for work also changed. We settled into a routine that was unique to us. If Dad was at work, we had beef noodles and green beans for dinner. It was our favorite but my Dad hated it. We would watch terrible movies and laugh at the main character while eating Fiddle Faddle. But most importantly, we would talk. The police scanner became our white noise and we kept an open line of communication with each other about what was going on. The importance of a "Dad is at work" routine is beyond measure. Find a common meeting point and stick to it. It will make the time away from Dad more acceptable. In fact, sometimes it will come to the point that when Dad is home and *his* favorite meal is for dinner, your child will wish for beef noodles and green beans.

As I grew up, more than worry, I felt a longing to be with my Dad. He was my protector, my mentor, and in a lot of ways, my best friend. He was a superhero in my eyes. He still is. My Mom was amazing and filled that opening in every way possible. But there is something special between a dad and daughter (or dad and son, mom and son, mom and daughter or whoever the police officer is in your family). My greatest memories growing up were the days I had with my Dad. Just as my Mom and I settled into a unique routine, so did my Dad and I. My Dad loves being a police officer but he is also always up for a good hustle. My grandfather and he were flea marketers who constantly had some business or project going on. So as I grew up, we were avid pawn shoppers and project entrepreneurs. We would start our day at our favorite fast food breakfast stop and then hit the road. We'd stop at different pawn shops, catch up with an assortment of friends, pick up supplies for various projects, stop for lunch, and head home with our treasures. Now, to many, this does not seem like the dream day out. But to me? Oh my! It was my favorite day. It was the day I would look forward to for a month. My Mom helped foster that relationship and would push us out the door some days. In retrospect, it was likely that part of her enthusiasm was the house to herself but nonetheless, she helped make those special days what they were. It is important for a police officer to forge that same routine and relationship with their child. Help them find something that is special to just the two of them. Great things will happen, I promise you that! It takes planning and control of time but the memories are worth every second.

As law enforcement spouses, we learn quickly how to manage time. If I can bestow one last piece of advice, it is to ensure that your significant other also learns the demands of organizing time. I often looked into a crowd at a school function and only saw my Mom smiling and waving at me. It is the life, I understand that. My Mom is absolutely selfless and made it to every school function, no matter how insignificant. But do you know the times I remember most? The ones where I looked into that crowd and saw my mom and Dad both smiling and waving. While my Dad couldn't make it to every school function, he made sure to help with every school project. Three very clearly stick out in my mind. I am a history junkie, who later became a history major and teacher. Because of that, I tended to want my school history projects to be larger than life. The good news for me was that my Dad is far craftier than he looks. I came home in early middle school with a project over ancient civilizations. The class had to make a model of a native tribe's home. I immediately took the project to my Dad (after he woke up, of course). Together, over the course of a week, we spent hours finding materials, researching environment, and putting together an amazing model. It had blue glass beads for water, legitimate thatching for roofing materials, and delicately placed twigs for walls. On another, we used three dozen tiny green army guys and materials from the yard to reconstruct the Bataan Death March. But our greatest feat? A miniature wooden sarcophagus that, when opened, had little wooden mementos that would have been important in Ancient Egypt. It was outstanding! And the best part? It was made with my Dad. He taught me how to make the wood pieces, helped me paint each piece, and didn't yell at me when I burnt him with hot glue. As I grew older, class projects were smaller but I was an athlete who craved the sideline cheerleading of my parents. I was a competitive swimmer and loved it. I wasn't great but good enough to secure a scholarship to college my sophomore year of high school. Do you know who was there the day the scout approached me after a swim meet? My Mom *and* Dad. Do you know who was there the day I swam my personal best and secured our team's win on senior night even though the odds were against us? My Mom *and* Dad. My Dad made the time. Police officers aren't off work at 5pm and they can't take long lunches. But sometimes those comp days are worth more than the extra pay that was offered as an alternative. The bills will get paid but the time can never be replaced.

So what is the snapshot? What is the overarching idea of my little trip down memory lane? Learn to adapt to your spouse's schedule and guide your children in the same. Find a routine that fits even if it doesn't seem special from the outside. Make time. But above all else, be open. Be open to questions and concerns. Be open to changes and attitudes. Be open to your child about everything. Fear is bred from ignorance, not understanding. Help your child understand. And be patient while they get to that point. It won't happen overnight but it will happen. And if all else fails, just survive the day with your child and have a glass of wine after bedtime. I have some good recommendations if you ever need them!

Living in a Fishbowl, As The Child of a LEO

There must be times when being the child of a LEO puts a bit of a damper on your "teen fun years" or at the least, threatens to put a damper on what might not always be innocent fun. Several years ago my then high school aged nephew was taking a train into the city to see a parade with his friends and a train full of teenagers from his school. My nephew was always a really good kid and we never worried about him getting into trouble. My LEO husband and I were also going into the city to watch the parade and planned to catch a train. While on our way to the train, a friend of my husband's from work called and advised us to avoid the train for a little while because a hot line had just gone out for a riot on a train full of kids. The riot started as the train pulled into our station stop! Not wanting to put his wife in the middle of a riot of teenagers, my husband advised that we should hold off on going for a few minutes. Being the worried aunt and uncle that we are, we immediately called my nephew. We knew that he would not be one of the rioters but we were worried that he could have been in the wrong train car and possibly had gotten hurt. As my mother used to tell me (repeatedly when I was a teen) "When you are near trouble, you are in trouble." Thankfully, my nephew immediately answered his phone and said that yes, the train he was on was indeed the train with the riot but that he was not in the train car with the problem kids. A very happy uncle and aunt were relieved that he was not hurt and we wished him a fun day at the parade. After hanging up the phone, we both laughed and talked about how hard it must be to be our nephew and not even have a little time when his LEO uncle wasn't aware of what he was doing, even though my nephew was miles from home at the time. "The very long arm of the law."

Being the child of a LEO sometimes comes with its own pressures. Stricter parents with stricter rules are the norm. A LEO's child may also have the "in the public eye" pressure. Be it your friends, teachers or neighbors, you are known by all as the child of a LEO. Some people will expect you to "behave better than that!" "Don't embarrass your father!" "I'm calling your father if you keep that up!" "Did someone see me say or do something that my father will not be happy about?" And on the list goes of things a LEO child has to keep at the back of his or her mind. LEOWs need to be aware that they are always in the public eye but it could be even more pressure on the child of a LEO.

Thoughts from kids over fifteen.

Was it hard being a "Leo's child?

Up until I was eleven or twelve I thought having a Father that was a police officer was the best thing in the world. He was around to coach all of my baseball games and was a constant presence in mine and my sister's lives. This leads me to my preteen and teenage years, where I hated having my Father as a police officer (minus the perks of the PBA card) because he was a constant presence in our lives.

Scott B.

It wasn't necessarily hard when it came to being a LEO's child but it did come with hardships. I had really early curfews compared to my friends which always seemed to get me made fun of. Also, many of my friends were and still are very intimidated by my father which means they do not come around the house often. My father is a genuinely nice guy, I just feel that the police officer tag is what intimidates some.

Luke C.

Personally, it wasn't hard being a LEO's child. My father was able to make it to my sports games and important events in my life that I wanted him there for. The schedule itself is the only hard part about being a LEO's child. When I was younger I wouldn't see him for a week if he was working the 3-11 PM shift because I would be in school during the day and come home when he was at work. Overall there hasn't been any burden on our relationship.

Trey N.

I never found living the life of a police officers' child difficult. In fact, I've had a great life because my parents provided for my sister and me and made sure to be around. While my Dad worked, my Mother was around to be with my sister and me. And when my Dad was home he spent his time with us. It never felt like we were living some challenging life when our parents showed us very little neglect.

Andrea V.

Growing up, I did not find it hard being a LEO's son because I usually saw my Dad every night and he always had weekends off so there was plenty of time to see him plus my Mom was always home when we were, even when she went back to work.

Connor L.

Did you get into "trouble" as a teen to prove you were not too much of a cop's kid or did you feel you had to behave better than other kids?

I don't think I ever felt the need to prove how bad I was nor did I ever feel pressure to behave better. I think my bad behavior did come to a shock to many people because I was the child of a police officer.

Scott B.

Growing up I was always taught to treat people the way I wanted to be treated. I never really was the one to get in trouble growing up through grades K-8. When high school came, I was with a crowd of kids that did like to party and have a good time. I may have partied a little with them to feel somewhat rebellious against my parents, but it wasn't necessarily because I wanted to prove I wasn't much of a cop's kid.

I still do feel like I have to behave better than the others around me. I don't want to embarrass my parents by getting in trouble. Since my Dad's a police officer, I feel that I was always looked at to be well behaved and well-mannered by others. So yes, while growing up, I definitely feel like I had to behave better.

Luke C.

I didn't get into trouble as a teen because I knew right from wrong. Plus, I always wanted to be a police officer myself so I stayed out of trouble and on the right path because I knew it could only benefit me towards my goals in life. I didn't feel like I had to behave better than any other kids my own age due to my Father's job.

Trey N.

I always worked really hard not to get into any trouble. I was never the rebellious type to go out and prove that because my Father was a cop I could get away with anything. I may have a lead foot when it comes to driving but that's the worst of it when it comes to breaking the rules.

My parents raised me to follow the rules and if broken, consequences would be the initial reaction. We're no better than any other child who has a parent with a serious profession. Being an officer's child maybe made us more aware of what happens when rules are broken, but the rules should always be followed.

Andrea V.

There were always strict rules in our house that my brother and I obeyed but at the same time we had plenty of freedom. Just like any teenage boy, we did get ourselves in a little trouble every once in a while but nothing too extreme. Most of the kids we hung out with came from strict homes as well, so that kept us all out of trouble. Having a police officer as a father did stop us from getting into trouble because there were always rules to go by but nothing too strict.

I never felt I had to behave better than other kids, I just behaved the way that I thought was right for me and what the right thing to do was. Like I said, most of my peers come from well-rounded families with Fathers who are police officers.

Connor L.

What did your Mother do that helped you cope with your Father working nights, weekends etc.? What did she do well as a Mother and what did she not do that you wish she had?

From what I remember, my Dad always managed to be around. He would work days or midnights, so we never really had to deal with him not being home. There were definitely times when he would have to work overtime or double but compared to most of my friends' parents, he was around a lot more which I'm sure made it a lot easier on my Mother. I think my Mom did a great job catching me coming home drunk/high or getting into trouble, in fact I think she would have made a great detective.

Scott B.

When my Dad worked evenings or weekends, my Mother made it her first priority to make sure we were safe and to make sure we always were where we needed to be. I played a ton of sports and she seemed to make every single game and drive me to every single practice. The support system from her was incredible.

Luke C.

My Mother always cooked dinner for us. My two brothers and I would all sit at the kitchen table and talk. The family that eats together, stays together. My Mother was always there for us as well. I have great parents. Any time I wanted to go to a friend's house, ask for advice, homework etc. she was there to help the best she could.

Trey N.

My mom was always there for my sister and me. She stopped working when I was born so she could be around and be attentive. We were never those kids who had to go to after school activities until sundown because the parents were working. My Mom made sure to always be there for us so we wouldn't notice that Dad was at work. But the memories I hold from my childhood always place my Dad at the dinner table or home at night. I'm sure there were plenty of times that I can't recall where he was gone or had to work, but it was nothing that affected my childhood or growing up.

Andrea V.

Whenever my Dad was working my Mom was always there. If it wasn't for her, I don't know what we would do. She always had a good meal on the table at dinner and always was there if we had to be at a school or sporting event if my Father wasn't home.

Connor L.

What did your Father do that you liked and what did he do that your wish he had done differently?

My Dad was sometimes overly cautious or protective due to the nature of his job and the things he saw on a daily basis.

Scott B.

What my Dad did that I like was that he was also extremely supportive. He always was there to give me a little extra practice in my particular sport. Even if he worked all night he somehow had enough energy to hang out with my brothers and me the next day. What I didn't like was that sometimes he brought his work home through emotions. Sometimes he would get angry very easily after a rough day but this was rare. Now that I am older, I definitely understand more why sometimes he was short tempered.

Luke C.

I loved that my Dad made time for the family. Family is who he is and he enjoys going on vacation, taking trips and doing anything family oriented. Every summer we'd go on two vacations as a family. Most of my friends never went away on vacations or even sat down to dinner with their families because they were too busy working. My Dad took the time out of his schedule and made family important. And that's a lesson I'll carry with me throughout the rest of my life. You work hard at your job to provide for your family because they are the most important part of your life.

Andrea V.

One thing our Father did that we liked was the he made us into hard working men while we were growing up. He always had me and my brother working during all circumstances. I think that made me and my brother become the hard workers we are today.

Connor L.

Did you fear your Father being hurt and if so, how did you cope with your fears of your Father getting hurt?

I had the opportunity to witness my Father interact with some of the more "colorful" members of the community he protected. His side job was in the same town and I would always ride along with him. It was always a positive interaction and it seemed as though mostly everyone seemed to like him. I'd imagine there were people that didn't but I was never witness to this. So as a child, I can honestly say I do not remember any instances of being scared for his safety or well-being.

Scott B.

As a LEO's child I think that it is natural to always have a little fear in your mind. He works in a profession where people hate him and the majority of the population he deals with are new found or veteran criminals or drug addicts. Also, every once in a while you see on television that a police officer was killed in the line of duty. So yes, I do fear him being hurt. I cope with my fears by trying to avoid thinking about them. I can't go through a day constantly worrying about my Dad because then I would not function properly. I trust his training and his knowledge of the situation to make sure he keeps himself out of trouble and stays safe. I like to think of him as invincible.

Luke C.

I did fear that my father may get hurt on the job. I was taught from a very young age that he has a unique job and a job that he may have to put his life on the line to save another. It has been embedded in me for as long as I can remember.

Trey N.

It's not something I dwell on because that thought can drive a person crazy. It's in the back of my mind that something could happen, but it's been almost thirty years and I've had no reason to believe that my Father will be put into a situation he won't be able to get himself out of. But I also believe that if anything were to happen, that he would be the hero and ultimately my family would be taken care of.

Andrea V.

I never feared my Dad getting hurt on the job growing up although my friend's father got hit by a drunk driver while pulling another vehicle over. This changed my thoughts on my Dad getting hurt but I never stressed it.

Connor L.

Did you think about becoming a LEO yourself? What made you decide it was or was not the career for you?

I did think about it and it was purely out of pressure from my Father. He painted such a pretty picture and would talk about all of the perks of the job that he knew I would love. He always failed to mention witnessing deaths, physical damage, verbal abuse etc. Ultimately, I did not go into law enforcement.

Scott B.

I am studying Justice and Law right now in college with aspirations of becoming a LEO. What made me decide is that I love helping people and I love knowing people run to me for help. I also understand the difficult life it puts you in because I grew up in a law enforcement family. I almost feel as if it is in my blood.

Luke C.

I did become a police officer because I looked up to my Father. I decided I wanted to because of the stories he would come home with. It sounded very exciting and very rewarding. The job is not for everyone but I feel I have made the right choice.

Trey N.

When I first entered college I was a Criminal Justice major. I thought law was interesting and becoming a cop would be a nice job to have. But as I got older my decision changed, and not because I didn't like law enforcement or because I didn't want to be like my Dad, it just wasn't my passion. I found something else I enjoy and love and followed that through. I know that going into law enforcement is always a back-up plan but for now, it's not for me.

Andrea V.

I always wanted to be a LEO growing up and I feel that I'm interested in doing it because I grew up around police officers.

Connor L.

Do you have any other thoughts that you would like to share?

For the most part, I loved having a Father as a police officer and his job gave him flexibility to always be around my Sister, Mom and I. As I look back now and think about how being a police officer was not just a job for my Dad, it's in his DNA. Ten plus years after his retirement and he still talks as though he is "on the job." Seeing his passion day in and day out was a great life lesson and really taught me that finding happiness in your career and personal life is what's important in life.

Scott. B.

Thoughts from kids under 15.

What do you like most about your Father being a LEO? What do you like least?

I like that my Daddy arrests bad guys and that he turns his lights and siren on for me. I don't like missing my Daddy.

Kyle P. age 4

I like that he protects our county. I don't like that he misses a lot of what we are doing such as my basketball games and stuff.

Jared P. age 11

I like that he protects us from the bad. I don't like that we don't always have him here with us.

Wyatt P. age 13

I like that he helps protect me and others. I don't like how much he has to work.

Gabriel T. age 12

I like that he can protect us. I don't like that he has to send people to jail.

Liam D. age 8

What I like most about my Dad is that he protects the city and what I like least is that my Dad might die on duty.

Hailey A. age 10

I like that my Father helps protect people and that he is dedicated to his work. What I like least about it is that I don't know what could happen out there, if he would come home or not.

Alexis A. age 13

I like the fact that he helps people and saves lives. I don't like that it is dangerous and he might get hurt or killed.

Olivia A. age 11

The thing I like most is when he is at work, he is doing something to help save the world. The thing I like least is that he works night shifts instead of days like normal so he sleeps during the days. I don't like that he works out of our city so it's a long ride if he has to go to get something.

Adam R. Age 11

I like the police car most. I don't like when Mommy isn't home to put me to bed. (Gregory's Mother is a LEO)

Gregory C.

Are you proud of your Father and do you tell your friends that he is a LEO?

Yes, I tell my friends that my Daddy is a police because I love it.

Kyle P. age 4

All my friends know he is a police officer and think it is so cool. I am proud of him.

Jared P. age 11

Yes I am proud of him and tell my friends that don't already know.

Wyatt P. age 13

I'm very proud of him. I tell my friends that he is a police officer.

Gabriel T. age 12

I am proud of my Dad and no, I do not tell my friends. I never tell anyone because I might blow my dad's cover.

Hailey A. age 10

Yes I am proud of him and sometimes I tell my friends and sometimes I don't.

Liam D. age 8

Yes, I am extremely proud of my Dad. Sometimes I tell my friends about my Dad, only if I'm really close to them. I don't want them going off telling bad people about him and so his cover will be blown.

Alexis A. age 13

Yes I am very proud of my Dad and I tell some friends but not all of them.

Olivia A. age 11

Yes I am proud of him but I only tell friends that I trust.

Adam R. age 11

Yes I am proud but I don't have time to tell all my friends that my Mommy is a Policeman.

Gregory C.

What do you do that helps when you are missing him?

When I miss my Daddy I sleep with Mommy and sleep on his side of the bed and get Mommy to call or text him for me.

Kyle P. age 4

When I miss him I send him texts or call him.

Wyatt P. age 13

I just miss him. I do nothing.

Gabriel T. age 12

I go into my Mommy's room at night and sleep on Daddy's side of the bed.

Liam D. age 8

I think of me and my Dad's happy times when we were alone at the beach playing.

Hailey A. age 10

I think of the positives and picture him just doing boring office work and on the weekends I stay up really late until he comes home.

Alexis A. age 13

I keep pictures of him in my room or my iPod but my favorite one is in my wallet.

Olivia A. age 11

Somehow when I miss him he always ends up in my dreams so I try to think about him while I sleep.

Adam R. age 11

I think of my Mommy.

Gregory C.

Retirement: It's a New Chapter in Your Lives together and The Future is Wide Open!

One morning over breakfast coffee, while you are still shaking off a good night's sleep:

LEO: Hon, I'm thinking about retiring soon. (Pause) Maybe even by next month. What do you think?

LEOW: What!!! ??? When did you decide this? I had no idea you were thinking about going so soon.

LEO: It just feels right. I can't give a long list of concrete reasons. I'm tired of getting up for work every day, the rotating shifts and I want to do something with my life before they throw dirt on my face so I guess those are my "reasons." It's been weighing on my mind lately. When I first got the job, an old hair bag Lieutenant told me at his retirement party that everyone on the job knows when it's time to go. Nothing too concrete to point to but you just know when the time is right for you. I now understand exactly what he meant. I just feel like it's time. Ya' know?

LEOW: I love you and if that's what you think is right for you, I'll support you. Let's set some time aside to figure out our finances and how we can make this work. (While inside your mind is racing about what this means for you and the life and routine you two have built.)

In many ways, it's been a long haul and yet in other ways it feels like the academy days were just yesterday, but finally your LEO is going to retire. Now you can finally do all the things the two of you talked about over the years or perhaps you plan to keep working and your dreams of retirement as a couple will have to stay on hold. Maybe your LEO's retirement date has been decided years ago, maybe it seems like a sudden decision or maybe it's due to an injury. Perhaps he is still young and will start a second career or perhaps he is ready to stop working completely. It's a big change no matter the timing. You might be terrified or you might be filled with relief and happy anticipation. A little of both? Maybe your first thought is to do a happy dance in the middle of the street followed by sheer panic. No more fear of the dreaded knock on the door with life altering news. No more dinners put on hold when your LEO calls to say he will be late. No more nights sleeping alone. But, even "wanted" change can be stressful and a bit scary. Can you really afford it? Will you lose your independence? You have to give up your "me time" that you have learned to love and cherish when he works four to twelve. What if he's bored and drives you crazy? What if he regrets it? Will he miss the camaraderie of being with the guys? If he still needs to work, can he find a new job? The life of a LEOW is all you have known for most or all of your marriage, it's a huge lifestyle change and your emotions and feelings may run the gamut.

Start making the list of things to do. Review the pension or his 401K. Make an appointment with the financial planner. Your husband needs to talk with his boss and fill out any needed paperwork. Tell your families! Thinking about moving? Talk with your husband about where to move and then start planning a visit to the area and research real estate agents. If your husband still wants to work, he needs to start pounding the pavement and lining up a new job. Going out with an injury? What are the benefits available? Can your husband work again and if so does your husband need training to be marketable? Your head starts swimming with all that needs to be done.

First things first! Oh the retirement party he is going to have! Best get planning right away and make sure everyone has enough notice to attend. Pick a location but not too expensive because we all know LEOs won't be able to afford too much. Can you get a deal if you have the party mid-week? After all, his LEO friends don't need it to be a Saturday night when their day off might be a Tuesday. To have it at a fancy banquet hall or just a few guys from work at the usual bar? He is too modest to ask for a big bash but it definitely has to be the big bash! This is a big deal and needs to be celebrated in style. Buy a new dress (but you want to look smashing so you need to work to drop a few pounds for a size smaller than you now wear dress), get comfortable dancing shoes because oh yeah, there is going to be lots of dancing, your husband is going to need a new tie and probably even a new navy blue suit to go with his big baby blues, reserve a hotel room so you don't have to drive home after a few drinks, line up some speakers to toast your husband, making sure he gets a little "roast with the toast" and the "to do" list grows. His best friend "on the job" will surely want to help plan the party. Best give him a call as soon as your husband officially gives his boss the news. It is going to be a party to end all parties. Your husband has earned it and deserves it! This is going to be fun!

How did you help your husband decide if it was time to retire?
He had been volunteering at a local park and could walk to work, share history and chat with visitors, work with animals and operate an eighty passenger boat etc. when a seasonal park ranger position became available. He hadn't been seeking other law enforcement retirement opportunities and didn't just want to retire because he was only fifty one at the time. After twenty five years with his agency, he had come up through the ranks to a very high rank. After 9/11 he grew a little discouraged that the agency, being close to a major metropolitan city, was increasingly pre-occupied with national security/site security/government interoperability etc. and seemed less concerned with the tenents of community policing... this together with the opening of the park ranger position provided the opportunity for "transition."

Eve P.

My husband was in the youth division for the later part of his career and it was getting quite apparent to him that the frustration with the young adults he was arresting and their parents was wearing him down. The court appearances were feeling as though he were on trial rather than the youth he had arrested and his patience and enthusiasm for his job was becoming non-existent. We both knew it was time to "change it up."

Julie J.

I did not help my husband decide if it was time to retire. It was solely his decision and it surprised me a bit but we both agreed it was time.

Sheila E.

Did your husband find a new career after retiring as a LEO? If so, what does he do? If not, how does he fill his day?

My husband has worked security before retirement and now even more so. He also does some limousine driving.

Julie J.

My husband has completely retired from all work. He has been catching up with the neglected honey do list, catching up on unread books, taking long walks and exercising.

Sheila E.

Has your life changed since his retirement?

I've continued in my own career in the media business so he was either working for the park or now completely retired and not working with the park. He tends to do all of the house management, shopping and cooking. He also does a tremendous amount of volunteer work within our community.

Eve P.

I was working at the time my husband retired so we were really never both home during the day together.

Julie J.

What if anything did you do to help him adjust to retirement?

I spent some time both as a volunteer and later as a part-time employee of the park as well.

Eve P.

"Civilian" life was a bit of an adjustment for my husband. He knew he would always be a part of a brotherhood of policemen, but actually not "clocking in" at headquarters and seeing everyone on a daily basis was tough to get used to.

Julie J.

Was it hard for you to adjust to his retirement?

No, since I was working and had my own "distractions."

He had gone about as far as he could go with the agency, he probably was never going to be promoted any higher because we never moved into his department's jurisdiction.

Eve P.

Yes, I am happy that he is looking forward to his time off and that he is healthy to enjoy himself. With a positive outlook, everything falls into place.

Sheila E.

Were you nervous prior to his retirement?

No because he had a couple of years with the park environment as a volunteer and there was no reason to suspect that a full-time position wouldn't be successful.

Eve P.

I was happy that he retired, but of course nervous about the change.

Julie J.

No, I wasn't nervous because I didn't know it would be so soon. I did not have time to get nervous!

Sheila E.

Does your husband keep in touch with "the guys" and if so, how?

Yes, via email, phone, lunch and dinners.

Sheila E.

My husband made a lot of great friendships in the department and keeps in touch with many of them. He attends many of the retirement parties, Christmas parties etc. He loves a party!

Julie J.

Stories That Make Us Smile

"Pea-Oh-Knees": Very beautiful flowers and it's hard for me to pass up an opportunity to photograph them. My neighbor Ed, of chicken coop owner fame, has several peonies lining his walkway and I could not resist the lure to take photos of them. Ed was outside and after approaching him with camera in hand and chatting a bit, I asked if I could take photos of his peonies. Apparently, I need to work on my enunciation because he spun his head around, he glared at me and said "WHAT?!" I stammered "Your flowers, your flowers, the flowers in your yard!" He laughed and said "Sure." Well, thankfully he didn't immediately say "absolutely" and get himself ready for the photo session.

I share this story about myself because LEOWs love to laugh. We can laugh at our husbands and the crazy parts of their jobs, we can laugh at our kid's antics and most of all, we are happy to laugh at ourselves. We need a good old fashioned laugh as frequently as possible.

We all know the fear, the annoyance and the inconveniences of being a LEOW but let's be honest, there are also a lot of "I can't believe that happened" smiles and often belly laughs.

Whether it's our kids, ourselves or our husbands, we find a smile and humor in situations that probably don't exist in a civilian home or our civilian counterparts might not find so funny. Yes, we can have an off-beat sense of humor and find humor where others might not. It's just another crazy day in the life of a LEOW!

With my own head now on a platter, I can freely and without guilt share stories from fellow LEOWs and their families.

"Roses are red, violets are bruisingly blue, I will never commit violence against you." Thanks, I think? Oh, cop humor. Think he went on some domestic calls last night?

Cristina T.

My husband had been out of the police academy for only about a year or so and we hadn't been dating too long. We decided to go away for a nice weekend at the beach right after the fourth of July. My husband brought along some fireworks and suggested we set them off on the beach after dark. A bit of his wild youth remained despite the police shield in his pocket. I really wasn't keen on the idea and once I saw the wind blowing, I really wasn't keen on the idea but my husband was not to be deterred. He set off the first round and things seemed to go okay so he continued to set off a few more rounds. All of a sudden we heard a voice from the sand dunes screaming "Hey moron (not the exact word the guy used), what the heck (another word again) are you doing?" Up popped a half dressed young man and a young woman from the dunes and we could see that flames were all around them. Apparently, the wind had blown the fireworks into the dry dune grass. We breathlessly ran to the dune and immediately began throwing sand on the flames with the help of the young man and woman. We had visions of the entire dune burning and the flames reaching some nearby homes. My husband saw his dream job going up in smoke and his much feared arrest featured on the evening news. Somehow, we managed to put out the fire without too much damage to the dune and slinked away without an arrest. Whew! That was surely a close call and embarrassing at that. Despite his crazy antic, I married him and have never been sorry. At the time it was very scary but we have since learned to laugh at our poor decision to light off the fireworks and our mad dash to put out the flames. An even happier ending: My husband has since retired from his job and had a long and very successful career, attaining a very high rank.

Kimberly K.

The funniest story related to the job had to do with an invitation to our wedding. We couldn't afford to invite everyone we wanted and we couldn't invite a lot of people from our jobs. We kept our wedding and our honeymoon pretty simple because we were paying for a good chunk of it ourselves and we wanted to save for a house. I had never met him but my LEO really wanted to invite his Police Chief to our wedding. I agreed that would be the appropriate thing to do, however, the Chief respectfully declined because he was going to be on vacation with his family. For our honeymoon, we kept it simple and drove up to a beautiful place in a nearby state. While we were on our honeymoon and while touring one afternoon, my LEO says, as our tour van was coming into the main building; "That's the Chief's son." I said to my LEO, "it can't be, you think you know someone every time we go somewhere." We step out of our van and there stands my LEO's boss, the Chief with his family, whom I had never met. I have no idea what came over me. As my LEO stood there with his uncontrollable giggling, my mouth opened and out it came; "Sure, you don't come to our wedding but you show up for the honeymoon, NICE!" Looking back at me was this man, not very tall, chin down with two eyeballs peering at me over the top of his eyeglasses. Thinking to myself, "Oh crap, did I just really say that? Did I just say that to someone I never met? To my LEO's boss? Yes, I did!" He turned beat red and we all started to laugh. That story however would follow me for years, all the way to my LEO's retirement party. Hey, if you saw your husband's boss on your honeymoon, trust me, you'd at least be thinking what I said. Admit it.

Doreen O.

So...hubby's department has a new team...ready for this? The T.W.A.T. team. Tactical weapons and technology. No joke.

Leslie N.

Our 13 year old was talking with her Dad last night about upcoming things at school, and if with his schedule he would be able to come. He responded that he would be able to make most. She then asked that he NOT come in uniform because he will scare all the boys away. Hubby then looked at me and said....."Uniform it is!!!" While we were laughing, she was running to her room saying she will NEVER get a boy!!!!!

Trish S.

My three favorite stories that make me laugh:

I buy my Girl Scout cookies from the daughter of a fellow LEO. I teach high school Science. When the order came in I was joking with a colleague of mine who knows my husband is a LEO about how I was meeting my dealer in a parking lot after work for the hand off. One of my students whispers to another "Is she (meaning me) talking about *drugs*?!" So I whispered back "Yeah, *Girl Scout Cookies!*" The class had a good laugh over that one as once again, their teacher's peculiar brand of humor caught them off guard.

While watching Jeopardy there was a question that began "In this novel about a serial killer..." my young son Kyle jumps in with "Who would kill cereal??!!"

As is typical, my LEO often has a lead foot and we were making some good time on our two hour drive when he blew past a black sports car parked on the shoulder. Immediately the blue lights came on and my LEO pulled over in a safe place. The state trooper approached our vehicle on my side of the car and introduced himself after I lowered the window. In those days, I was young and liked a good low neckline to accentuate my "girls". Well, apparently it worked...during his entire do you know why I pulled you over speech, his eyes never left my "neckline". He didn't even notice when my husband handed him his I.D. alongside his badge! This is still a fond memory for both of us as my "girls" were almost as guilty of him getting a ticket as was his speeding!

Maggie F.

I was told by a random stranger who must have seen the plates on my car that I'm part of a "scary underground subculture of police and their families" I laughed and said, "Really? I am?" He replied with "uhh yeah" so I said "well if that's the case and we are so scary why are you even talking to me and giving me your unsolicited opinion?" He looked at me blankly and walked away. People are so funny. I've been threatened and cornered etc., but never been told that! I just laughed extra loud as he walked away. Oh I love this life!

Emily W.

One time my husband was clearing a house on a possible burglary call and almost shot a stuffed Bobcat. Another time he had a call where the wife was accusing her husband of having a girlfriend who the wife said lived under their mobile home and would sneak into their mobile home when they were asleep.

Bjae K.

Non-LEO related but it was hilarious!! I often help out in my son's 4th grade class and today I was helping them with this week's spelling words. One of the words was "extinct", so after giving them the meaning I asked "what were some things that were extinct?" The kids were shouting out things like dinosaurs, mammoths, etc. This one boy yelled out "Dildo's!!" I was like "What????" He said "You know those birds with huge wings." I said "Honey, I think you mean Dodo's." Still laughing!

Brittany G.

My husband responded to a traffic accident of a woman who tried to take a left too early in the turn and took her left turn right into a tree. Thankfully no one was hurt at all. He walked up to the passenger, who looked shaken, and asked him about the accident. The passenger told him he worked for the DMV and the woman was on her driving test to get her license! My husband looked at the car and then back at the passenger and asked "Did she pass?"

Meredith K.

After a long day, I received a call asking me to prepare a solution that would neutralize skunk odor. My husband had talked to the ER nurses and had gotten a list of agents needed. I forget the particulars but in an effort to capture a rabid skunk, my husband had gotten the wrong end. Luckily, he keeps an extra uniform at work. He had that skunk smell in his nostrils so even when we reassured him that we didn't smell anything, he could barely stand himself. The guys in his department have a few nicknames for him based on the types of incidents he finds himself in. He will share some of the ribbing with my older boys who love to feel part of the club. We have heard on occasion, my middle son call him by one of his co-workers nicknames for him. It's always good for a laugh.

Annemarie J.

My husband and I were living in the town where my husband works and he was working 4-12. It was a beautiful late afternoon and I decided to take our one year old son outside to play with bubbles. I got some soapy bubbles in my eyes and the pain was awful. I couldn't see a thing and a neighbor panicked, called HQ and asked for help. The dispatcher recognized the address and immediately sent an ambulance, the fire department and what seemed like every patrol car working that day, including my husband. By the time my husband got there my eye was fine and I was laughing with all the responding guys.

Another time my husband and I had gone out the night before and as he often did, he put his off duty gun in my purse because he couldn't conceal it well with his shirt. The next day I forgot that the gun was in my purse and as I was at the grocery store check-out counter I removed the gun to find my wallet. I immediately realized what I had done, stuffed it back in my purse and removed my wallet. I looked around in a panic, imagining someone calling out the SWAT team for the crazy lady with the gun at the check-out counter, but fortunately no one noticed or if they did, they pretended not to.

Elarie S.

We don't usually buy doughnuts, but did for a sleep over this weekend. My five year old says to me, "mom, do you know why I LOVE doughnuts? .... It's because I'm a police officer!" I couldn't help but laugh!

The other thing my boys say to my husband (on his days off) is they ask "dad, when are you going to put on your super hero uniform?" Or they tell him how much they love his super hero uniform before he leaves for work.

Brittany G.

Per our nine year old's morning routine, he woke up, and came and snuggled with me a little bit, and then went to look in our bedroom to see if his Dad was home and sleeping yet. When he didn't find him, he asked if he was home yet.....When I answered no, he just shrugged his shoulders and said "He must have busted a lot of bad people last night. I sleep Mom and he busts people!!!" Only out of a mouth of a LEO kid!

Kathy H.

My husband worked a fatality wreck the other day and was talking to our son about it. My son's only question was, was his brain hanging out. The things our LEO kids ask.....

Ashley P.

My eight year old is playing with his Legos and he has two figures he's playing with, one he says is himself and the other is cat woman. I asked what he was playing and he said he and cat woman were cops and she has a purse to keep all the marijuana that she buys undercover in and he goes in and arrests the bad guys.

Missy R.

Chick stole a banana and danish from 7-11, proceeded to get chased by the store clerk, dropped the danish and was eating the crumbs off the parking lot pavement when hubby showed up. Took her to lockup (she was already banned from the store so she was trespassing and had other warrants) where she was allowed to use the bathroom and proceeded to wash her hands in the toilet AFTER she used it and BEFORE she flushed it. Uh-huh... I got nothing.

Connie M.

What was I thinking? I needed a dozen donuts for Saturday and found a box of donuts on sale on Tuesday. I figured I'd buy them on sale and keep them until Saturday because the sale date was good for several days past Saturday and buying them early would save myself a trip to the store on Saturday morning. Why did I think a box of donuts would remain unopened and uneaten in a LEO house for more than one day? Duh! Off to the store I went on Saturday morning for the donuts I now needed again.

Carolyn W.

LEOs share their stories

One summer I had the opportunity to spend 100 hours of ride-alongs as a civilian going through the hiring process for police constable. I had the privilege of riding with many awesome police constables and have several stories to look back on with fondness. However, there is one story that sticks out in particular. One evening shift I was out on the road with PC "D", who had the best sense of humor and I enjoyed our shifts together immensely and learned a lot from him. We often patrolled rural areas and areas known as cottage country due to the thick forests, lakes and cottage style homes in the county. We were patrolling an area near a highway and as we headed northbound we started to cross a bridge and when we looked to our right we saw six bare rear ends!! PC "D" threw the cruiser into reverse and landed beside the now six fully dressed young people who had looks of horror on their faces due to the fact that they had mooned a police car. PC "D" proceeded to inform the individuals that they were receiving a verbal warning for public nudity and not to do it again. After PC "D" finished his lecture he got back into the car and as he pulled away the two of us laughed so hard I had tears streaming down my face. Talk about bad luck when you choose to moon cars going by and you manage to get a police car!!

Rochelle J.

Mrs. Sheridan (not her real name) was an elderly widow and a lovely woman who lived in a very large old house on the wealthy side of town. Mrs. Sheridan lived alone and often heard those "Things that go bump in the night." Things that only older people, who live alone, hear at night.

Mrs. Sheridan was somewhat unique in that she heard the "Bumps" during the day as well. When she did, it would usually result in a call to headquarters.

One problem Mrs. Sheridan would call about is that she was often "Bombarded by rays" from outer space. Each time she would hear a news broadcast that NASA had launched a spacecraft, manned or unmanned, she claimed they punctured the atmosphere and by doing so, allowed rays from space to penetrate the ozone, enter her house and "drive her crazy."

Officers would routinely be called to check her house inside and out and top to bottom with Mrs. Sheridan close on their heels. Nothing would be found out of place and she would admit that she no longer felt the effects of the rays, and the officer would mark the call "unfounded." Mrs. Sheridan would thank the officer politely and go on with her life until NASA launched another spacecraft.

One otherwise uneventful afternoon, while on routine patrol in Mrs. Sheridan's neighborhood, I received a radio call. I was directed to respond to Mrs. Sheridan's address by a relatively new dispatcher. He put out the call as "Request for police, in regards to suspicious activity." The dispatcher followed up with a computer message that read "She said something about rays." I advised the dispatcher that I was familiar with the address and no additional units would be needed.

Upon arrival, I was met at the front door by Mrs. Sheridan who appeared a little upset. She explained that once again NASA punctured the atmosphere and she was again being "Bombarded by the rays." I advised her that I would be glad to check it out. As usual she followed close behind me. I inspected each room for any sign of something amiss. As usual, I found nothing. While on the second floor, I opened a door I had forgotten about since my prior visits. Behind what appeared to be just another closet was a narrow and seldom used flight of stairs. The stairs led to a third floor attic. The solution to our problem came to me like a bolt from space... one might even say a "ray" from space; Aluminum foil!

I asked Mrs. Sheridan "Do you have a roll of aluminum foil?" She said "Of course, in the kitchen." I asked that she get it immediately.

When she returned, I went to the attic alone. I proceeded to cover everything with sheets of aluminum foil until the roll ran out. I came back down, handed her the empty roll and announced with pride that I had fixed her problem once and for all. I explained that because of the facets in the aluminum foil, the rays would be deflected and would no longer be able to penetrate the house any further than the third floor attic. And as long as she didn't go up there after a launch, she would no longer be bothered by the rays.

She hugged and thanked me with tears in her eyes. She asked "how did you know what to do?" I explained that "I had to do the same thing at my house because the rays were making me nuts." The rays were never again a problem at Mrs. Sheridan's.

I returned to my vehicle and called in a 10-16 "Condition corrected" and resumed patrol.

From that day on, I was guaranteed all of Mrs. Sheridan's police business. She would call headquarters and ask for me by name.

Another time I took a prisoner over to the court for arraignment in front of a no-nonsense judge. Judge Greene asked the defendant "Young man, do you have $75.00 on you?" Dude said "No." Judge said "Good, bail is set at $75.00. Officer take him away." "Next." Dude said "What the hell did you ask me for?" Judge said "Next"

Tommy G.

I went on a car accident call and when I got there I found the car was up a pole... I mean literally up a pole. When the other responding Officer and I got there we realized we couldn't even reach him to help him and had to wait for the fire department to respond. While waiting for the fire department, I asked the guy if he had been drinking. He replied "Do you think I could get this _____ing car up here sober?"

I had another funny incident, or at least it is in hindsight.

When you are working patrol alone in one of the most remote sectors of town in the middle of the night, three A.M. seems a little darker for you than anyone else. Add to the darkness a dense fog and mist that makes it difficult to see the hood of your own patrol car and the night becomes almost spooky. All of your senses are just a little more hyper as you adjust the defroster, headlights and wipers in an effort to see where you are going. For me, this was that kind of night.

At about 3:15 A.M. I received a radio transmission from a no nonsense desk sergeant who ordered me to respond to the nearest call box, right away, for an assignment that could not be broadcast over the radio.

I responded immediately, I sped up and made a sharp right turn in the direction of a call box I knew was about three miles away from my location. When I made the turn, I heard something roll from one side of my car's trunk to the other. I ignored the noise and kept going.

My route took me down a dark two lane road, one lane east bound and one west bound. To my left was nothing but woods, to my right, behind a security gate and high fence was a long driveway that led to a chemical plant that operated twenty four hours a day, seven days a week.

As I proceeded past the chemical plant, as fast as I could, given the driving conditions, my eyes began to tear badly, my nose and throat became very irritated and I started coughing and choking. My first thought was "Oh my God, there's a chemical leak at the plant." My vision was obstructed and I couldn't tell if I was seeing fog or smoke. All I knew was if I was having such a reaction driving by quickly, in a closed vehicle, conditions could not be good at the plant.

I arrived at the call box and before the sergeant could give me the assignment he had for me, I excitedly informed him of the "Emergency" I had just discovered. I advised him we needed the nearest fire department with a hazardous material team. We needed to contact the chemical plant security right away. The sergeant advised me that he would handle the notifications and I should return to the plant to meet the responding fire units. I said "No way! The fire department has breathing apparatus and I don't." Until we found out what the heck I was breathing, I was staying as far away as I could. Luckily, he understood and advised me that he would have the responding units meet me at the call box.

Within minutes a fire chief, who had obviously just been awakened by our call met me at the call box. I explained about the tearing eyes, nose and throat irritation and coughing. He said he would check it out and I said "I'll stay right where I am!"

While I waited, I thought it might be a good time to see what had made the noise in my car's trunk. I popped the trunk, looked inside and found the entire contents covered in a while powder. My eyes began to tear again and my nose and throat became irritated. In the middle of it all was an industrial sized dry chemical fire extinguisher and lying beside it was the locking pin which had fallen out. Apparently, when I made the sharp turn, which took me past the chemical plant, the extinguisher rolled, the pin fell out and discharged its entire contents into my trunk making its way into the passenger compartment.

As I stood behind the car reading the extinguisher's label, which included such warnings as; "Do not spray at a person's face, avoid inhaling the chemical agent and may cause skin irritation", the fire chief returned.

He looked much more awake than he had earlier. He informed me that no one at the plant had seen or smelled anything unusual and the fire department had checked the premise with negative results.

I apologetically explained to him what I had discovered in my trunk and that the "chemical leak" had been confined to my vehicle. He drove away without much further conversation.

It took me about an hour to vacuum out the trunk and another hour to write the incident report and requisition another extinguisher.

I never did find out why the sergeant wanted me to go to the call box in the first place.

Cliff L.

I was sent on a car accident call involving three cars during a heavy rain storm. One of the cars needed to be towed so I offered the driver of that car the use of the backseat of my patrol car to stay dry until he could catch a ride with the tow company. I was out dealing with the accident, directing traffic for a good fifteen minutes and then got back in the car to do the paperwork. I had worked on my accident report for another fifteen minutes when dispatch sent me to another accident. I left the first accident, lights and siren and after about two blocks the guy in the back seat spoke up. I had completely forgotten he was there! I jumped at the sound of his voice and apologized profusely to the guy. He was fine, but my heart had to be beating about two hundred beats per minute.

Another time I was out with the SWAT team working the job of "Breacher" at a "house with a fugitive." My job for that particular day was to go to the back of the house, break a window and throw a stun grenade inside, thus distracting anyone inside so that the SWAT team could make their entrance through the front door. In this case the window sill was about seven feet off the ground and I am not that tall! I managed to throw/drop the grenade without looking inside the window. I heard a muffled bang but all seemed well as the SWAT team made their entrance through the front door. I went around to the front door and heard laughter from the back of the house and my name being mentioned in not so complimentary terms and then someone said "What did you do?" I looked in the kitchen and saw broken glass, water and fish everywhere. Apparently, I dropped the stun grenade into a very large fish tank. For my retirement party the PBA gave me a fish tank.

Ron S.

My husband was out for his bachelor party and his friends rented a bus. I was about to get off night shift and received a call from his friend stating that they were DONE and wanted me to pick my fiancé up. He told me they were in his vehicle and in a parking lot. They had left the party to go sit in the truck. When I pulled up I was still in uniform. As I approached the truck, several men yelled "Hey the stripper is here!" and "Did we hire a stripper?" I came back with "NO, it's the fiancé coming to pick up her man." Some of them finally recognized me and were quite embarrassed.

Once I pulled over a man who presented me with a Sheriff's business card. On the top of the card the words "get out of jail free," were handwritten. I asked what the card was for and he said "It says right there. I was told if I give it to you, I can get out of a ticket." My reply, "Ahhhhh, NO."

I took a drunk man home one night. He had just broken up with his woman and was quite upset. We were busy so instead of arresting him I took him home so he would not get hurt or hurt anyone else. I listened to his heart wrenching breakup story and I tried to give good advice as best that I could to someone under the influence. I opened the car door to let him out and he thanked me for listening. Then, as if we had been on a date, he puckered up his lips and closed his eyes for a good night kiss. "Not tonight, lover boy."

Lori T.

Stories That Make Us Proud of Our LEO

We all know the annoying LEO bashing that goes on in social media, comments from strangers in public and at parties we are invited to, in the news media and sometimes even in our own families. It seems that every LEO mistake and often wrongly perceived mistake is discussed ad nauseam but very little heed is paid to the daily good our LEOs do for their fellow citizens. If a "LEO does good" story makes the news, it's usually short, gone in a day and it's usually a spectacular act of heroism that a LEO commits to make a news story that isn't anti-LEO. The day to day "making a difference in other's lives" stories are known only to the other LEOs working that shift and maybe the LEO's family, if he shares his daily stories. If he talks about it, it will be done with modesty and as an after-thought to his day, not the headline of his day.

Like many LEO's, my husband is a fairly private person. He doesn't like to make a big deal out of his profession and prefers to remain under the radar, so to speak. I have only seen him show his badge off duty a few times in seventeen years. The first time was after a long day at the state fair and two really drunk guys were fighting it out in the parking lot near our car. Of course he stepped in until local LEOs arrived and took over. The next time was a similar situation- a domestic argument in the parking lot of a big box store. Then there was the time that we were at the mall and a woman was walking out of a department store simultaneously dragging and smacking the daylights out of her two year old. He called out to her that she needed to stop what she was doing and she graced him with a few choice words culminating in "Who the h--- do you think you are?" He pulled out his badge and responded, "The guy who is going to take you to jail if you touch your child again." On each occasion I watched my LEO do his thing with a real sense of pride. I am so proud of him and the way he does his small part to make this world a better place.

Filled with pride and beaming from ear to ear! Yes stories of our husband's doing a good job make us all smile and we fill with pride. It doesn't have to be a "race into the burning building" story or a "disarm the bank robber" story for us to feel pride in our LEOs. The day to day work that they do fills our hearts with pride every time. When they are not working, LEOs continue to share their compassion and desire to help others, making us proud to be their wives. If someone who was helped tells the story, we just about burst with pride. We also love to hear about the good that other LEOs do, feeling pride for the entire Thin Blue Line. The feeling of pride in our husband's daily mission of making a real and positive difference in people's lives is one of the perks of being a LEOW.

At my current job, one of my co-workers was telling me a story about how she was a victim of identity theft, how terrifying it was and how the officer that handled her case was really great. It turns out it was my guy!

Meredith K.

When my daughter was just learning to walk, she took my husband's radio and managed to push the button and began talking on the radio. It's a small town so all the LEOs and dispatchers knew her so they just talked back to her.

Patty R.

I was looking through our nine year old son's pack of papers that he left on the counter this morning. One of the papers had a question about safety.....They had to answer it as to what made them feel safe...Our son said..."My Dad makes me feel safe. He's a police officer, he has everyone's back!!!!!" Yep, that's our LEO kid!!!!! The teacher's response was......"Tell your Dad thanks for keeping us all safe!"

Kathy H.

The other day my husband was sitting in line waiting to pick up my youngest from school. As he was sitting there he heard a loud explosion. As all police do, he left the school line and went to investigate. A truck had struck the power pole and pulled the line down. The line was arching and had set a ladies yard on fire and the fire was lapping up on the brick on the outside of her home. On the front porch was a caretaker screaming Help! My husband ran up to her as the fire was burning and running under her parked car. When he got to the caretaker she told him that there was an elderly lady inside and she couldn't get her out. My husband ran in, picked the elderly lady up and ran with her outside. The lady was so thankful. Today she sent flowers and called my husband's sheriff. I'm so very proud of him.

Tracy Y.

While this may never make the news and might seem small, I think it has a big impact on kids. Whenever my husband sees a kid's lemonade stand, he always stops to buy a cup and chats with the kids for a little while and lets them check out his "cool" car.

Lauryn P.

My husband's detective squad recently worked on a homicide case in their usual methodical manner because it is their sincere and deeply held belief that they never ever want to arrest the wrong person. The local newspaper reported on the conviction of the killer by saying "It took (blank) police department some time, but, working with the District Attorney's Office, they arrested..." Ah, yeah it took the police "some time" because they didn't want to arrest the wrong person! Imagine if the police rushed to make an arrest and the wrong person was arrested or the case was lost at trial due to sloppy police work... the news media would have a field day with negative coverage then. I smile with pride when I know how hard my husband's squad works to do things by the book, follow the spirit and the letter of the law, leave no stone unturned and will not even consider an arrest until there is no possible way they have the wrong person. They work hard to make sure the people they arrest are guilty not just to the "probable cause for arrest" standard but are guilty beyond the "reasonable doubt" standard. They have yet to lose a case in court and have never been over turned on appeal!

Terri W.

My husband keeps items for kids in his gear bag. If he has a child that is on a scene or in a bad situation, he will give them a stuffed animal, snack or sticker to let them know he's there to help. He does anything to make the little ones as comfortable as can be.

I can't tell you how many times he has not eaten his lunch because he's given it away to someone or spent our money on buying baby bottles or something a victim needed. He has the biggest heart and I am so lucky to be married to him.

Shannon V.

My mother is in a nursing home and my husband Frank and I spend a lot of time at the nursing home with her. Frank is well known and very well liked among the residents and staff. He has a great sense of humor and always has everyone smiling. My mother loves Bingo Day and we always attend with her. Frank always sits with a man in his 80s, who has a severe disability but so enjoys Bingo. Frank helps him play the Bingo card and despite this patient's limited communication abilities my husband and he have bonded. Watching my husband interact with such kindness and compassion for the elderly and infirm, the dignity he always treats them with and the friendship he has with this gentleman fills me with pride.

My husband also helps out our elderly neighbor by clearing the snow off of her driveway and sidewalk with his snow blower. She has never asked for help but my husband has taken it upon himself to assist her in any way that he can.

Frank has a huge heart and he makes a difference every day in so many lives at work and at home.

Jessie D.

Many years ago, there was an elderly woman Mrs. Jackson, who my husband's job got to know very well because she was a "frequent caller." She would imagine things like a fire in her living room and the officers would come and "stomp out the imaginary flames" for her and then check the rest of the house to give her peace of mind that the "fire" hadn't spread. They would often be called to the home because "someone was in my house." They would slowly walk around the house to let her know it was safe. One day, they were shocked to find that someone was indeed in the house. Mrs. Jackson's son lived a few hours away and had allowed someone to live in the attic room as a way to keep an eye on his mother. His mother had forgotten he was there and became frightened. The guy in the attic left soon after that incident. Another time Mrs. Jackson called and said someone was harassing her with phone calls about a piano. She complained that they wouldn't stop calling no matter how many times she told them she did not have a piano. While the guys were there taking a report about the phone calls, a piano truck showed up to deliver her piano. She used to teach piano and her son thought she would like to play again so he ordered a piano for her as a surprise. The delivery guys said they had been calling all day to arrange delivery and she kept hanging up on them. Poor Mrs. Jackson almost had a heart attack but the police officers taking the report had a good laugh.

The guys in the "crew" soon became concerned about Mrs. Jackson and also a bit attached to her. They began to check on Mrs. Jackson without being called and would often bring her hot meals. She had plenty of frozen and canned food that her son kept stocked for her but the guys wanted to be sure she had a "nice meal" whenever they could. They would share their Sunday lumberjack breakfasts, lunch pizzas, takeout dinners and everything in between. The guys were pretty rough around the edges and full of testosterone but were so kind, thoughtful and generous with Mrs. Jackson. I don't even know if her son ever knew all that the guys did for her but eventually she agreed to move in with her son and Mrs. Jackson was no longer a frequent caller.

Sue K.

Managing On a LEO Paycheck

Budget: Ugh! Do we have to? Yes! A must discussion for any LEO and LEOW!

"Sergeant Blacking, you cheap bastard! You didn't give the delivery guy a tip!" The desk Lieutenant's words echoed throughout the Police building, thanks to the intercom system. Sergeant Roger Blacking immediately thought, "I gave the guy a ten dollar tip, what is he talking about?" He put his glasses on, which he should have done when he paid the guy, looked into his wallet and turned a thousand shades of red as he realized his mistake. The bill was thirty dollars and he meant to give the delivery guy two twenties, which included a very generous tip. Instead he gave him a ten and a twenty.   Roger immediately ran down to the desk and gave the Chinese food delivery guy the remaining twenty dollar bill that was in his wallet, too embarrassed to ask for ten dollars back. Moral of the story: Wear your glasses when reaching into your wallet and always pay attention to your money. And yes, his crew makes sure to remind him of this from time to time with some good natured ribbing.

While small mistakes such as Sergeant Blacking's can make us laugh, financial issues are serious business and can bring both happiness and pain.

Police salaries are not known to be extravagant. Add a few kids into the mix and it's hard to make ends meet. A budget is a must to ensure you achieve all of your financial and life goals. A budget will also help you decide if it is time to add children to your marriage or if you need a sounder financial foundation on which to afford all of their needs.

It can be a good idea for husbands and wives to sit down and work on a budget together. Both need to understand all financial matters in the marriage and agree on the final plan of attack. Heaven forbid one of you should die prematurely, the other will need to know and understand all financial information.

Are you and your husband on the same page financially and if so, do you have any advice to help other couples discuss and agree on finances? Do you have a formal budget?

We have a budget but we live paycheck to paycheck for the most part. We are not on the same page! I love to shop. He wishes I'd save more. Cassie S.

We are on the same page financially. We both are not big spenders and long ago my husband set up auto-withdrawals from his paycheck to investments. It is a great way to save. We also save additional money from each paycheck. We don't have a budget per se but always save more than we spend. We have been to a financial planner to ensure our retirement goals are within reach and this helped us to understand our finances better.

Terri W.

We are on the same page but we are honestly on the same page about everything. The only advice I can give is you have to always have open communication and absolutely no jealousy about anything.

Bjae K.

Yes we are. We talk about finances and work our budget together. All purchases that are not in the budget are discussed and those that cost $25 or more are discussed again even if they are with money that is just for our own spending pleasure.

Beth C.

In his line of work, we absolutely have to have a budget. We go through and calculate each bill and his paycheck and subtract everything out. On those weeks we have a little extra, we buy a little more food and it all seems to even out by the end of the month. We bought a chest freezer which has allowed us to stock up on meat when we find great deals and we also buy in bulk at one of the "box stores," to help stock up on items that can keep. Don't go crazy when extra money comes in and look at the best place to put that money to use. Be frugal and coupon (you don't have to go to extremes but using coupons here and there really does help) and watch for sales.

My husband leaves me in charge of the finances because I stick to the budget and make sure we can pay for everything that we need to. He came from a marriage where his ex-wife spent more than he made and he never made ends meet. Since we got married we talk about money; money is not a taboo subject for us. We're open about what we spend and how much we spend on something. If the item we want to buy is over one hundred dollars we discuss the purchase and once we're both in agreement we purchase it. We do try to have an "allowance" (I hate using that word but that is what it is) each pay period that we can spend on whatever we want. We also each put money aside during the year to save for Christmas so we can buy the other what we want to and not have him/her know what it is. There has to be communication when it comes to finances and neither person can be hot headed about finances.

Patty R.

We have a very very tight budget. It took some getting used to, but I'm thankful for it now. We have really learned to place less value on material things and I feel like we are happier for it. We discuss everything about money and disagreements are very rare.

Colleen R.

Financially, we tend to wax and wane. I do the books and keep our bills paid. We have planning meetings about the week and purchases that are coming down the line. We try to do our best to stretch our resources and plan for seasonal spending including kid's activities and school needs. We don't always agree how to proceed but usually one of us will rethink our position and compromise. Our sacrifice is for the greater good of the family. We have a hard time with the poor decisions we made early on in our married lives, before we had children. We'd do a lot differently if we could go back. That seems to be a theme in our financial health. We are still paying for poor choices we made as well as credit card debt.

Annemarie J.

I would say on most things my husband and I are on the same page financially and that's because our big goals are the same. It's bad enough that LEO's have a high divorce rate, the stress of money is another leading cause. There are many resources available, often for free for public service or at a nominal fee to help manage your financial portfolio and help get or keep you on track. Ask at your local bank if there is anyone in house that can help. Many banks have free checking services and other financial services, including good interest loans for police officers.

Budget? When I met my LEO, he didn't know what a budget was. He had been on his own from an early age. He was responsible in paying his bills, but planning for the future or specific budgeting was not his forte. My father, who had multiple degrees in finance made sure I knew the basics of money management and has always been available when advice was needed. I think my LEO was happy when I took the money aspect over but he is always in the loop.

Denise N.

A quick look at your spending prior to making a formal budget.

For a quick financial picture of what you are saving, compare your bank and investment statements from one year ago with statements from today. Have you saved or lost money? Once you have a quick shot, it's time to understand where your money is going. You may do a budget using the many apps that are available or the old fashioned way by hand. Apps or computer programs can make the budget process very easy. Physically writing everything down helps some people get a better sense of exactly when and where they spend money. It's more time consuming and arduous but you might find the "by hand" method yields more impactful results, hitting you in the gut each time you spend a penny.

Making a budget.

1) Make a list of all your monthly expenses. Check your bank statement and credit card statements to make sure you have them all. Go back at

least six months to be sure you do not miss quarterly or bi-annual payments. Don't forget, utilities, car payments, mortgage or rent and union dues.

2) Make a list of all yearly expenses such as magazine subscriptions, life, healthcare and car insurance, average yearly dental and eyeglass bills, dues for organizations you and your husband belong to and taxes. Divide that by twelve for the monthly cost.

3) Make a list of all out of pocket cash for at least two months. Every time you spend a dime, even if for a cup of coffee on the way to work, write it down. Keep your grocery receipts for two months. Make a monthly average for cash payments. Review your credit card receipts for several months and get a monthly average.

4) Add together all your monthly bills, cash payments average and credit card bill average, your yearly expenses that you averaged out for the twelve months, to determine what you are spending each month.

5) Go through the complete list of expenses and determine what is necessary and what is discretionary. Review your cash payment list and credit card bill to determine what is necessary and what is discretionary. Needs vs Wants. For example: Food and shelter are needs although they can possibly be purchased for less. Video games, vacations, designer clothes and fancy cars etc. are wants, not needs and can be eliminated or cut back on to save money. Divide the total expenses list into these two categories for later use.

6) Make a list of all monthly income. To add any income paid on a quarterly or yearly basis, divide the yearly income by twelve and the quarterly by three to determine the monthly portion.

7) Subtract your total monthly expenses from your total monthly income. Do you have any money left over? Are you spending more than you make?

8) Make a list of what you need to be saving for. Are you fully funding your IRA and any retirement savings programs through work? Do you

have kids to put through college? Will you need a new car soon? Do you plan to buy a house and need a down payment? Do you have children's weddings in your near future? Do you have six month's salary as a cushion for an emergency? If you have a special needs child, do you need to establish a fund or trust for long term care?

9) Add to your monthly expenses what you need to be saving per month for your future needs. For example, if you need to fund your IRA at $6,000 per year, you need to put aside $500 per month per IRA or if you want a new car down payment of $10,000 in two years, you need to set aside $417 each month.

10) It is also important to speak with an insurance agent to determine your individual life and homeowner or renters insurance needs. You may also want to discuss with your insurance agent an umbrella policy (liability insurance) to help cover potential law suits from inadvertently acting outside the scope of your job and therefore, not indemnified by your job or other potential lawsuits, for example false arrest. An umbrella policy may also cover lawsuits that exceed your coverage on other policies, such as car or homeowner's policies you may have. Do you want long term care insurance for your senior years? It's cheaper to purchase when you are younger than waiting until you are older. You will need to budget for these insurance expenses too.

11) While reviewing insurance needs, keep in mind that some police jobs or unions will offer legal counsel for job related legal issues and also some offer discounts on legal counsel for non-job related issues such as divorce, real estate closing etc. Check with your union and job and if this is something you think will be beneficial to you but not offered at work, you may want to join a fraternal police organization that includes such legal discounts as part of your yearly dues. These additional dues will need to be a part of your budget.

12) Review your necessary and discretionary spending to see where cuts can be made if needed.

When you are satisfied with your new budget of spending and savings you may want to speak with a certified financial planner to determine how best to achieve all of your financial goals.

Stretching a budget.

Sometimes, no matter how good you are at budgeting and controlling your money, things just happen. Unexpected job loss, medical expenses or car repairs can cause a snowball effect of destroyed savings and tattered budgets. The stress money troubles can cause often feels insurmountable but fear not, often it is possible to reverse the troubles with a little bit of hard work and dedication to getting out of debt and squaring your finances once again.

If finding a part time job or supplementing your income in some other way is not an option then you need to look around your home for answers. The first thing I got rid of when we had some budgetary issues was cable. The price of entertainment in the twenty first century is out of this world. We were paying nearly $250 per month for cable, internet access and phone service. In one ten minute phone call, I cut those things down to less than half. We have basic cable, no long distance calling and a mid-grade internet connection. I use the internet for work so we had to remain connected but I opted for the slower, sometimes more annoying connection for about half the cost. Our cable is basic and the phone line is really only used now for the house alarm system. I wouldn't think twice though about totally dropping our cable connection if we needed to save even more money.

Another cash black hole is cell phone/data plan service. I have lived my whole adult life without the ability to access my email from my cell phone. If finances are an issue, drop the data plan and lose the smart phone. Pick up a pay as you go phone for emergencies or basic communication but cell phone service is a luxury, not a necessity and should be one of the first things to go in a financial emergency.

It should also go without saying that in a financial crisis, coupons should be your best friend. Stick to store brand items and forgo fancy snacks and treats. If you want a cookie, bake one at home. Homemade is cheaper and tastes so much better than preservative laden store bought treats. Eating take out, fast food and restaurant meals should come to an end as well. Make rice, pasta and beans your best friend for a while. There are many creative ways to cook them, they are filling and nutritious and cheap! A five pound bag of rice is less than five dollars and doubles in amount when you cook it. Toss in a can of tomatoes and some kidney beans with garlic and spices and you will be surprised what you can do. Again, it won't be gourmet but in a financial crisis, that doesn't matter. When you are faced with debt collectors, defaults and repossessions, a few rice dinners are insignificant. Not to mention, it is so much healthier for your family than eating fast, processed foods all the time. You might find you like the challenge of creating inexpensive, healthy, great tasting meals.

Another way to boost your budget is to go on a downsizing, de-cluttering spree. You would be surprised how much *stuff* you have in your house that you can sell and how much it might be worth. One year I decided to pay for Christmas with only things I sold online. It was a very good Christmas! There is a lot of money in your kid's outgrown clothes, tools the hubby hasn't touched in five years and even random items you keep holding onto "just because".

Finally, consider changing your living arrangements. In desperate times, extreme measures may be necessary. Is it possible to move to a smaller, less expensive rental? Should you think about selling a home that is more than you can afford and moving to an apartment?

When things feel like they have spiraled out of control, consider the things you can control. You might be surprised at what you can accomplish with just a few changes to your spending habits.

What tips can you share to help stretch a budget?

I shop for my daughter at consignment stores and through Mom swaps on Facebook. I also use discount sites online.

Cassie

I try to make casseroles so we can have leftovers. I have a Christmas club account to help put money aside for Christmas and I also have a small savings account that takes out a little each check for rainy days.

Bjae K.

I shop the grocery store fliers to plan my meals. I make most things from scratch so I am not spending a lot a prepared food. I hate to shop for clothes so I don't buy things unless I really need them.

Terri W.

I buy generic, on sale and meats in bulk. Most of my kitchen planning meals are heavy on prep but I feel that is part of the burden since I stay home. I try to make baked goods for our house that freeze well. I try to have a few dozen cookies in the freezer.

Annemarie J.

I honestly have no clue how ends meet sometimes. We've looked at our bills and things we want and decided what we can live without and what we can't. We put a little aside in our safe each paycheck to have in case of emergencies. We look at sales and make menus so that we buy what we need for the two weeks in one trip so we don't go to the store multiple times and spend more than we truly are able to.

Patty R.

I make my own laundry soap, make enough supper for lunches the next day and shop sales for everything.

Colleen R.

I find direct deposits and taking advantage of pre tax deductions help. While I may not be extreme, I am a coupon clipper. I never realized how much money you can save by preplanning your shopping, sticking to it and using those coupons! When you first start clipping, learn the rules of each store. It does take some time, but once you get it down, it doesn't consume that much time. There are so many phone apps now, it's becoming easier and faster to compare prices and make your shopping list and save your coupons right at your finger-tips. I use store cards and other coupon apps which cover the major retailers. The key to using coupons and budgeting, is sticking to the list of items that you really need. I find when I do this, I save more and then I don't feel guilty when we take some of that "savings" money and go out.

Denise N.

You really need to be willing to look at what is a priority in your life. You also need to be willing to discuss finances with your LEO. Every relationship is different and to who is the person that keeps the family on track financially, but communication is a key ingredient for us. Also we use the Dave Ramsey method and it has saved us more times that I can count!

Beth C.

Already too Far into Debt?

Are you already too far into debt to see any end in sight or do you want to revamp your financial life by saving more money? Dave Ramsey has written several books on how to cut expenses to get out of debt, the best way to pay down your debt and how to save money once out of debt. Many police wives have used his methods to help them find freedom from what felt like crushing debt. There are many "get out of debt books on the market and Dave Ramsey is just one author. He has been mentioned by numerous LEOWs as having advice that was helpful to them. You may choose to do your own research to determine what resource would be best for your own circumstances. When you are finally in a position to invest, it may be a good idea to get professional investment advice from a certified financial planner who can review your individual circumstances and tailor a plan to meet your needs.

The Total Money Makeover Workbook by Dave Ramsey (Jan 21, 2003)

Dave Ramsey's Complete Guide to Money: The Handbook of Financial Peace University by Dave Ramsey (Jan 10, 2012)

The Financial Peace Planner: A Step-by-Step Guide to Restoring Your Family's Financial Health by Dave Ramsey (Jan 1, 1998

The Total Money Makeover: Classic Edition: A Proven Plan for Financial Fitness by Dave Ramsey (Sep 10, 2013)

What is an umbrella insurance policy, as mentioned in item ten of the budget?

There is a saying in police work, "one oh crud (although crud is not quite the word LEOs use) wipes out all your atta boys." It works in life too. One oh crud moment wipes out a lifetime of hard planned for and fought for savings. We buy insurance to plan for and protect us from those "oh crud" moments.

A liability Insurance policy is often referred to as an umbrella policy. It covers above and beyond your homeowner's, car, boat etc. insurance policy for liability. You may commonly purchase an umbrella policy to cover from one million to ten million dollars above what your other insurance has as liability limits. For example, if your homeowner's policy has a three hundred thousand dollar limit and you are sued for seven hundred thousand dollars, your umbrella policy will pick up the difference for the additional four hundred thousand. An umbrella policy may also protect you financially up to your chosen limits in the event you or your spouse commits a false arrest, slander, libel or malicious prosecution. If the police department does not cover you for these events, your umbrella insurance may cover your liability. Umbrella policies only cover actual damages and generally do not cover punitive damages. An umbrella policy may also cover any legal expenses incurred up to the limit of your policy. It is an important policy for police officers to consider purchasing. As with all major financial and life decisions, please speak with a professional and in this case, a licensed insurance professional. Your individual life circumstances, assets and coverage needs, determined in consultation with an insurance professional, will help you determine if an umbrella policy is right for you and exactly what will or will not be covered.

LEOs eat too!

LEOs are often asked questions from the public and from time to time the question might leave the LEO shaking his head. Sometimes the head shaking question is just a statement.

True story:

Yes! LEOs Eat! While working in uniform and eating at a diner, a middle aged woman approached a LEO and said "oh my gosh, it never occurred to me that police officers have to eat too." Really? How did she get this far in life and miss that whole cops and donuts thing? The LEO had to break it to her gently that LEOs are human and need food at regular intervals just like civilians.

Meal periods are usually short to begin with and become even shorter when duty calls and so more often than not, LEOs choose a meal spot based on speed of food service and convenience of location. This usually means expensive and unhealthy on a Monday day tour when a fast food restaurant or diner is the usual spot to grab a quick bite and even more so when the only thing open at three in the morning is the fated donut shop or gas station market. Sometimes, your LEO prefers something from home and it's a great way to save money on the cost of your LEO eating out while he is working.

Brown bagging can seem a hassle but when one weighs the savings and health benefits, it really is worth it and your LEO will definitely appreciate it, but sandwiches can get boring. Do you have any suggestions to make a brown bag lunch more interesting?

My husband loves tuna boats... tuna fish or chicken salad stuffed in celery stalks. He also likes tuna or chicken salad in a tomato or pepper. The tomato can be a bit messy to eat but I put it in a small round Tupperware to keep it from spilling everywhere. You can also just cut the tomato or pepper up and mix it with the salad.

Donna J.

I make homemade soup once a week and put large batches in individual portion containers in the freezer. I take out what I need, microwave and then put it in a thermos to keep it hot for his lunch. Having several different kinds of soup in the freezer keeps him from getting bored.

Krissy N.

My husband is kind of a health nut so I make his food every day. He takes chicken and broccoli to work. They have a microwave available to them.

Cassie S.

I go to the store and buy stuff for salads. My husband loves having salad for lunch and I can add ham, chicken, steak or anything else. I put the items in little bags and put them all in a bag for him; this is his favorite lunch. We are also blessed to live in the city he works in so he can come home and grab lunch or dinner and have homemade pizza, roast or whatever else I've made. He also takes leftovers from meals the night before and heats them up. If I'm making lasagna, I make more than we'll eat and cut up the extra, portion it in containers and freeze it so that he can grab a container out whenever he goes to work and he's good to go.

Patty R.

I send meals with my husband daily. This can be a simple packet of oatmeal and fruit, a sandwich, chips and granola bar for a day shift. For a night shift, a hot meal of whatever dinner I am cooking and snacks for overnight. We save lots of money by doing this.

Annemarie J.

He usually has leftovers from the previous night's supper.

Colleen R.

Working your job around his schedule / Working from home.

He works 4-12 and you work 9-5. He is gone when you come home from work and you are asleep when he gets home and he is asleep when you leave in the morning. Ships passing in the night. He is off Tuesday and Wednesday and your days off are Saturday and Sunday. Have a few kids and it can be extremely stressful to juggle it all. You feel like a single parent working all day, coming home to a house with kids but no husband to help and you miss him like crazy. What to do? Some wives have very lucrative careers that they would rather not give up and have to find a way to work around their LEO's difficult and often erratic schedule. Some wives love their job and don't want to give it up. Some find that by the time they pay for child care, they have little left over from their pay check and working makes very little sense/cents and some wives prefer to be a stay at home Mom. A stay at home Mom has a chance to see her husband on his weekdays off and before he goes in to work on night tours. If your choice is to stay home, it can often be difficult to make ends meet on a LEO's salary. A work from home job is a great solution for some women.

Do you have a job that works around his crazy schedule? Can you suggest careers or work from home jobs that are flexible?

I am a therapist and I work for the same County that my husband does. I work Monday to Friday nine to five (ish) and he works evenings. Our schedules work now, but we are concerned about what we are going to have to do once we start having a family. I am working part time in private practice as well. I am hoping that I can do private practice full time so that I can be in charge of my own schedule and work whenever I can around his schedule so that we don't have to put our kids in daycare. We shall see!

Meredith K.

When I first met my LEO, my schedule was the normal Monday through Friday, 9am-5pm. There were those weeks when my LEO worked overnights, I just had to accept that I was just not going to see him for a week because he needed to sleep. After we got married and life went on, we did our best to make our work schedules work. Granted, before kids, it was easier. I worked in the health and fitness industry. I tried to take shifts and give lessons at times when he would be working so we could be together. Shifts were shifts, but as a private swim instructor, I had some flexibility as to when I taught my lessons and I would try to teach those when he was working. They also paid well. The downside, they are tiring and while I had been doing it for a while and had a large client base, it can take time to build up and you need an available pool to work out of. Then your clients don't always show up. It can be hard to be in the water for hours day after day for a long period of time and if you're out sick and can't work, chances are, you're not going to get paid unless you're a salaried pool director, which I did become but the hours were long and the chemicals long term, unpleasant to be around.

Then as they say, if you can't beat them, join them. Well I didn't really join my LEO but I was a volunteer EMT and went on to become a Paramedic. I had been taking the minutes of the monthly ambulance call audits for the local hospital and medical director of the ambulance corps, when the new EMS director at the local hospital approached me. He asked if I would be interested in a job working in the Emergency Education Center with him. I literally was nine months pregnant about ready to have my first child and I already had a job I liked. Who expects a job offer when you're that pregnant and all you're thinking about is what color Winnie the Pooh sheet you're going to have in the crib? That was totally out in left field. He went on to say he needed someone who knows all the local EMS providers and he would be willing to be flexible. After I had my son, as it happened, the hours at my old job weren't going to work out. The gentleman approached me again but I told him I needed daycare because my LEO worked days. He said he would do what he could and if there was any availability in the hospital day care center, which was right next door to the office. I ended up taking the job, which I admit, didn't pay the best, but it was 2 miles from my house, my 12 week old son was in the building next door and I could go visit him anytime I felt I needed to. The best part, the new boss was willing to work and be flexible with hours as long as I got my time in and got the work done.

Unfortunately, someone isn't going to walk up to you every day and just say "Hey, come work for me and let's work out the hours." However, I do believe, with a well thought out plan and a commitment to work, sometimes you can work something out with your boss. When I was offered the job, my LEO was working in community policing, which at the time was a daytime job. My new job would have had me put my newborn into daycare 5days a week and really almost cancelling out going back to work. My LEO knowing how important it was to me to get back to work and what a great opportunity it was, sat down and evaluated his own job. Because he was not in a usual rotation, he went back to his chief and made the argument that they could save on some overtime and actually made a schedule that made better sense to meet the department's needs if they allowed him to come in later 2 days a week and work a Saturday. Ultimately they agreed and my LEO was home on Mondays and 2 mornings a week with our newborn. The afternoons he had to go to work, I would leave work early and make up the hours on other days. Everyone won. I got a new job with some income. My LEO got to be home a couple of mornings with his newborn and we didn't get totally killed with day care expenses.

I would later take a grant position that initially would let me work from home. You just need to be careful with this. You have to be very disciplined to work from home and make sure you don't let anyone distract you. Even if you are disciplined, others will interrupt. This only lasted for a while before the boss got a new boss and the deal was reneged. It's too bad, I ended up spending so much time traveling back and forth instead of really focusing on what I could have been doing. Egos, that's the overly polite way of putting it. (I'm being really nice and they don't deserve it)

Denise N.

I started out as a stay at home Mom but I recently took a job with a food store part time and they are working with me around my husband's schedule. I go to work when he gets home at night so he can be here with our daughter. There are medical billing jobs that allow you to work from home and create your own hours and many jobs are willing to work with you when they learn you are a LEOW.

Patty R.

I stay at home with our three year old. I've never worked full time and quit, or as he says, retired when we got married. Flexibility is key with their job. I can't imagine working nine to five and him working midnights. It would put a stress on our family that we are fortunate to not have right now.

Cassie S.

I was fortunate enough to take over my Mom's job once my youngest started school. Medical billing from home. I had someone who worked for me so my husband and I were able to go to a movie or out to lunch by ourselves if he worked on the weekends and was off during the week.

Elarie S.

I currently am a stay at home Mom so that I can be with our four boys. My LEO is never sure what his day will hold and cannot really commit to being somewhere at a certain time. Due to this, it works best for us right now for me to be home. I was working full time as a medical transcription editor from home previously, which was flexible to a certain extent.

Vicky C.

I stay home and don't work but know of some stay at home jobs including the decal business, t-shirt embroidery, dog walker, graphic artist and writer. Some LEOWs do pampered chef parties or Tupperware parties to bring in some extra money.

Terri W.

The next few pages contain a list of money saving tips and tricks shared by fellow LEOW's. These pages are intended to be removed from the book so that they can be notated on as needed.

Some money saving ideas

Grocery shop the sales by checking the flier before shopping and plan meals based on the sales.

Use coupons, checking online coupon sites prior to shopping. Buy the Sunday newspaper for the coupons if you save more than the cost of the newspaper. Use coupons/apps on your phone for ease.

Check sale dates at the grocery store, checking the back of the shelves for better dates to cut back on throwing out expired food.

Speak to the butcher at your grocery store to determine when meats are marked down so you can get the best selection.

Use your plastic grocery bags for your garbage eliminating the need to buy garbage bags.

Wash out your plastic zipper food storage bags and reuse.

Buy store brands when possible.

Make your own cookies and baked goods.

Make your own laundry soap and cleaning products.

Cut back on morning coffee at the café and bring your own from home

Brown bag your lunch and snacks.

Eat out less often for dinner and cook things that you know will make left overs for the nights you know you won't have time to cook.

Eat vegetarian several nights a week, making pasta, rice and beans your go to meals.

Cut your phone bill by eliminating your land line or keep your land line and use only a basic pay as you go cell phone for emergencies. Keep your cell phone but eliminate data plan.

Cut back on your cable bill by using the most basic service or eliminating it all together and turn off your television.

Use an internet connection and service for any television you want to watch via your computer.

Watch movies with Netflix or free on demand instead of going out to the movies.

Get free DVD movies and books at the library instead of buying or paying for books or a rental movie. Books can often be downloaded to a Kindle for free from the library website.

Check your local library to see if they offer free passes to local attractions.

Check your local library for free music concerts, lectures, book discussion groups and movies.

Iron your husband's uniform or dress shirts or teach him to do it to save on dry-cleaning costs. Even some poly blend shirts benefit from a quick iron.

Check yard sales and thrift shops for gently used clothing, toys and household goods.

Have a clothing, toy and sports equipment swap for yourself and kids with friends.

Clean out your house and hold a yard/tag/garage sale.

If using your credit card for day to day buying make sure you are paying the balance off each month and any "points earned" are worth it. Reaching into your wallet and using cash will make you rethink your daily purchases. Using plastic can make it a little too easy to spend money.

Buy a home repair how-to book for basic repairs and save on the costs of a professional.

Put off buying a new car and fix your old one or buy a pre-owned car.

Check with your insurance agent to determine if you can cut down on monthly insurance premiums by increasing your deductible. Make sure you can afford to pay any increase in the deductible if needed.

Do you have a skill to barter with? Can you do the dentist's accounting in exchange for dental care for your family? Tutor his kids? Can you paint his office or paint artwork for his office?

A stay at home Mom may be able to add a working Nom's errands to her own daily errands for a fee. Walk the neighbor's dog for a fee.

Set up a babysitting club with friends to save on babysitting costs. Exchange babysitting for each other.

Cut back on Christmas/ Hanukkah and birthday presents. Speak with family about not exchanging gifts with adults or pick only one person to exchange gifts with. Make a gift such as baking cookies instead of buying a gift. Offer to provide a service such as a months' worth of errands in place of a store bought gift. Give money to a charity as a family gift instead of buying individual gifts.

Take mass transit when feasible.

Skip the vacation and have a stay-cation at home, playing tourist in your own back yard.

Start a garden and grow some of your own vegetables and can them for the winter.

Refinance your mortgage.

Move to a smaller home or sell your home and move to an apartment if the rent is less than your monthly home expenses.

Move to a smaller apartment if you already live in an apartment.

Use all tax deductions possible, a tax consultant/preparer may be worth the money but not in all cases.

Laundry

If your husband is in charge of laundry, "atta girl!" Give him a hug from all the wives out here and share this section with him.

Law enforcement officers often eat in their cars causing many food stains on the front of their shirts and ties. We also have the added joy of cleaning all sorts of bodily fluids from victims, suspects and crime scenes that end up on our husband's clothing and all the other imaginative stains our husbands manage to bring home after a "day at the office."

What are your worst laundry stories?

On more than one occasion, my detective husband has been to a particularly bug infested home. Ugh! I hate the creepy crawlers and dread the thought of him bringing any of that into our home. While standing on the back porch of our home and out of view of any neighbors, he has been known to turn his pockets inside out, turn the cuffs of his pants out, get undressed, while leaving his clothing in a heap on the porch, and run to the shower. I first shake out all clothing in the woods across the street. I put the dry cleaning in a plastic bag, seal it and leave it outside until the next day when I can get it to the dry cleaners. The machine washable stuff gets put in a bag, brought into the house and immediately washed in the hottest water possible.

Terri W.

I didn't realize a pair of my brand new pink lacy undies had gotten mixed into the laundry pile with my husband's light gray polo shirts and I washed the pile. Three of the shirts came out pink. I was horrified.

Patty R.

I washed his uniform for him last Christmas while I was in the middle of making some very sparkly ornaments for our tree. Well, long story short, I put his uniform in the wash with the cloth I had on the floor to catch my glitter mess. He was "Officer Sparkles" for quite some time.

Colleen R.

Long story as short as possible... hubby overslept this morning. When he realized how late it was he jumped out of bed, took a quick shower, grabbed his clothes out of the basket of laundry I had just taken out of the dryer and ran out the door. I get a text message from him stating that he had stopped a car and could smell that there was a large amount of marijuana in it. As he and the K-9 are doing a search going around the outside of the car, our five year old daughter's pink Doc McStuffin underwear falls out of the bottom of his pants leg in the middle of the street. He said he was horrified but it seemed like no one else saw so he kicked it under the car and kept on with the search.

Joleen O.

Laundry stain removal tips.

There are many stain removal methods and these are just a few that seem to work for tests done on a 100% white cotton t-shirt. The companies of the products listed do not in any way endorse this book. These are simply products that worked well in our stain removal test. The authors do not guarantee results and do not endorse any specific techinique.

When removing stains, always make sure that the stained part of the fabric is not touching a clean part. For example, if the stain is on the front of a shirt, make sure the front is not touching the back of the shirt when treating the stain or the stain will bleed onto the clean back of the shirt. You may place an old towel between the back of the stain and the rest of the clothing.

Always check a part of fabric that does not show for signs of damage from the cleaning agent prior to cleaning. Use these cleaning methods on washable fabrics only.

Always use cleaning supplies in a very well-ventilated area and avoid any fumes, mixing of chemicals and/or contact with skin.

Suggested stain removing items to keep on hand:

Hydrogen Peroxide: Check for color fastness on any fabric you use Hydrogen Peroxide on.

Dawn Ultra Dishwashing soap, green bottle doesn't leave green stains

Baking Soda

Ammonia

Dynamo Toss Ins Mountain Mist brand laundry detergent

Whisk Laundry liquid detergent

Fels Naptha Bar (available at most grocery stores along with discount "box" stores.)

Nature's Miracle pet stain remover (available at Pet stores.)

Old toothbrush for scrubbing stain

Vacuum cleaner

The authors of this book do not guarantee results nor do they or any contributors endorse these techniques. These are things that have worked for other women and are merely suggestions.

All- purpose homemade stain removal

1 teaspoon Dawn Dishwashing detergent, 3-4 Tablespoons of Hydrogen Peroxide and 2 to 3 Tablespoons of Baking Soda.

Specific Stains and cleaning remedies. (All stain removal methods have been tested on a white 100% cotton t-shirt, after allowing the stain to dry for at least twenty four hours):

Blood*:* Hydrogen Peroxide can act as a bleach so make sure to check an inconspicuous place on your fabric prior to using. Pour hydrogen peroxide directly on the stain, let it soak and then blot with a clean dry white cloth such as an old t-shirt. If the stain remains, repeat as needed.

For many body fluid stains (blood, vomit, feces and urine): Nature's Miracle, a pet stain remover available at Pet stores, does a great job. It's made for animal urine, feces, vomit etc. Gross but it works really well. If a stain is dried and is visibly sitting on top of fabric, use a putty knife to gently remove as much of the dried stain as possible. Test treat an area that won't show, for color safety. If no fabric discoloration, saturate the stain with Nature's Miracle, let soak 5 – 10 minutes, blot with clean dry white fabric such as an old t shirt. If needed, repeat but let it soak 30 minutes or more.

For those with pets, including K-9 partners:

For cleaning a pet vomit stain on carpet, it is going to sound gross but what works best is to let the stain dry if the carpet has stain protective coating. The stain will sit on top of the carpet and not soak in. Rubbing it while wet will push the stain further into the carpet. If need be, cover the stain with a paper towel so that you don't have to look at it while it dries. Once dry, use a putty knife to lift off as much of the "item" as possible. Vacuum off any remaining loose material. Check for color fastness and if safe, saturate with Nature's Miracle and let soak for ten minutes. Rub with clean white cloth and repeat, soaking longer if needed until the stain is removed.

Tomato sauce, barbeque and salsa stains: Run cold water from the faucet through the back of the stain, forcing the stain back out the front. Pour some white vinegar onto the stain, rub with toothbrush and then pour some dish soap designed to remove oily stains (Dawn Ultra works well) onto the stain, rub in with an old toothbrush, add more vinegar, rub with toothbrush and run cold water through the back of the stain. Repeat as necessary and launder in cold water.

Oily Stains: Test a small area first for color transference. Pour dish soap designed to remove oil (Dawn Ultra works well) directly onto the stain. Wet a tooth brush and gently brush in the soap. After 15 minutes rub with a tooth brush again. Pour cold water from the faucet through the back of the stain while holding the fabric taut. Repeat as needed until stain removed.

Salad dressing: This is similar to an oily stain and treat as you would an oily stain.

"Brown sauce" from Chinese food: Most likely the "tasty brown sauce" is made with soy sauce and oil. You need to tackle the two. First pour cold water from the sink faucet through the back of the stain. Next, pour on Dawn Ultra dish soap, rub with tooth brush to remove some of the oil. Next you need to tackle the soy sauce. Soak the stain in a bowl with Nature's Miracle for as long as needed. It might take up to thirty or forty five minutes. Once you have removed as much of the soy sauce stain as possible, you need to retackle the oil stain and any remaining brown sauce with Dawn Ultra dish soap. Pour Dawn Ultra on remaining stain and rub with a toothbrush to remove all oil and any remaining brown sauce/soy sauce. Pour on more Dawn, rub and launder. Nature's Miracle works best but, if you do not have Nature's Miracle on hand you may rub with Dawn Ultra and then soak in equal parts ammonia and water. Scrub with toothbrush. This may take some elbow grease and more Dawn. Remove as much as possible and then pour on a final dose of Dawn Ultra, rub and launder.

Mustard: Gently scrap off any dried on mustard with a butter knife. Dampen with water and rub on Fels Naptha. Use a tooth brush to work out much of the stain. Pour on some Dawn Ultra dish soap and rub in with a wet toothbrush, wetting as needed until the stain is no longer visible. Run cold water through the back to the front of the stain.

Mud: Let dry and use a vacuum cleaner with no attachment to suck up any loose dirt. Spray with Resolve foam carpet cleaner and work in with a toothbrush. After working in Resolve, pour Dawn dish soap directly on the stain and work in with a wet toothbrush. Continue working until most if not all of the stain is removed. Run cold water through the fabric from the back of the stain to the front. If any stain remains, use more Dawn and work in with the toothbrush. Let soak thirty minutes and launder.

Chocolate: Gently remove as much as possible with a putty knife. Check an inconspicuous part of the fabric to make sure ammonia will not discolor fabric. Mix equal amounts of ammonia and water in a bucket, bowl or sink and soak the stained item for 10 – 30 minutes, rub with old tooth brush and continue soaking and rubbing until the stain is removed. Wash as usual. Ammonia fumes are powerful so make sure to use in a well-ventilated area.

Red wine: Occasionally a LEOW might find herself watching girl TV or reading a book with a glass of red wine while her LEO is working four to twelve. If the wine spills, first check for color fastness and then immediately soak in Nature's Miracle for as long as it takes to remove the stain. If the item is a piece of clothing, place the section of clothing with the stain in a bowl and soak in Nature's Miracle, adding more as needed as the surrounding fabric will soak up the Nature's Miracle. Blot the stain with a clean white cloth from time to time. Wash as soon as the stain is removed by Nature's Miracle. You may pour some liquid laundry soap on any faint remaining stain.

Fingerprint powder: Warn your husband in advance to never ever rub fingerprint powder into the fabric or to use water on it in an effort to remove it. These methods will only spread the powder and make it harder to clean. Gently fluff off as much powder as possible as soon as you realize the powder is there by shaking the shirt, pants or whatever fabric it is on. Now, leave it alone and do not rub stain. As soon as possible, vacuum the stain from the front of the stain until as much of the powder as possible is removed. Use the hose of the vacuum without any attachments. This should remove most of it. If some stain remains or if it was inadvertently rubbed in, vacuum and then use Resolve High Traffic Foam carpet cleaner making sure to place a piece of plastic such as an old white grocery bag (without print on it) or an old towel between the stained part of the fabric and any other part of the fabric. For example, the front and the back parts of the shirt. A foam cleaner traps the fingerprint dust particles better than regular soap. You need to remove as much of the dust as possible. Let fabric sit a few minutes after applying foam cleaner and then very gently blot with a clean white cloth. Repeat as needed until the blotting doesn't pick up any more color. If stain still appears, use a combination of Dawn Dish soap and more Resolve carpet cleaner and use a toothbrush to scrub. Repeat as needed several more times. The foam may appear to have some of the color in it. When no more color shows in the foam, run cold water from the back of the stain to the front with the fabric pulled taut. If not completely gone, repeat Resolve and Dawn. When you have removed as much as possible and a slight hint of stain remains, use Shout Advanced stain removal spray. Do not launder until the stain is no longer visible.

Shirt collar grunge: Spray/mist collar with water or wet lightly and rub Fels Naptha on the collar. Launder as usual. Whisk laundry detergent applied with a toothbrush also works well.

Rust: White Brite Laundry Whitener brand laundry additive by Summit brands, Fort Wayne N.J. Use according to package directions.

To clean those lovely polyester uniform ties: Treat the stain as listed for specific stain. Hand wash in a sink and air dry. To iron out the wrinkles, cut a piece of cardboard to the size and shape of the tie, place inside the tie and iron on the coolest setting possible.

Bullet proof vest smell: Your husband probably keeps his vest in his locker, causing the damp sweat to sour overnight. If possible, he can air it out at home each night. If he fears he will forget it at home or if he finds this too onerous, give him a bottle of non-floral scented Fabreze to keep in his locker to spray on the vest after each tour. He may also use a non-floral scented fabric softener sheet or hanging car air freshener or a cologne soaked small rag tucked into the vest inner pocket. Make sure whatever you use, it is not a floral scented or the other guys will break his chops. The outer carrier is washable and should be washed at least weekly. Remove the bullet proof panels, fill washer with water, add laundry detergent, and baking soda or Oxyclean, agitate and then add the outer carrier. "Dynamo Toss Ins Mountain Mist" brand detergent works well for odor removal. Let soak at least 30 minutes and wash as usual. Hang up to air dry.

Smoke smell from a fire scene, cigarettes or cigars: Check fabric in an inconspicuous spot to ensure that the cleaning method will not damage fabric or color. Add 1 cup baking soda and 1 cup white vinegar to the washing machine. Let soak 30 – 60 minutes and wash as usual. If you worry the vinegar will harm fabric, use baking soda alone along with your detergent. "Dynamo Toss Ins Mountain Mist"Brand detergent works well on items with heavy odor. You may want to use extra strength Fabreze on his outer coat if not washing right away. Fabreze also helps with cigar or cigarette odor if riding in a car with smoker. Spray clothing with Fabreze and if possible, leave item outside for a few hours.

Smelly exercise clothing: After too many quick grab take-out meals, donuts and home baked goods, many officers find they need to work-out to keep in shape for their job. Unfortunately, their work-out cloths can get pretty nasty smelling. Soak work-out clothes on the longest washing machine cycle possible with one "Dynamo Toss Ins Mountain Mist" Brand detergent.

Alcoholism, Domestic Violence and Suicide

The authors of this book are not professionals and do not claim to be. All resources provided are readily available online at various government sponsored websites or have been suggested by other wives because they were successful for them. None of the information is endorsed by any contributing member of this book but provided as merely one resource you may choose to use.

Not subjects to be discussed in polite company. With apologies to "polite company," they are subjects that need to be discussed.

There are many times when police wives experience things unique to their lives but there are times when our issues are the issues families from all walks of life experience. Try as they might, our LEOs cannot always protect us from our past or the abuses of today and our Police families are not immune from the painful subjects of alcoholism, suicide and domestic violence. Perhaps our LEO is even the person in need of help. We tackle these painful and difficult subjects in an effort to help other LEOWs recognize what may be impacting their lives and to help them know that other LEO families share in their experiences.

We are especially grateful to those who have shared their personal stories in this section. While it was painful and difficult for them, they did so in belief that by sharing their stories, other law enforcement families may be inspired to seek help.

If you read this section and it touches a painful nerve, we urge you to seek professional help, if needed. Resources listed are only a few of many available. This book is not endorsed by any resource mentioned; we share them because other LEOWs have found them useful. We urge you to do your own research and make choices that are best for your own individual circumstances. Once again, the authors and the contributors are not experts and do not offer expert or professional advice.

While we have broken the issues down into three sections, in real life experience some people may find that the issues overlap. An alcoholic may become abusive when drinking. A depressed person may self-medicate with alcohol or illegal drugs and become more depressed and eventually suicidal. A person who is physically abusive may also be suicidal. Tackling and solving the "underlying problem" may be a difficult process and even more reason to seek professional help.

Alcoholism

www.safecallnow.org is a website that was started to specifically help public safety employees, current and retired and their families with various issues including alcohol abuse and suicide. Their Mission Statement is: "Safe Call Now is a confidential, comprehensive, 24-hour crisis referral service for all public safety employees, all emergency services personnel and their family members nationwide." Their phone number is: 206-459-3020. They have confidential referral services for suicide, alcohol abuse or other substance abuse. You will speak with a retired police officer, public safety officer or other mental health professional who understands the issues unique to the law enforcement officer. This is just one resource mentioned to us by several sources and we cannot vouch for its usefulness

No one plans to grow up to be an alcoholic. Most people don't even see the disease in themselves early on in their drinking but their family and friends usually do. You may be a great parent or spouse in many ways but alcohol will take its toll on your family and friends. You would never intentionally harm your family but your drinking can harm them just as much as if you intentionally hurt them and in some cases even more so. We share these stories in the hope that if you see even a tiny bit of yourself or a loved one in the lives of others, you will seek the help you need.

An alcoholic and retired police officer shares his thoughts.

Pete C.

Statistics are important if you are writing a term paper for school or you have a need to impress someone with how much research you have done. If you are the family member of an alcoholic, do you really care about statistics? Do you really care that 88,000 people die every year from alcohol related illnesses? Do you care that he is twice as likely to abuse alcohol or drugs as the general public? No, you do not. If you are the family member of a police officer who is having a problem with drugs or alcohol, one hundred percent of your family is suffering. One hundred percent of your family is being affected by the actions of the substance abuser. One hundred percent of your family needs help. These are the only statistics that are making an impact on your family.

Not every police officer who stops for a couple of beers after work has a drinking problem. In fact, going out after a shift is common among us. It's a way of relieving stress and a method of bonding. It is a part of the camaraderie that comes with the brotherhood that most police officers feel for one another. The point at which it becomes a problem is when the drinking continues to excess. It doesn't stop after everyone else has gone home.

If you are a family member of a police officer and you suspect that they are having a problem with alcohol or drugs, you are probably right. You know if their behavior has changed. You know if their life is beginning to center around a drink or drug. You know if they are staying out late, missing family functions, missing work because they are too hung over to make it in to work. You know if they are drinking alone or isolating from friends and family. You know if they get hostile when you question their consumption. These are just a handful of symptoms, you probably have a list of your own.

The problem is what are you going to do about it? The answer to this question is extremely complicated even for medical professionals. Alcoholism is a disease for which there is no cure. When it involves a police officer it gets even more complicated. The good news is dealing with it is not impossible.

I am not a doctor or counselor and I have no formal training in alcoholism or drug addiction. I am a retired police officer and an alcoholic. I have been in recovery for more than twenty years and living proof that alcoholism can be managed. The only way I manage my disease is to not take that first drink. By doing so, I don't need to battle the whole bottle every day. If I don't take that first drink, the rest of them don't matter. I didn't get to this point in my life alone; I had a lot of help along the way. I have been through two rehabilitation centers, a county hospital detox program and I still didn't stop until the alcohol almost killed me. I was fortunate. A great many alcoholics and addicts are not. The cold fact is; that left untreated addiction to any chemical can be fatal.

This brings us back to the question; what are you, the family member of an alcoholic police officer going to do about it? The answer is, get help, not only for the alcoholic but for yourself. If the alcoholic is not willing or able to stop their behavior, you will need help to know what your options are. As sad as it may sound, your only option might be to walk away. The person you are trying to help may not want that help.

Alcoholism is a disease. I don't know of anyone who has beaten this disease by themselves. If a member of your family were diagnosed with diabetes, heart disease or any other major illness would you try to treat them by yourself or would you get help from a professional? I think you know the answer.

Alcoholic or addict and I use the term interchangeably because the disease is the same, only the chemical is different. The treatment is the same; abstinence. The only way to beat it successfully is to stop using completely. There is no controlling it half way. There is no drinking socially for an alcoholic. Will power does not work. The only thing that works is a willingness on the part of the alcoholic to get help and the desire to stop. Withdrawal will not only be unpleasant but in some cases can be fatal. The physical detox should be medically supervised. The mental part could last a lifetime. I still get the urge to have a drink over twenty years later. I've learned I only have to resist the first drink just for today. I know I don't ever want to go back to living the way I did before I stopped drinking.

Confronting a substance abuser can be dangerous and is another reason it should not be attempted alone. There is a very good chance that the alcoholic is well aware that they have a problem. They are as confused and as frightened about what to do as their family is. An alcoholic or addict will only consent to help when they are ready to recover and stop using and change their behavior. In some cases this may never happen. If forced to get help to recover by a court, peer pressure or a family member, recovery might work short term but relapse is almost certain.

Why is getting help more difficult for police officers? Step one of Alcoholics Anonymous states "We admitted we were powerless over alcohol and our lives had become unmanageable." Can you imagine how difficult it is for a police officer to admit that? To admit that they are powerless over anything? People who knowingly put their life on the line every day, admitting that they are powerless? It goes against the grain of everything they stand for. And to admit in the same sentence that their lives are unmanageable. The same people who manage the problems of the public at large on a daily basis, admit their lives are unmanageable? It is very difficult to admit and sadly for some it's not possible.

Police officers feel that if they come forward and ask for help their colleagues are going to find out they have a problem. This might be viewed as a sign of weakness. The truth is by the time their drinking gets to this stage; the alcoholic's colleagues already know there is a problem. The weakness really comes from not doing something about the problem, because they are not living up to their full potential.

Help is available for both the alcoholic and their family, but you have to look for it. Most police officers are not going to trust anyone to help them who is not a police officer. That is okay, there are plenty of cops in recovery who are willing to help others. Most municipalities have employee assistance programs. Most health insurance plans will cover in-patient and out-patient treatment. Today with the internet, help can be found right at your fingertips. Alcoholics Anonymous is another option. AA is an organization made up of alcoholics who meet for the purpose of keeping each other sober by sharing their experience, strength and hope. AA is free of charge. An AA meeting can be found in just about any city on any day of the week.

I don't know what the statistics are for addiction recovery. I can tell you help is available and recovery is not impossible. It will not be easy but it will be worth it.

A daughter and now LEOW shares the impact her mother's drinking has had on her.

Sandy D.

My mother's problem with drinking did not start really until I was in ninth grade. It started out with just having a beer every now and again and then it grew. As time went on and even to this day, she drinks a gallon of whiskey. The only positive thing that I can say is that my mother has never let her problem keep her from going to work. She will still go to work every day. My mother would come home from work and start drinking and would not stop until she passed out. At first this did not affect my brother and me, but after a while it got to the point that we would not invite any friends over because she was out of control and would act stupid and it would embarrass us. I remember on one occasion she came into my room when I had a friend over and peed in the middle of my room. When I said something, she said that it was okay. Because it got out of control, once I hit high school, I stayed gone as much as possible and when I turned sixteen, I became pregnant with my oldest child. It did not seem that my mom cared that I got pregnant as long as it did not interfere with her drinking. Even though I finished high school, my brother dropped out of school. I married and had two more children and left home. My children have never and are still not allowed to be around my mother if I am not there. My kids are between the ages of twenty one and fourteen and it has impacted them as well. They know what is wrong with their grandmother and they understand why they are not allowed over there alone. I do it for the protection of my children. I rarely drink anymore because I am afraid I will turn out the same way as my mother. When I was in school I would drink and party but after I had my first child, I stopped and to this day, I might have a drink once a year. My mother's drinking has made me who I am and in some ways, it's a good thing. I am more aware of people who are around me and who I let into my circle. If they are going to drink and carry on, then they are not allowed around me. My ex-husband and I divorced after nineteen years together because he started drinking and would not stop. I have been with my present husband, a LEO, two years now and he does not drink because he knows how important it is to me. I worry about my children because they see what impact it has had on our family, but it scares me that they will try it and then fall into the same pattern as my mother. My brother and I have begged and pleaded with our mother to stop drinking and she has said that she does not have a problem and can stop at any time. I know that this is a sign of someone who has a problem. My mother is not allowed to attend any functions that happen in our family because she will not stay sober enough. I do not think that she does not care, but rather that she cannot stop. I worry every day for her health and I am scared that one day I will call and find out that she has passed away. Everyone has tried to help my mother but if someone does not think they have a problem then it does no good. It has caused a strain on our relationship. I do not talk to my mother as much as I should, I will sometimes go months without speaking to her. Please do not get me wrong, I love my mother and want nothing bad to happen, but for my sanity I have to limit my interaction with her. If I knew someone who had a problem today, I would beg and do whatever it took to get them help. I pay attention to my husband because he is in law enforcement. He has a drink every once in a blue moon, but if I think that in one day he has had too many, I let him know and he will stop. He knows how upsetting it is to me and what I have been through. Please pay attention to your spouse or loved ones. Know if there is alcoholism in their family and if so, keep an eye on them because it can get out of hand. Do not let it go on because I know that it impacts all my relationships with people. I have cut ties with really good friends because they drank. My mother has not allowed me to have a healthy relationship with people who drink. If someone has a problem, I would tell them to seek help and let others help them, they cannot do it alone and they do not have to do it alone. If they say that do not have a problem, I would tell them that if you cannot go one day without a drink then you have a problem. I would let them know that the drink does not fix problems, it only makes it worse.

A LEOW whose sister is an alcoholic answers questions.

Erica O.

How has the alcoholic in your family's behavior negatively impacted you and the rest of your family?

The alcoholic is my sister. She turns thirty-one this year. It runs in our family on my Dad's side. Many of his relatives have problems with alcohol. My father is an alcoholic who has been sober for over twenty years. I was too young when he was drinking to remember much or I have blocked it out. He threw away my toys once, my favorite doll.

As far as my sister goes, she really drained my family in many ways. Financially, she owes my parents, in my estimation over fifteen thousand dollars if you counted all the money my parents have given her for the past fifteen years. They have paid many of her bills including auto insurance, lawyer bills and other basic living expenses. She was unable to save any money for a big retirement party for my father that all of us kids were going to pay for. My other sister paid her part. She owes her for that plus for other bills she has paid for her.

My husband and I tried to help her. We let her stay with us in our finished attic so that she could save money to get herself back together.

She had a bedroom, sitting area and half a bath so that she had some privacy when she did not want to be with our family. She was supposed to pay a small amount for rent, utilities and food but at the end of a year, she had not paid anything and had no money to pay it with. She saved nothing while living with us. She was hiding alcohol in various parts of the rooms she lived in. My husband and I rarely fight, other than the normal ins and outs, but we were having huge arguments over my sister. It was impacting my children as well. My oldest, now in high school, was wondering why she was in our attic, knowing her age. My other teenaged child often heard us fighting.

My mother is very much someone who keeps things to herself and no one knew the severity of my sister's problem. Most people had an idea that something was wrong but did not know exactly what the problem or the extent of it was. My sister, was at a dead end job and no prospects for a romantic future. Also, her looks have been declining. Her teeth are broken and brown from smoking and lack of dental care. Eventually a relative who did not know about the problem was told and the entire family decided on an intervention. This opened a can of worms that can never be closed. My relatives all now think they have the right to interfere with everything.

I had been telling my mother for many years that my sister had a problem because she never seemed to outgrow the college party stage of her life. She would claim to envy my house, family etc. but she never did anything to improve her circumstances.

Is your family member aware they have a problem and have they tried to get help?

After each of her two driving while intoxicated arrests, she did attempt court ordered rehab, which she actually laughed at because it was such a joke. The intervention our family tried went very badly and she was uncooperative and angry. She called me later and yelled at me for over two hours. She claims that she wants to change but has missed court dates and is currently driving on a suspended license. Luckily she does not live in our town or my husband's police jurisdiction.

How has their drinking impacted your relationship with them?

Simply put, we don't have a relationship. Almost like social media friends who never actually meet. We were very close and it hurts that we are not anymore. I do not trust her and what she says. I worry about her but I have learned to distance myself. Almost like a police officer who can sit and eat lunch right next to a dead body. I have spent so much time and effort trying to tell everyone that I am tired of hearing it now. Oh, poor Diane, she has a disease. I have yelled so many times, "That is what I have been telling you for years and no one listened." It's hard to explain but it's like I have been on the roller coaster for years and now that everyone else is on, I'm getting off. Except, unlike a roller coaster, alcoholism is not fun!

What would you like to say to someone who might be an alcoholic or other families dealing with someone they love who drinks too much?

I really don't know the answer to that question. It is such a terrible disease that no one wants to admit to. I guess I would say to involve professional help sooner than we did. My mother kept saying that she has to want to do it, which is true but the disease is powerful and all consuming. It is not a race, it is a marathon and I got tired of running.

A LEOW and child of alcoholic parents answers questions:

Wendy F.

Who in your family abused alcohol and how did that impact you growing up?

My mother and her husband were both alcoholics. It had a very major impact on my childhood because my mother was the type of drunk who would pick fights and my father would fight right along with her. On Monday mornings, when we were riding the bus to school, the other kids would laugh at us because you could see the tire tracks across our front lawn and the kids knew it was my father who had been drunk driving. He always drove drunk with us in the car. Both of my parents and their families were major marijuana smokers also. I was able to start smoking pot at a very young age. I remember smoking pot with my paternal grandmother at the age of ten. Smoking pot at home was also something that was allowed at a very young age. We also began smoking cigarettes at a very young age. At ten years old, I was caught with cigarettes and instead of taking them from me and keeping me away from them, my mother and father decided it would be a good idea to make a deal with me. They decided if I could smoke an entire cigarette in front of them without getting sick, they would buy cigarettes for me. Of course my sister and I had been smoking for about six months already so this was not hard for either of us. At the tender age of ten, I was allowed one half of a carton of cigarettes per month. They had to be light cigarettes because regular cigarettes were too unhealthy, in my mother's opinion. I still shake my head at their logic. By the time I was able to quit smoking cigarettes for a major length of time, I had been smoking for fifteen years of my life and I was only twenty five years old. Very sad indeed.

How does their alcohol abuse impact you now?

I do not allow my kids around people who are drunk and I rarely drink. I talk to my kids about people in our family who have addiction problems and how they need to make wise choices for themselves.

Do you think alcohol abuse had made you the person you are today and if so, in what ways?

I think everything anyone experiences in life makes them who they are. I could choose to let my past define me, but if I did then I would be no better than those people who would have cast me aside because of my family. I am not my parents and I am not doomed to be just like them. I really hate when I hear people say, "Oh that kid has no chance. Do you know who their parents are?" Or, "That kid will be a druggie just like his dad." What an unfortunate thing in life that we all can't have the chance to make our own path. No one should ever doom someone to a reputation that is not their choice.

Do you worry about your children and alcohol due to a family member abusing alcohol?

I definitely do. Alcoholism is a definite worry for me because there are family members on both sides of my husband's and my family tree. I hope that my husband and I have set a good example of what should really happen when it comes to consuming alcohol.

If you could speak with others who might have an alcohol abuse problem, what would you like to tell them?

Your addiction and choices affect more people than just you.

General information about alcoholism.

Alcoholism is a disease that impacts all walks of life, including law enforcement. About eighteen million people in the United States of America have an alcohol use disorder. You probably know someone who drinks too much, has an alcohol abuse disorder or is the most serious of the spectrum, an alcoholic. Perhaps you find yourself drinking a bit too much when you're home alone during your husband's four to twelves. Unfortunately, police wives are not immune from alcohol abuse. Perhaps your husband has a few too many at the end of work each night?

Research has shown that alcoholism may be hereditary, especially among males. This genetic link does not guarantee that one will become an alcoholic but it gives those with a family history of alcoholism a warning to be aware that they may have a predisposition to alcoholism and may want to be vigilant. A family history of alcoholism may also influence a person to abuse alcohol because it seems "normal" to them due to being raised with alcohol abuse. While research shows that there is some genetic link among family members, one need not become an alcoholic due to a genetic predisposition. On the flip side, not having a family history, parent or grandparent who suffers from alcoholism, does not guarantee that you won't have a problem because genetics only accounts for 50% of the risk.

What is considered too many drinks?

According to the United States Center for Disease Control too many drinks/ at risk/ heavy drinking are for men more than four drinks on any given day or more than fourteen in a week. For women, the amount of drinks is three drinks on any given day or more than seven in a week. Twenty five percent of people who exceed these limits have alcoholism or alcohol abuse. If a person drinks beyond these guidelines, he or she may not be an alcoholic yet but increases his or her risk of developing the disease.

The Centers for Disease control (CDC) website gives the following Symptom check list that may help one determine if they have a problem with alcohol:

Had times when you ended up drinking more, or longer, than you intended?

More than once wanted to cut down or stop drinking, or tried to, but couldn't?

More than once gotten into situations while or after drinking that increased your chances of getting hurt (such as driving, swimming, using machinery, walking in a dangerous area, or having unsafe sex)?

Had to drink much more than you once did to get the effect you want? Or found that your usual number of drinks had much less effect than before?

Continued to drink even though it was making you feel depressed or anxious or adding to another health problem? Or after having had a memory blackout?

Spent a lot of time drinking? Or being sick or getting over other after effects?

Continued to drink even though it was causing trouble with your family or friends?

Found that drinking—or being sick from drinking—often interfered with taking care of your home or family? Or caused job troubles? Or school problems?

Given up or cut back on activities that were important or interesting to you, or gave you pleasure, in order to drink?

More than once gotten arrested, been held at a police station, or had other legal problems because of your drinking?

Found that when the effects of alcohol were wearing off, you had withdrawal symptoms, such as trouble sleeping, shakiness, restlessness, nausea, sweating, a racing heart, or a seizure? Or sensed things that were not there?

The National Institute of Alcohol Abuse and Alcoholism gives the following guidelines for the disease Alcoholism:

1. Craving. A strong need or urge to drink.
2. Loss of control. Not being able to stop drinking once drinking has begun.
3. Physical dependence. Withdrawal symptoms, such as nausea, sweating, shakiness and physical anxiety after stopping drinking.
4. Tolerance. The need to drink greater amounts of alcohol to feel the same effect.

If you find the above symptoms fit your life or your LEO's, you/he may want to speak with your/his Doctor to assist you in finding treatment appropriate for you/him. Some but not all law enforcement jobs and Human Resource departments will provide assistance in getting help. Know the health plan benefits and the rules, regulations and guidelines of your LEOs job.

Drinking to the point of it being a problem that you or your LEO needs to address does not have to fit into any of the symptom lists above. Many jobs will not fire an employee for alcohol abuse but will fire the employee for the behavior such as driving while intoxicated, failing to come to work, coming to work under the influence etc. It may be best to seek help prior to the behavior becoming a problem at work or home. You/your LEO may want to consider speaking with your/his doctor to find a program that is right for you/him to assist you/him in stopping drinking.

If your spouse is drinking to the point of it being a problem for work or home, you cannot make that person stop. You may want to seek out a support group to help you make your own decisions for what is best for yourself and your family.

Domestic violence / Intimate partner violence

The authors and contributors of this book are not professionals in this area nor do they claim to be. The information provided and all resources are readily available to the general public in a variety of venues. Please seek help if you feel unsafe.

The National Domestic Violence Hotline. 1800-799-7233.

A LEOW shares her story.

Domestic Violence- You Can Turn Your Life Around

Kathleen B.

I am a domestic violence survivor and am now telling my story to help others be able to get out of a bad situation. The number one thing DV victims feel is that they cannot make it on their own if they leave. Well, I am here to tell you that you can make it. I kicked my now ex-husband out of the house and filed for a divorce leaving me a single mom of two boys, ages 7 and 10 months. I am not going to paint a pretty picture and tell you that it was easy because it was far from easy but well worth it. I am sure you probably say to yourself "if I leave I will never love again because no one will ever love an abused woman"; well, again I can tell you that is not the case. I went from being in a marriage that was great to start with then went down the road of mental, emotional, and physical abuse to getting a divorce and a few years later falling in love with my Prince Charming (my husband now, who is LEO). I honestly hate that I went through what I did but I feel that it made me appreciate my LEO way more than I probably would have had I not gone through all that I did. I am not going to sit here and tell you it is all a walk in the garden in my current marriage because it's not. Our marriage has to go through obstacles most marriages do not have to tackle such as insecurities, low self-esteem, not fully trusting at all times, and not knowing how to react to certain things because you still have that fear in the back of your mind from your previous marriage. Until I went through abuse I was a very trusting person who would express my opinion on things. After the abuse started I began going into what I call my "shutdown mode". To avoid conflict I would just shut down instead of expressing my thoughts. This has been a major struggle for me to move past. I still, several years later, find myself shutting down to avoid conflict even though I know that there will not be any abuse if I disagree. Thankfully, my LEO is very caring and attentive to me and is usually able to tell if I am going into shutdown mode and he will do everything he can to keep me from going there. He has been my biggest supporter and part of the reason I chose to go to a counselor, which has helped me tremendously. I had a negative experience with a counselor when going through my troubled marriage and I said I would never go again. I found a wonderful new counselor after my LEO and I started dating seriously so that I could give our relationship my best. I knew I was broken from all of the abuse and did not feel that it was fair to my husband to suffer because of my ex's mistakes. As a result from all of the violence I endured I went through a very bad depression and was also diagnosed with Post Traumatic Stress Disorder (PTSD) during my counseling sessions. I knew what all I went through but never really thought about how bad it was until I finally got out. I think that is because at the time I was just doing everything to survive and keep my children safe and not truly realizing what I was actually enduring.

My ex-husband made a bad choice to use a dangerous drug that I was unaware of and it completely changed him. He was truly a different person before the drug. Since I am a Christian and took my vows seriously I made the decision to try to help him in his battle but it was ultimately unsuccessful because he did not want help at the time. I have always been the person to try to fix problems and thought I could fix his. If my ex had wanted to, he could have gotten the help he needed and turned his life around. I stood by him way longer than I should have because I did not want to go through a divorce and feel like a failure. I, as most abuse victims do, hid the abuse from my family and friends for as long as I could. I did not want people to tell me what to do because I wanted to give my marriage my all. I went through some of the worst nightmares a person should never have to go through. I was shoved, hit, grabbed, choked, taunted, and the list goes on. When we would be split up he would break in the back door of our home at all hours of the day and night causing me even more stress to the point I started having panic attacks and not being able to sleep. This happened off and on for a few years. Then I actually took my stand against him and told him to get out and kept my word. That same morning, a couple that I grew up with and their son died in a double homicide/suicide incident. I was heartbroken and realized that could have very well happened in my home. Later that day I was headed to my Mother's home for the boys and me to get a break, when my Dad called and told me that my husband had caused a wreck, hitting two other cars head on. The big thing was he was high on some pills and had ingredients in his vehicle to make drugs. I was so angry but glad that I had kicked him out the night before. He of course was arrested for the drugs and paraphernalia and had to sit in jail. I went the very next morning and met with a lawyer who drew up divorce papers for me. I took them myself to the jail to serve him with the divorce. He began trying to convince me to not do that to him and then started saying he refused to sign them and I could not make him. Thank goodness that I knew all of the jail staff and they helped me talk him into signing the papers without us having to go before a judge. I honestly do not know if I could have handled going through that. Our divorce papers were signed and waiting for the judge to sign off on them. That same night I went to the funeral home for my friends I mentioned earlier and know that God had a hand in my being there. I stood there looking at two caskets, one a husband/dad who took his wife and son's lives followed by his own and the other was holding the wife and baby. I grew up with both the husband and wife and would have never thought I would see something like that happen to them. They were both great people. My Dad and a my friend stood beside me and made me really think about the fact that I could be there with people coming to pay their respects for my children and me. My friend said something to me that made a huge impact on me and I have caught myself saying the same thing to others- "It is better to come FROM a broken home than to be IN a broken home". I really needed to hear those words because that was my hardest thing about getting out, not wanting to break my promise to God that I would love this man and be committed to my husband. I did some deep soul searching and praying to be able to keep my divorce proceedings going. I cried and went through all of the emotions a normal person going through a divorce goes through even though I was relieved to be going through the divorce. At that point I finally was going to get some peace and was happy with my decision. I prayed a lot and felt that God did not want me staying in a dangerous situation. I know the Bible does not condone divorce but I also know that God would rather us be safe and divorced than to stay in a very unhealthy marriage that could take someone's life. My divorce was final while he was still in jail for the drug charges which made me feel safe. I could finally breathe again or so I thought. After he got out of jail he began calling, texting, and showing up at my home again. The panic attacks and not being able to sleep were back again. I honestly do not know how I managed to function on the little sleep I was getting during that time. Every noise I heard had me on edge. I did not like for my sons to be away from me out of fear of what might happen to me if he showed up and I was home alone. I felt a little sense of security when they were there because I did not think he would cause major harm or kill me in front of them. I did not like them seeing me the way they were seeing me either because I was not the fun, happy Mom they were accustomed to. I remember one particular day after the divorce he started calling me at noon and since I had caller I.D. I would let his calls go to the answering machine and he would leave very threatening messages. Then he would hang up and text my cell phone, then call it as well. He did this cycle every few minutes for about 12 hours. I thought I was going to lose my mind from that day alone. I was sitting up working late that night around 1 A.M. when our dog started barking and I knew that meant someone or something was out there. I always kept our screen door locked so I would have that protection between whoever was on the other side and me. Thank goodness I did that because he was on the other side of the door. I wanted to call 911 and have them send a deputy out to make him leave but did not want him to know because he would then leave before they got there. I was finally able to call and they sent an officer out who laid the law down, telling him he was either going to leave and go back to the county he was living in (next county over) or he was going back to jail. He decided to leave and never came back to my home again. He still continued to call and try to torment and harass me but I no longer answered his calls and he eventually quit. To some, the journey would have had a happy ending there but for me it didn't. As relieved as I was to finally be out of that marriage I still had a lot of work I needed to do to regain my life. I started focusing on my sons and myself again for a change and threw myself back into my job to try to numb the pain of all that I had been through. I did not seek counseling until later so in all honesty I was still being controlled by my abuser even though we were no longer in contact. I finally realized that in order to have myself back and be able to have a happy home, be it with another spouse or just my children and me, I had to start rebuilding my life and finding ways to get over things I had endured. As I said earlier, my counselor has been a huge part of my life and for that I am very thankful. She showed me what all I had been through and how it tore me apart on the inside. I no longer felt good about myself and thought no one could ever want to be with me after I let someone treat me the way he did. I didn't respect myself so how could I expect someone else to respect me. During my time of trying to regain my life I came back in contact with a wonderful man and friend who knew what all I went through because he was an investigator in our Sheriff's department. We began chatting and catching up then decided to take things to the next level and date. I now call this amazing man my husband and my LEO. He was definitely a God send. He turned my broken heart back into a whole heart that could actually love again. I did as I'm sure most abused men and women do and tried to push him away out of fear of getting hurt. I knew he would not physically harm me because I had known him my entire life and knew he was a good man. I learned to open my heart again and love someone that loved me just as much. He was what I had always wanted in a husband; the person who would do everything in their power to protect me and not be the person causing me harm. After we were married I finally started sleeping again at night and not constantly worrying that someone was going to break into my house or appear at places I went to. As much as I hate it, my LEO didn't get the best deal because he became a husband to a broken woman and Dad to two boys that had been let down by the man in their life. I do not mean to let things from my past into our marriage but there are some things I just have not gotten out of me yet. I still find myself going into shutdown mode when I think there may be a disagreement on something and it is just out of habit. Once you have done something for so long it becomes second nature and we have to retrain our minds. I am blessed enough that my LEO does not let me go into shutdown if he can help it. He constantly reassures me that I am in a safe environment and do not have to worry that he will react in a bad way if I disagree with him. He listens to me when I am having a tough day and my past is beating me up again. He shows me that he is right there beside me through it all. He can sense when I need extra attention and love from him and will pull me close to let me sleep in his arms instead of ending up having panic attacks during the night. He also lets me have some time for just me if he feels that is what I need at a particular time. I never thought I would be able to let someone in my life again after all of the pain and hurt I had gone through. I am so glad that I let my LEO into my world because I would not be as far as I am with my healing if I did not have him. I know from experience that once you have been abused you put a wall around yourself to try keeping yourself from ever being hurt again. All it takes is for that one special person to come into your life at the right time and show you that true love does exist and love does not hurt.

Everyone is affected by the abuse they receive in different ways so there is not a perfect remedy for everyone to heal. For me, the thing that has helped the most is realizing that I did not deserve any of the abuse. An abuser thrives on controlling their victim. By telling the victim it is their fault and not the abuser's, it makes the victim start to believe they deserved the abuse. This is far from the truth. No one deserves to live in fear especially in your own home and by the ones who are supposed to love you the most. Most victims want out but cannot seem to get out or know how. People that have never been through abuse ask how you could stay with the abuser knowing they will harm you again but as a survivor I know it is not that easy. During the time you have been abused you have a different mindset. Your abuser has brainwashed you to think you are the reason for his violence and if you will just give him one more chance he will promise to stop. You are dealing with a manipulator that you obviously loved at some point so you want to think it will stop. Well, you stay and things are great for a few days, weeks, months, then all of a sudden the violence is back. Another reason a victim may stay, is out of fear. In my situation I was told that if I left him he would harm the people closest to me which were my children and parents. My mind told me that if he was hurting me then why wouldn't he go through with his threat of hurting my family. So as crazy as it sounds to others I stayed longer than I should have in order to protect my family. Someone that has never gone through a situation like that honestly cannot understand why you do the things you do instead of doing what you know should be done. I knew I had to get out of my marriage before someone was seriously hurt or worse but at the time I felt I was protecting my family by me staying. I did not like being on the receiving end of abuse but I thought rather me endure it than someone I loved being hurt by him. Yes, it caused some of my friends and family to become upset with me thinking I was trying to protect him when in fact it was them I was protecting. I will be the first to admit that before I went through being abused I made judgments and said there was no way I would stay in an abusive relationship. It is a lot easier on the outside looking in. It has to be a decision made by the victim to get out and done in the right way so that no one is hurt worse. Once you have made the decision to get out make sure you have a good escape plan to ensure your safety. Let someone you trust know your escape plan and keep in contact with them so someone knows you are safe. I am not going to sit here and say that once you get out everything will be perfect because there will still be trials and moments of weakness. You will have to rebuild your life and in that you may have to step outside of your comfort zone. There will be times you feel that you just can't go on but you have to wake up each day and claim it as a new start. A lot of abuse victims end up depressed or become addicted to some type of substance. The reason for this is because they are trying to numb the pain of what they have gone through during the abuse. Their bodies ache and hurt from being hit or thrown across the room, etc. To ease the pain they use something to help with the mental and physical pain. The biggest advice I can give someone that is going through a domestic violence situation is to rely on family and friends and get out. If your state does not do a protection order automatically I highly suggest getting one. If the abuser wants to get to you bad enough they will ignore the protection order but they will also be charged with breaking the protection order if they come near you. Once you have gotten out then you can focus on getting your life back. Do not try to accomplish everything in one day because it will stress you out even more. Wake up every day and live for that day. The added stress of trying to fix everything all at once could make things worse on you mentally. If you have children, make sure that they are okay and get them any counseling or doctor's appointments that you feel will benefit them. You need to remain strong for the children but when they are not around or are in bed feel free to cry, be angry, or whatever emotion you need to get out. If you keep the emotions in, it will only make it harder on you and take longer for you to regain your life. I found over time that if I was having a bad day I could cry or do something to get my frustrations out and would feel so much better. Another thing I highly recommend doing is to find a good self-help book that will help you "escape" and deal with everything you have going on. The hardest thing for me was to get through all of the emotions that were flooding me. One day I would be angry about having to go through all that I did; the next I might cry all day. Each person is different and has to figure out what is the best way for them to move forward. I found a book when I was first having problems in my marriage with my ex-husband and it became my best friend. It is a Christian based book that helps deal with different types of problems in life, Stormie Omartian's Just Enough Light for the Step I'm On, Trusting God in the Tough Times. I have the majority of my copy highlighted with my favorite parts. It has chapters on dealing with specific types of problems and goes into how to move out of the past and into the future. One of my favorite passages is "In order to live successfully in the present and move into the future God has planned for us, we have to step out of the past. If we don't, it will color everything we see and affect all we do." "When you make Jesus Lord over your past and are willing to forgive yourself and everyone else associated with it, He can set you free." There are multiple passages in this book that I have written down somewhere to be able to see them when I am having a bad day. This book along with prayer, my family, and friends were what helped me through the toughest time in my life. Yes, you are/have gone through something that no one should ever have to go through but do not let that steal the rest of your life from you. The saying "that which doesn't kill us, makes us stronger" is so true. I went through some terrible times and would not wish them on anyone but those tough times made me the person I am today. I still have days that I want to stay in bed and just cry but I remind myself that I have a great life now and do not need to punish my family for something someone else did to me. I am so blessed that my husband is such a caring, understanding man because he has been a big help in my regaining my life. He knows to be patient with me but to not let me shut him out. He made a point to know things that would bring back bad memories and does his best to try not to do those things. Things that would not be a big deal to most people can do damage to someone that has gone through abuse. One of the things that can be a setback for me is a lot of yelling and arguing so in our home those things are not allowed. I know it seems small but to someone that has PTSD a small thing can be a big thing. I heard yelling and screaming followed by other actions that left deep wounds so when I hear a lot of yelling and arguing I feel like the world is caving in around me and can go back to having panic attacks. I had never had panic attacks until I started going through abuse and I still have them from time to time if I have something major going on. Every day is a new day and in our home we take things day by day. If you are in an abusive relationship please reach out to someone you trust for help.   If you do not say anything and continue living in it you are only causing yourself more harm. Things can be better and my life is proof of that. You do not have to suffer nor do you have to suffer alone. I made a promise to God that if He helped me get out and regain my life I would help others in similar situations to get out. Do not suffer in silence; let your voice be heard.

Below are statistics shared by Kathleen B.

Domestic Violence Facts:

One in 4 women will experience domestic violence in her lifetime.

Women experience more than 4 million physical assaults and rapes because of their partners, and men are victims of nearly 3 million physical assaults.

Every year, 1 in 3 women who is a victim of homicide is murdered by her current or former partner.

Every year, more than 3 million children witness domestic violence in their home.

Children who live in homes where there is domestic violence also suffer from abuse or neglect at high rates (30%-60%).

According to the U.S. Department of Housing and Urban Development, domestic violence is the third leading cause of homelessness among families.

Without help, girls who witness domestic violence are more vulnerable to abuse as teens and adults.

Without help, boys who witness domestic violence are far more likely to become abusers of their partners and/or children as adults, thus continuing the cycle of violence in the next generation.

Domestic violence costs more than $37 billion a year in law enforcement involvement, legal work, medical and mental health treatment, and lost productivity at companies.

#1 FACT:

Most domestic violence incidents are never reported. Help change the facts. Speak up, speak out, and make a difference for victims of domestic violence.

The statistics listed above were pulled from www.safehorizon.org.

A LEOW and victim of an abusive ex-boyfriend answers questions.

Jenny T.

Who was your abuser and how long did the relationship last?

I was given a broken arm and choked by an ex-boyfriend. The relationship lasted about two years but was only physically abusive for the last day. Critical and hurtful comments... much of the relationship.

Was it a gradual escalation? What warning signs do you see now looking back that you missed at the time?

The abuse was emotional and verbal after the first few months of the relationship. He would criticize my clothing, what I said and just about everything about me. I thought if I just would do as he wished, he would be happy. I should have seen early on that things were not good but at the time I had zero self-esteem and thought all his criticism was valid. I didn't like myself as I was so why should anyone else, or so I thought. The abuse got physical in an instant. We were fighting, as usual and he suddenly pulled me by my arm, breaking it and then he choked me. I started to black out before I really knew what was happening and could not do anything to stop him. Thankfully, he realized what he was doing and stopped. Of course, he blamed me for getting him so angry that he hurt me. I think it scared him as much as me because he let me go at that point and we never spoke again. I changed my phone number, email and door lock and never looked back.

What if anything, could others have done to assist you?

I'm not sure there was much anyone could have done to make me see that constant criticism wasn't healthy or "normal" in a relationship. I thought his criticism meant he loved me enough to want me to be "better." I now know that love feels good and if you love someone you lift them up, not tear them down. The relationship was full of emotion, just not healthy or good ones.

Did you think of yourself as in an abusive relationship or did you rationalize the abuse to yourself?

I didn't think I was being emotionally abused. I thought in my heart that I was not acceptable the way that I was so I saw his criticism as valid. I knew all the made for TV movies about abuse but when you are in that situation, you just don't see things clearly or that you could be the victim. The abuser is some other guy and the woman is some other woman. I don't think it's easy to see yourself clearly in those situations.

Did you seek help to leave and if so, where?

I did not seek help to leave. Fortunately, I found the strength to leave on my own. I think knowing I could have died was a wake-up call. The broken arm also was a daily reminder for a long time. I am grateful that he did not kill me and that I walked away with only a broken arm. I'm also grateful that he let go so easily because I know many abusers do not let go.

General Domestic Violence Information

The authors are NOT professionals in this area, nor do they claim to be. All information provided is readily accessible on the internet and in a variety of sources. Please seek help if you feel unsafe.

Domestic violence, or also known as Intimate Partner violence, is a problem in all walks of life, including police families. Domestic violence is not limited to husband / wife and other intimate relationships but may include abusing children or an elderly dependent relative. It crosses all socio, economic and ethnic lines Being married to a LEO does not make you immune to domestic violence and can, at times, make the victim feel less safe in seeking help for fear that the abuser will have " the law" on his side. A LEOW victim may fear that her abuser's fellow LEOs will stick up for her abuser and not do what is needed and required to protect her. While it is the duty of all law enforcement agencies to protect a victim and this should not be a concern, a LEOW may report the abuse directly to another agency, expressing her concerns. She may choose to report the abuse to her local district attorney or county or state police.

A LEOW may also fear that her husband will lose his job if she reports abuse. This is not an unfounded fear and may exacerbate the difficult choice a woman feels in seeking help. She may fear her LEO will have no means to support her family along with continuing to inflict violence on her. There are shelters and women's groups that will assist her to be safe from abuse along with some possible programs to assist her in becoming financially self-sufficient. .

Domestic violence is deadly serious and whatever special and unique problems with reporting the abuse a LEOW may feel she faces, she may choose to first protect herself by reporting the abuse and seeking professional help. Help is available! Please seek it out if you are in fear of your safety.

According to the domestic violence statistics website (www.domesticviolencestatistics.org), every nine seconds in the United States of America a woman is assaulted or beaten and every day more than three women are murdered by their husbands or boyfriends. Domestic violence is the leading cause of injury to women; more than car accidents, muggings and rapes combined.

The National Violence Against Women Survey, November 2000, found that twenty two point one percent of women surveyed reported that "they were physically assaulted by a current or former spouse, cohabiting partner, boyfriend or girlfriend or date in their lifetime. "

These statistics are alarming! When one factors in that not all domestic violence is an assault but may include emotional abuse threatening words, the numbers surely rise. Emotional abuse and threatening words may lead to physical abuse and help should be sought sooner rather than later. Often the abuse starts emotionally and escalates over time. The situation will not get better on its own. Some signs to be aware of include but are not limited to the following: Your abuser isolates you from family and friends, gives excessive criticism, controls your freedom and movements, controls your work life or lack of, your money, your clothing choices, threatens you with violence, controls your reproductive choices including raping you (no husband has the legal right to rape you), and blames you for his violent or controlling behavior. This behavior may be interspersed with times of gentleness, kindness and promises of change on the part of the abuser. Without professional help an abuser is very unlikely to change and even professional help is no guarantee of change.

The National Domestic Violence Hotline is an available resource and their phone number is 1-800-799-7233.You may choose to call this number from a phone for which your abuser does not have access to the call records. You may choose to do computer research from a computer that your abuser does not have access to the search history, such as a public library.

Based on research of available resources, it is suggested that if you feel you are in imminent danger, you need to call 911 immediately or leave, if possible to leave safely. Sadly, leaving is often the most dangerous time for a victim of abuse and you may want a police agency to assist you in leaving the home, even if the threat level is not escalated prior to you leaving. If possible, you may choose to have a back-up plan in place so that you have a safe place to go to. You may want a cell phone, phone numbers of agencies to call, copies of important documents, keys to your car, money and a set of spare clothing if possible to be kept at a separate location, such as with a family member or friend. Spare keys for your own car may be needed at a secret location in your home to ensure you can flee in your car if your abuser takes your everyday keys. Police agencies have access to women's shelters if you need protection from your abuser. Orders of protection may also be granted by the courts, although this will not protect you if the abuser is unconcerned with going to jail.

Domestic/intimate partner violence is not limited to a male abusing a female. Women may be the abuser at times. Husbands may choose not to hit back for fear of arrest or chivalry or embarrassment that they have been beaten by a woman. If you see yourself as an abuser in any of the signs or symptoms list or if you hit your intimate partner, children, parents or others, you need to remove yourself from the situation and seek professional help.

Domestic Violence Involving Children

The authors and contributors are not professionals in this area, nor do they claim to be. All information provided is readily accessible to the general public in a variety of venues.

Child abuse is a subset of domestic violence and a subject that can bring tears to the eyes of every job hardened LEO. We all outwardly cringe when the subject is brought up. We share a story as told by a LEOW who was abused as a child and some basic child violence abuse information in an effort to help others who might recognize abuse in their own family or the abuse of someone they know and feel compelled to get immediate help.

To report abuse that needs an immediate police response, call 911.

The Government Center for Disease Control and Prevention gives a hotline for child abuse: To report abuse or get help, contact the National Child Abuse Hotline at 1-800-4-A-CHILD (1-800-422-4453). The phone is staffed twenty four hours a day, seven days a week. All calls are confidential. The hotline offers crisis help, referrals, literature and support resources.

A LEOW and victim of child abuse at the hands of her step father answers questions.

      April K.

Who was your abuser and how long did the relationship last?

I have never been hit by a boyfriend or husband. I have always had a very honest discussion with any boyfriend I have ever had that went like this, "If you ever feel the need to hit me, please know that I will fight back. I will physically fight for my life and then I will fight against you through the criminal justice system."

I was physically beaten by my mother's husband, my stepfather when I was a child. He would hit us, kick us, pull out handfuls of our hair and slap us. He would tell us if we didn't do exactly what he told us to do, then he would take us out behind the house and kill us. He would hit us when our mother was not looking and then when we told our mother that it happened, he would deny it and call us liars. Then we would be in trouble and sent to our rooms. This went on for years.

Did the physical abuse start right away in the relationship or did it come sometime later?

My mother moved us from a different state, following this man to the state that I currently live in. The abuse did not start until we got to this state and she was far away from anyone she knew. Along with my sister, brother and I, he beat my mother too. He held a gun to my mother's head to force her to do what he wanted. My sister became pregnant when she was a teen and he repeatedly kicked her in her stomach with steel toed shoes in an effort to make her miscarry. When we went to school the next day, we called child protective services and we never went back to live in that house again. I wanted to leave before then but my sister and brother wanted to stay. It was my sister's idea to go to school that day and call for help. That was a very good move on her part.

Were there warning signs of potential abuse that you see now but did not see at the time?

There were no warning signs that I remember. He was and is a con artist.

What if anything could others have done to assist you?

When my sister, brother and I would have to run over a mile away to the nearest phone to call the police when my mother was beaten or asking us to help her, the police really should have done something to get us out of that house. My mother's husband was very good at making outside people think he was super nice, calm, and a wonderful person and that everyone else was lying. He could con people into doing things they would not normally do. A good example of this would be that when we went to the house with the social worker and told my mother that we were leaving, she said, "Well, you will be leaving eventually anyway so I am staying." Her husband had convinced her that this was the logical choice to make.

Anyone who knew what our home life was, could have stepped in and got us help years before we had to get help for ourselves. My sister, brother and I had to go to school and beg for help from social services. It should never have been put on us to get ourselves out of the violent life we lived.

How did the abuse your mother suffer impact you?

My mother's own abuse at the hands of her husband impacted me because it caused me to no longer look at her as a mother. It caused me to see how truly weak she is. It made me a very strong person though.

Have you had any kind of support or professional help to deal with the physical abuse and if so, did the support or professional impact you in a positive way?

The only counseling I had was after my brother, sister and I left home when we called CPS. I had some counseling while I was in foster care. It was extremely helpful to me and I think if I had not had adults that I could trust to talk to as a teen, I would probably not have made it past sixteen. I felt betrayal of my mother, anger towards her for not protecting me and my brother and sister and anger towards all of my family for abandoning me and my brother and sister

What else would you like to share?

At first I was afraid of my step father but after a couple of years I learned how to turn off my emotions and turn off my responses to his abuse. It is a survival tool that helped me through many beatings as a child. No emotion however, caused the beatings to be more severe for me because he did it for the reaction. I refused to give him that reaction he was looking for. I'd like to tell other people in this situation that you need to find the strength within yourself to get out. No one can do that for you. If you have children, get them out of that situation!

.

According to the United States Government Centers for Disease Control and Prevention website, 1,570 children died in the United States from abuse and neglect in 2011. 681,000 children were found to be victims of maltreatment by child protective services in 2011. It would seem that with this many children abused, some adults had to have been aware of the abuse and may not have done all that was needed to assist. If you suspect abuse, as a responsible adult you need to call 911 or if the threat to the child is not immediate and you are not sure if there is an abuse situation, you may call the police or the National Child Abuse Hotline at 1-800-422-4453. They are on call twenty four hours a day, seven days a week to offer confidential crisis help, intervention, support resources, referrals and literature. Do not stand by and do nothing! Report abuse and if you feel it best, do so anonymously but report it. If you are abusing a child, remove yourself from the situation immediately and seek professional help.

Suicide

The authors and contributors are not professionals in this area, nor do they claim to be. All resources and information provided are readily available to the general public in a wide variety of venues. Please seek help if you or someone you know may want to hurt themselves.

A resource that has been suggested by others but not the only resource available. www.safecallnow.org is a website that was started to specifically help Public Safety Employees, current and retired and their families with various issues including alcohol abuse and suicide. Their Mission Statement is: "Safe Call Now is a confidential, comprehensive, 24-hour crisis referral service for all public safety employees, all emergency services personnel and their family members nationwide." Their phone number is: 206-459-3020. They have confidential referral services for suicide, alcohol abuse or other substance abuse. You will speak with a Police officer, retired Police officer, Public Safety Officer or other mental health professional who understands the issues unique to the law enforcement officer.

24 hour /7 days a week "Suicide Prevention hotline: 1-800-273-TALK (8255)

A Deputy shares his thoughts on answering the call for a suicide.

Paul M.

I've been a deputy for twenty nine years and I've had more suicide calls than I can remember. My wife's uncle shot himself and I know the pain her family went through so I tend to get angry when called to a suicide. As with all calls, you can't let your emotions get to you and you can't dwell on this type of call but I remember a few. There was a fourteen year old kid who hung himself, the twelve year old who shot himself, the woman executive who hung herself and the guy who shot himself in the head knowing his son would find his body when the kid came home from school. That is the one that pissed me off the most. Making your family live with your suicide is bad enough but to make your kid find your body is selfish and unthinkable. The worst or hardest suicide to deal with was the suicide of a fellow deputy. I didn't know him but a lot of the guys I work with did. It was hard knowing how painful it was for all of them to have to go to that call, to see their friend lying there dead. The guy got into a fight with his wife while his kids were sleeping in the next room. He had been drinking and put the gun to his head and pulled the trigger. I still think it's possible he never meant to actually pull the trigger but was too drunk to know what he was doing. My wife thinks I have a lot of wishful thinking and that he knew what he was doing. She thinks people don't "accidentally" commit suicide but that it's a long thought about process until they get to that point. I'm not sure about it and I guess it doesn't make much difference at this point. The pain on the faces of his co-workers, his wife and family is etched into my mind. His co-workers did an extra caring and respectful job of taking care of the scene and their friend's body out of respect for him but it didn't change what happened. You never want to go to a fellow officer's suicide, especially if you knew him. I wouldn't wish that call on anyone.

A LEOW shares the pain of the suicide of her father.

Cathy J.

I was out to dinner with my husband and another couple a few years back. While I knew the husband Dave, I had never met his wife Michelle. Michelle and I got to talking while my husband Bill was talking police shop with Dave. Somehow Michelle and I got to talking about growing up in our respective small towns. She mentioned a girl she knew growing up and she talked in general terms about how her friend had a very difficult childhood. Michelle wondered aloud about how badly her friend's life must have turned out. I opined that she might have gotten over whatever difficulties she had as a kid, as many people do. Michelle said that she didn't think it was possible to get over "that kind of tragedy, a tragedy so awful that I could not even begin to imagine." Michelle lowered her voice and leaned in close to me and whispered "my friend's mother committed suicide when she was eight years old." I laughed to myself because Michelle unwittingly had just stepped into a social faux pas. In short, open mouth, insert foot. I turned to Michelle and said "oh but I don't need to imagine that, my father committed suicide when I was child." I assured Michelle that it was ok and that her friend has most likely grown up to be a well-adjusted adult.

I don't tell you this story to make light of suicide. On the contrary, I tell you this story to share that well-adjusted or not, you never ever get over it. You get on with the business of life but you never "get over it." The little girl that I was died on the day my father died. I sometimes wonder who she would have grown up to be. Would "I" live in Kansas, be married to a farmer and have six kids or maybe I'd be a lawyer or perhaps a computer programmer. Not my life today by a long shot. The truth is I'll never know who that little girl was meant to grow up to be. A "new but not better me" eventually emerged, the sweet and innocent "Daddy's little girl" was gone forever. The people left behind learn to survive and maybe even thrive in life but deep down, it's always there. The "what if" will never go away. Would he have been proud of me at high school and college graduation? What would it have felt like to walk down the aisle on his arm on my wedding day? Would he have wiped a tear from his eye? So many milestones spent without him. I wonder what his voice and his laughter sounded like as I have no memory of them. I remember the day I turned 42 and I knew I had lived longer than he did. What would he look like today? What would he have thought if he had held on just a little longer? How could he have left at such a young age? And my heart breaks for him for the pain he must have been feeling to choose killing himself over life. So many years later and I still can't bear to read a book about men being loving fathers, helping their children grow up because I know how much I missed out on. I can't rub salt in to that wound.

The "new me" that lived after my Dad's death was too young to understand. I thought that he hated me so much that he killed himself to get away from me. I knew it was all my fault and that I should have done something to help him. I utterly failed him. As an adult, I now know all of that was very wrong and that his suicide had nothing to do with me but to the child that was me, it was definitely my fault.

That kind of guilt led me to live my teen years "hell bent on self-destruct." I drank way too much, starting at the ripe old age of fifteen. I blew off my work at school and sank into a depression myself. I lashed out at my family but the person I was most angry at was me. I spent too many years not trusting love because the first man I loved, my Dad, broke my heart. Love meant heartache. I could go on about the difficult and painful time of finding my way to becoming the strong, well-adjusted and happy adult that I am today, but it's not important to the story of suicide I am telling now. I believe in my heart that if my Dad had a crystal ball to see the future on the night that he took his own life, he would not have wanted to inflict such destructive pain on any of his family. He could not have imagined the true fallout for any of us.

If you know someone who is depressed, if you are depressed, get professional help NOW! Do not wait, for the sake of those who love you, family and friends. If you commit suicide they will not be better off without you. They will not be okay. The pain and damage from your suicide will reach far deeper and last far longer than you can imagine in your lonely and depressed state. If someone you love commits suicide you will never stop wondering "what if?" You will never stop hurting or wishing things had turned out differently. Don't wait for that moment of regret. Help them get the professional help that they need NOW!

I have a very sad memory of telling my elementary school teacher of my father's death, soon after he died. I merely said that he had died and did not even say out loud how he died. She said "yes, I know" and immediately walked away. She taught me to keep my mouth shut about my Father. While times have changed since I lost my Father, many people still do not know how to behave around someone who is grieving the loss of a loved one to suicide. If you know someone who lost a loved one to suicide, please don't treat them any differently than you would if the person had died of cancer, a car accident or any other way. Those left behind after a suicide grieve just like everyone else and need the love and support of their family and friends. They do not need to have their pain compounded by being ostracized.

A LEOW whose brother committed suicide answers questions.
Natalie E.

Who in your family committed suicide and how has it impacted your life?

My brother took his life. It has impacted my life in so many ways. He was the only male figure in my life since our father's death when I was four and he was ten. He was my older brother and my protector. My kids have never gotten the chance to know him... and love him. The pain is still as fresh today as it was when he took his life ten years ago.

Do you worry that suicide or depression might be genetic?

I fear that depression or suicide is genetic. I myself have suffered from depression since his death.

Where there warning signs that you were not able to see at the time but in hindsight, you can now see?

I know there were signs. Ever since our dad's death from cancer, he became very angry and depressed. As he grew up many things triggered his anger and depression. I should have been there for him more!!!

If you could talk to someone who was contemplating suicide what would you like to say to them?

If I could sit and talk with anyone who is contemplating suicide, I would tell them that first and foremost, that they are loved and that they would be greatly missed. I would also talk to them about what might be triggering the pain that second.

What would you say to your family member if you could go back in time or if you could talk to them today?

If I could go back in time and talk to my brother, I would tell him it is not worth it. I love him and please stay with me!!!

Do other people treat you differently when they find out your family member committed suicide vs dying in a different manner and if so, what would you like to say to them?

I feel like I am treated differently because he took his life. More of like pity, and then treated like they can't be around me anymore. Most people do not know how he died because of the way they treat me.

Are there any other thoughts that you would like to share?

Hug your family members every time you see them; it may be your last time. Always tell them you love them, and if they are struggling, get them help!!!

General information about suicide as provided by several sources.

24 hour /7 days a week "Suicide Prevention hotline: 1-800-273-TALK (8255)

The American Foundation for Suicide Prevention is a good resource for information about suicide for the general population. *www.afsp.org*   Suicide is not just a problem for LEOs but also may be an issue for LEOWs or other family members. This site has warning signs, symptoms, risk factors, how to find help for someone who may be suicidal and other vital information on the topic of suicide.

Risk factors for suicide as reported by the Center for Disease Control and Prevention (_www.cdc.gov_)

"Risk and Protective factors" _n.d._

A combination of individual, relational, community, and societal factors contribute to the risk of suicide. Risk factors are those characteristics associated with suicide—they may or may not be direct causes.

Risk Factors

    Family history of suicide

    Family history of child maltreatment

    Previous suicide attempt(s)

    History of mental disorders, particularly clinical depression

    History of alcohol and substance abuse

    Feelings of hopelessness

    Impulsive or aggressive tendencies

    Cultural and religious beliefs (e.g., belief that suicide is noble resolution of a personal dilemma)

    Local epidemics of suicide

    Isolation, a feeling of being cut off from other people

    Barriers to accessing mental health treatment

    Loss (relational, social, work, or financial)

    Physical illness

    Easy access to lethal methods

Unwillingness to seek help because of the stigma attached to mental health and substance abuse disorders or to suicidal thoughts

What additional factors may contribute to a LEO contemplating suicide? Post-Traumatic Stress Disorder (PTSD) can be a factor.

Post-Traumatic Stress Disorder (PTSD)

The authors are not professionals in this area nor do they claim to be. All information provided is readily available to the general public in a variety of venues. Please seek professional help if you or someone you love exhibits signs of PTSD.

Isn't that what soldiers get? Yes, but PTSD is not just a "soldier's illness." Rescue workers and civilians can suffer from PTSD from such things as surviving a life threatening event, an injury, sexual abuse, violence, surviving a natural disaster and other traumatic incidents. For a LEO, it might not be one major traumatic incident but LEOs may experience a cumulative effect of trauma at work. LEOs are "tough guys and can shake it off" but not as often as they would like to believe. Everyone's genetic makeup, life experiences and psychological makeup is different and not everyone who experiences a traumatic event will experience PTSD. Many people can experience fear and trauma and not experience PTSD. Those who receive help from family, friends and/or professionals may be able to better survive the trauma. For some however, the fear and trauma continue in their brain.

PTSD usually appears within three months of the event but may not appear for years and therefore may not be the obvious cause of symptoms, leaving the sufferer and family unsure of why they are suffering and what they are suffering from. They might believe that the event was long ago and it can't possibly still be an issue. The LEO or his family might not realize that no one single event is the cause but that the cause is a culmination of events. For a single event, the person will often relive the incident in their mind. They might avoid places, people or things that remind them of the event. PTSD sufferers might have difficulty with relating to others, anger, guilt or shame, difficulty showing emotion or concentrating, memory difficulties, trouble concentrating, hopelessness. This can lead to isolation from family and friends. Physical symptoms include increased blood pressure, increased heart rate, rapid breathing, muscle tension, nausea, diarrhea, difficulty sleeping, alcohol or drug abuse and hallucinations.

PTSD may not be the diagnosis at the top of your list for the symptoms exhibited. The physical and emotional symptoms of PTSD can be confused with other physical and psychological issues and therefore, PTSD needs to be diagnosed by a professional. A thorough medical exam and discussion with a doctor will help determine if the symptoms are caused by a physical illness, PTSD or some other issue. A doctor can determine what treatment, medication and/or psychotherapy may be needed.

Another aspect that may contribute to LEO suicide is that LEOs are used to being the helper, not the one receiving help. Even if a LEO knows that something is wrong and that he needs help, he may be reluctant to ask for assistance when needed and problems can progress to unbearable. LEOs may also fear asking for help because they worry that their job "might not understand" and the LEO will be placed in the "rubber gun squad" (Have their gun taken away from them and be placed on desk duty.) Asking for help may also go against their masculine self-image and the peer pressure to be tough. Seeking help is the necessary step to prevent suicide but it may be a step LEOs won't allow themselves to take and they may need the assistance of family and friends to get them over the reluctance to seek help hurdle.

Suicide signs and symptoms from the National Institute of Mental health (www.nihm.gov)

"Warning signs of suicide" n.d.

Threatening to hurt or kill oneself or talking about wanting to hurt or kill oneself

Looking for ways to kill oneself by seeking access to firearms, available pills, or other means

Talking or writing about death, dying, or suicide when these actions are out of the ordinary for the person

Feeling hopeless

Feeling rage or uncontrolled anger or seeking revenge

Acting reckless or engaging in risky activities - seemingly without thinking

Feeling trapped - like there's no way out

Increasing alcohol or drug use

Withdrawing from friends, family, and society

Feeling anxious, agitated, or unable to sleep or sleeping all the time

Experiencing dramatic mood changes

Seeing no reason for living or having no sense of purpose in life

Developed by the U.S. Department of Health and Human Services – Substance Abuse and Mental Health Services Administration (SAMHSA)"

Dr. Richard Weinblatt wrote an informative article about Police Suicides at *www.policeone.com*

He gives some added signs of potential suicide of an officer:

"Police officer Suicide Prevention"

January 4, 2006

1) Spot risk taking. Officers who have ceased to care about themselves may take unnecessary risks on the job.

2) A rise in use of force incidents. Officers under pressure may become overly aggressive and take out their anger on arrestees.

3) A rise in vehicle collisions. Similarly, officers may start to drive in a reckless manner resulting in more cruiser crashes.

4) Substance abuse. Stressed officers may resort to an increased intake of alcohol or engage in substance abuse in order to "numb" their pain.

5) Downsizes. Officers that suddenly downsize by giving away valued possessions are giving a red flag indicator.

A very useful website for LEO suicide is www.badgeoflife.com from which the following statistics come.

"Debunking Suicide Myths" *n.d.*

Our 2008/2009 national study showed 141 LEO suicides in 2008 and 143 in 2009. This yields a suicide rate of 17/100,000, a figure that holds up under scrutiny and is consistent with CDC/NOMS data. The general public was 11/100,000.

The Badge of Life website is a great resource for dealing with LEO PTSD and suicide and has information about LEO training to prevent suicides. The site encourages stopping suicide long before the LEO gets to that point. The Badge of Life suggests "getting help before you need it." "An annual mental health check." This website also has links to books and organizations that might be of interest to LEOs and their families.

Also mentioned in the alcohol abuse section but it is worth repeating: www.safecallnow.org is a website that was started to specifically help Public Safety Employees, current and retired and their families with various issues including alcohol abuse and suicide. Their Mission Statement is: "Safe Call Now is a confidential, comprehensive, 24-hour crisis referral service for all public safety employees, all emergency services personnel and their family members nationwide." Their phone number is: 206-459-3020. They have confidential referral services for suicide, alcohol abuse or other substance abuse. You will speak with a Police officer, retired police officer, public safety officer or other mental health professional who understands the issues unique to the law enforcement officer. This is just one resources mentioned to us and we cannot vouch for its usefulness.

Recipes! Because We All Love to Eat

All recipes have been contributed by fellow LEOW's. Please pay close attention to the ingredients if you have food allergies or other special nutritional needs. The authors and contributors are not professionals and do not claim to be.

The old saying holds true for most LEOs: "The way to a man's heart is through his stomach." After eating so much quick grab junk food at work, a home cooked meal is especially important to many LEOs. To a LEOW, food is more than just sustenance for her family, it's often her way of saying "I'm so glad to have you home tonight. I've missed you, I love you and want to make you happy." We put a lot of love into our cooking.

Our LEOWs have graciously offered to share some of their family's favorite recipes. When known, the source of the recipe is given.

Main Course recipes.

A reheat and serve meal repertoire is a must for LEOWs because "normal" dinner hours are not the norm in many LEO homes. Unfortunately, Our LEOs are often unexpectedly late coming home for dinner when they get a last minute call or a call that started at nine in the morning and doesn't finish until late that evening. It's nice to have something waiting for them to eat which will heat up easily and still taste great. Or maybe they like to sleep a little late past the family's dinner time and have a quick bite to eat before going into work at midnight. It's also nice to have a good lunch from last night's leftovers for your husband to enjoy prior to going in for the four to twelve tour. He never knows what time, if at all his dinner break will be and therefor a home cooked and hearty lunch is often appreciated.

Sarah's Kielbasa Pasta

Turkey Kielbasa

1 good sized head of broccoli

1 package of shredded cheddar and jack cheese

½ box (approximately) of bow tie or penne pasta

Slice the Kielbasa into bite sized pieces and fry in a frying pan. While that's cooking, boil water for the pasta and the broccoli. Once all three are done, mix together and add as much of the cheese as you need to coat all of the ingredients.

Sarah A.

Egg Bake

1 box of croutons or 8 slices of day old bread cubed

2 cups milk

8 eggs

1 lb. ham or cooked sausage or cooked bacon cut into bite sized pieces

1 ½ cups cheddar cheese

1 tsp mustard

Salt and Pepper to taste

Layer bottom of 9x13 pan with croutons or bread cubes. Beat eggs, milk, mustard, salt and pepper. Stir in meat and cheese and pour over bread cubes. Refrigerate overnight. Bake at 350 degrees for 30-45 minutes.

Connie R.

Pork chops with raisins and brandy

This is the first dinner I cooked for my husband and he claims this is why he married me. When we were dating and I wanted to make a special first dinner for him, my step father recommended this dish to impress. He was right! It's also a great dish to make if you have company over for dinner because all of the work is done in advance and it cooks while you entertain your guests. You can also make it in advance and just reheat. It takes time and work so it's not a quick week night meal but if you have time on a weekend or you want a special dinner, it's worth it. The flavors meld and get even better when reheated.

Serve with mashed potatoes. They also can be made in advance and just reheat in Corning ware at 350 degrees for 20-30 minutes.

1/3 cup raisins

½ cup brandy

1 very large onion chopped

2 TBS olive oil

6 (1 inch) thick pork chops, bone in is better.

1 can (32 oz.) whole tomatoes, well drained

2 TBS red wine vinegar

½ tsp salt

½ tsp dried thyme

¼ tsp black pepper

1 TBS sugar

1 package baby carrots

Place brandy and raisins in saucepan and bring to simmer. Remove from heat and let stand 30 minutes. Brown chops in olive oil on both sides and then remove to large baking dish. Add onion to pan and cook to light brown. Sprinkle with sugar and cook 3 minutes to caramelize. Add tomatoes, vinegar, salt, thyme, pepper, raisins and brandy. Break up tomatoes with a spoon and bring to boil. Pour over chops. Add carrots to baking dish. Cover baking dish with 2 layers of foil and bake at 350 degrees for 1 hour and 45 minutes. Remove from oven and let rest for 15 minutes before serving. Great served with mashed potatoes or noodles to sop up the juice.

For Mashed potatoes, wash skins, prick with fork and bake directly on oven rack at 450 degrees for 1 hour and 15 minutes. Cut in half, scoop out skins, saving skin. Mash potato with warm melted butter, warm buttermilk, salt and pepper. Reheat mashed potatoes for 25 minutes in 350 degree oven if not serving right away. Reheat skins in 350 degree oven for approximately 10 minutes, until crispy and golden. Serve skins with butter.

Carolyn W.

Italian Sausage with Peppers and Onions

(All ingredients are approximate. You can add more or less to your taste. This recipe is a general guideline but there are no hard and fast rules with this recipe)

1 lb. Sweet Italian Sausage (or hot Italian Sausage if you prefer)

3 TBS olive oil plus more as needed

1-2 Sweet onions sliced (cut onion in half, slice and separate pieces.)

2 red pepper sliced

1 green pepper sliced or if you prefer, add another red pepper

1-2 cloves garlic, finely chopped

2-3 TBS dry white wine As with any recipe, if you don't like it well enough to drink it, don't cook with it.

Bay leaf

¼ - ½ tsp dried / crushed red pepper flakes (optional)

1 tsp fresh oregano

½ tsp fresh thyme

Fresh ground black pepper

Fresh cheese: Parmesan or Grana Padano or Romano or Asiago cheese (optional)

1 long Italian baguette or ¾ lb. dried Bow Tie or Gemelli pasta or small ravioli or tortellini

Fresh Basil sliced right before serving (optional)

Cook sausage in pan or on grill until browned. Remove from pan or grill and set aside, keeping warm. If using a grill place onion, peppers and garlic in a foil pan and grill over medium- low to medium heat with olive oil or add onions, peppers and garlic and olive oil to a clean pot on stove top. Cook vegetables for

5 minutes and add the white wine, bay leaf, (crushed red pepper flakes if using) thyme, oregano, and black pepper. While vegetables are cooking, if you would like, cut the sausages into slices to eat with sliced Italian bread. If you prefer, keep the Italian sausages whole. Add more olive oil as desired. Cook until the onions and peppers are soft. Serve on a plate with sliced Italian bread or cut the Italian bread into sausage sized lengths and place whole sausage, peppers and onions, on the bun sized bread, hot dog style. Or serve over pasta. If planning to serve over pasta instead of with sliced Italian bread, add more olive oil when cooking the vegetables. Sprinkle with cheese if desired or drizzle with additional olive oil. May top with fresh basil if desired.

Purists do not add basil, cheese or any of the below. I like all variations!

Variations in place of white wine:

Dry red wine such as Chianti.

May add 1 (14oz.) can of diced tomatoes or fire roasted tomatoes or chopped fresh plum tomatoes with seeds removed, if they are in season.

May add 2 TBs Worcestershire sauce.

May add a vinaigrette towards the last few minutes off cooking: Place in a jar and shake the following: 2 TBS vinegar such as balsamic, merlot wine vinegar or sherry wine vinegar, 4 TBS olive oil, freshly ground black pepper, ½ TBS honey, 1 tsp Dijon mustard.

May use ¾ cup of dry white wine and cook the sausages whole in a pan on the stove top with some olive oil. Remove sausages when brown and add onions, peppers, garlic and white wine to the pan. Scrape brown bits from sausage from the bottom of the pan. Cut sausages into slices and add to pan. Cook until vegetables are soft, adding herbs a few minutes before vegetables are done. Cooking the vegetables in the same pan as the sausage and using this amount of white wine will have a golden brown sauce/ gravy. Serve over rice.

If serving over pasta, you may add sliced celery when cooking the onions and peppers.

Carolyn W.

Sloppy Joes

1 pound ground chicken

1 onion chopped

¼ cup celery chopped

1 (8oz) can tomato sauce

1 (6 oz.) can tomato paste

2 TBS cider vinegar

2 tsp sugar

3 tsp dry mustard

2 tsp Worcestershire

1 tsp dried cilantro or marjoram

½ green pepper chopped

Dash of cayenne pepper

Burger rolls

Sauté meat, onion, celery and green pepper. Add remaining ingredients except burger roll. Boil and then simmer 45 minutes. Serve over rolls.

Carolyn W.

Chicken Enchilada Dip (doubles as a dinner)

1 lb. boneless, skinless chicken breasts, grilled and shredded. May use shredded rotisserie chicken if you prefer.

1 package softened cream cheese

1 cup Mayonnaise

1 (8oz) Mexican blend shredded cheese.

Combine the chicken, cream cheese, Mayonnaise and cheese, mixing well. Put in a baking dish and bake at 350 degrees for 30 minutes. Serve over crackers or chips or spread on French bread for a main course.

Connie R.

Chicken Casserole

(Family recipe)

3 chicken breasts

1 can cream of chicken soup

1 can cream of mushroom soup

1 cup sour cream

½ cup chopped onion

2 cups shredded cheddar cheese

1 roll of Ritz brand crackers

1 stick of margarine

Preheat oven to 350 degrees

Bake the chicken in the oven until done; set aside to cool and then cut into bite sized pieces. Place in casserole dish. Mix soup, sour cream, onion and cheese together in a mixing bowl and stir until well blended. Spread soup mixture over chicken until well covered. Melt margarine in a plastic bowl in the microwave. Crumble up crackers and spread over soup mixture and then pour margarine on top of crackers. Place in oven for about 45-50 minutes.

Nicolle H.

Spinach and Artichoke Bubble Bake

www.ohbiteit.com (by Amy September 6, 2013)

Pre-cooked chicken cut up (optional)

1 container of Pillsbury Grands Flaky Layers biscuits (8 count)

3 cups frozen and defrosted spinach

2 cups shredded mozzarella cheese (divided in half)

1 can artichoke hears

1 8 (oz.) container cream cheese

½ cup grated parmesan cheese

1 cup sour cream

1 tsp cayenne pepper (optional)

Salt and pepper to taste

9x9 square oven safe dish (Pyrex)

Rough chop the artichokes. In a medium bowl mix together the cream cheese, sour cream, parmesan, salt and pepper and cayenne. Add the sauce into the spinach and artichokes, fold in one cup of the mozzarella. Cut biscuits into fourths. Add cut up biscuits and chicken, if using, to the bowl and gently mix them into the saucy spinach and artichokes, coating them completely. Pour it all into your baking pan and top with that reserved cup of mozzarella. Bake at 350 degrees for 1 hour, making sure to cover it halfway through. May broil for a couple of minutes to get a golden brown top.

Carolyn L.

Touchdown Chili

(www.allrecipes.com by Jen Polk)

2 lbs ground beef

1 large onion, chopped

1/3 cup chili powder

1 ½ tsp ground cumin

1 ½ tsp dried basil

1 (28 oz.) can diced tomatoes with juice

1 (4oz.) can diced green chili peppers, drained

1 (15 oz.) can tomato sauce

1 (12 oz.) can or bottle of beer

1 TBS white vinegar

3 TBS brown sugar

1 tsp hot pepper sauce

2 tsp salt

½ tsp ground black pepper

Brown the beef, onion and garlic over medium heat. Drain off the fat and return to the stove. Combine the chili powder, cumin and basil; sprinkle over the beef. Cook and stir to coat the meat and toast the spices a little.

Pour in the tomatoes, green chilies, tomato sauce, beer and vinegar. Bring to a boil, stir and mix in remaining ingredients. Reduce heat and simmer for 3 hours. Remove lid for last 30 minutes of cooking.

Nicolle H

Lasagna

Lasagna is a great one to make for dinner because I can cook it when he calls me and he has time to come home, change and relax for a few minutes before dinner, plus it's a great one to reheat.

1 box of no boil lasagna noodles (Barilla)

1 lb. hamburger meat

1 jar of spaghetti sauce

Mozzarella

Layer the noodles in the bottom of a 13x9 inch pan. Brown meat and drain the grease. Add the spaghetti sauce into the hamburger. Pour half of the sauce mixture onto the noodles. Sprinkle mozzarella over the sauce. Add another layer of noodles over the sauce and then top with remaining sauce. Sprinkle mozzarella over the sauce. Cover with foil and bake for 40 minutes; remove foil and bake for another 10 minutes to brown the cheese.

Connie R.

Spaghetti Casserole

(Family recipe)

1 lb. hamburger

1 medium onion chopped

1 package of spaghetti noodles

1 can of cream of mushroom soup

1 (15 oz.) can of tomato sauce

8 oz. of grated cheese

Brown the hamburger meat and chopped onion, drain. Cook spaghetti as desired and drain. Place meat/onion in bottom of casserole dish and place noodles on top of meat. Mix soup and tomato sauce and place on top of the noodles. Place the grated cheese on top and bake in oven at 350 degrees for 30 minutes.

Nicolle H.

Crock Pot Chicken and Sausage Gumbo with Shrimp

(www.food.com   Rita Chef # 58104)

1/3 cup flour

1/3 cup cooking oil

3 cups water

12 oz. smoked sausage, sliced and browned

1 ½ cups chopped cooked chicken

2 cups sliced okra or 1 (10 oz.) package frozen whole okra, partially thawed and cut into ½ inch slices

1 cup chopped onion

½ cup chopped green sweet pepper

½ cup chopped celery

4 garlic cloves, minced

½ tsp salt

½ tsp pepper

¼ tsp ground red pepper

1 (14 oz.) can diced tomatoes, undrained

1 (12 oz.) package frozen shelled, deveined and cooked medium shrimp rinsed

3 cups hot cooked rice

For the roux, in a heavy 2 qtr. saucepan, stir together the flour and oil until smooth. Cook over medium heat for 5 minutes, stirring constantly. Reduce heat to medium, cook and stir about 15 minutes more until a dark reddish brown roux forms. Cool. In 5 quart crock pot, place water and stir in roux. Add sausage, chicken, okra, onion, sweet pepper, celery, garlic, salt, pepper, canned tomatoes and ground red pepper. Cover and cook on low heat setting for 6-7 hours. Add shrimp and cook for another 20 minutes. Skim off fat and serve over hot cooked rice.

Carolyn L.

Lemon Pepper Chicken in a crock pot

2 TBS butter

Lemon pepper seasoning to taste

4 boneless and skinless chicken breasts

1 bottle of lemonade

Melt butter in bottom of crock pot. Season chicken and place on top of butter. Pour bottled lemonade in the crock pot, making sure to cover the chicken completely. Cook on low 8 hours or high 3-4 hours, until chicken is done. The chicken will be so tender it will fall apart.

Emily M.

Crock Pot Beef and Rice soup

(Fix it and Forget it cookbooks by Phyllis Pelman Publisher Good Books)

1 ½ lbs stew meat

2 squash

1 cup onion

¾ tsp thyme

6 cups beef broth

½ cup quick cook rice

1 TBS oil

2 carrots cut up

1 minced clove of garlic

¾ tsp basil

2 cups Spinach

Cut meat into bite sized pieces. Brown meat in oil and drain. Put squash, carrots, onion, garlic, basil and thyme in a crock pot. Add meat and broth and cook 8-10 hours on low or 4-5 hours on high. Stir in rice and spinach. Cook 10-15 minutes more or until rice is done. (I cook the rice separately in a pot and just pour the soup over the rice.

Connie R.

Boneless Pot roast (crock pot)

1 (4-5 lb.) roast

3 cups water

2 beef bouillon cubes

1 can cream of mushroom soup

Garlic powder

Salt and pepper

Carrots

Onions chopped

Potatoes Chopped

Place water and bouillon in crock pot and heat for about 40 minutes. Add roast and cook about 2 hours. Add soup, garlic powder, salt and pepper and cook for another 2 hours. Add carrots, onions and potatoes and cook until tender.

Carolyn L.

Baking for the Bodega.

Bodega: According to the Merium Webster on line dictionary, *noun* \bō-ˈdä-gə\, the definition of a "Bodega" is: a usually small grocery store in an urban area; *specifically*: one specializing in Hispanic groceries.

> My husband Mike works for a medium sized department near an urban center with a high Hispanic population. The word, "bodega" is part of our regional language and often used to describe any small corner grocery store. Mike works in a detective squad with two other men and one woman, Suzanne. Suzanne often brings in boxes of cookies to share with the squad after dinner on the four to twelves. The guys cannot be trusted to eat reasonable portions of the cookies and left on

their own, they would eat a giant box of cookies meant to last a few nights, all on the first night. Suzanne keeps the cookies in her desk, also known as the bodega, and doles them out over the course of a few nights in reasonable portions. The guys know they are weak and appreciate that she is the "responsible adult" for them.

Mike and I were at a fancy award's dinner for a detective association and we were sitting at a table with Suzanne and her husband Tom. Mike was telling Tom about what a great Detective Suzanne is and how much the guys enjoy working with her. Mike then said to Tom, "the guys really love the little Bodega in her drawers." What? Fortunately for Mike, Tom knew what Mike was referring to and Tom was laughing too hard to reach across the table and punch him. Suzanne and I were laughing pretty hard ourselves.

Carrie B.

A LEO loves to share his wife's home baked goods with his fellow LEOs. It's his way of "bragging on his wife." And let's be honest; home baked sweets beat belly bomber donuts any day. "Baking for the guys" is a nice way for a LEOW to let her LEO and his squad know that they are thought of and appreciated. A LEO's co-workers are more than just co-workers in the normal civilian sense of the word. They would willingly lay their life down for each other. They spend the scariest, saddest, craziest and funniest moments of the job with each other and a LEOW understands this connection they have. A LEO will spend countless hours with his squad talking about the amazing girl he just met who soon becomes his wife, buying their first house, the birth of their first child, the repairs on their now ten year old home, how to work a LEO schedule to allow him to watch and maybe even coach their child's soccer and Little League games, what college their child is considering, the upcoming wedding of their oldest, they attend the wakes of each other's parents and they are there for all of the countless milestones of life while working together for over twenty years,. In essence, they "grow up in their adulthood" with each other. A LEOW's heart shares in a part of this wonderful life journey as her LEO shares his squad's stories and she attends parties and events over the years. Making baked goods is more than just baking a cookie. When a LEOW bakes for the squad, a lot of unspoken love, appreciation, friendship and thoughtfulness goes into that cookie.

Ice Cream Turtle Dessert

17 ice cream sandwiches

1 (12.25 oz.) jar of caramel topping

1 ¼ cup chopped pecans

1 (12 oz.) tub thawed Cool Whip

¾ cup heated hot fudge

Place 8 ½ sandwiches in a 9x13 pan. Spread evenly with caramel topping and sprinkle 1 cup pecans on top. Top with 2 cups Cool Whip. Top with remaining 8 ½ sandwiches and put leftover Cool Whip on top and then finally top with heated hot fudge. Eat immediately!

Connie R.

Honey Comb snacks

1 box honeycomb cereal

1 lb. white chocolate broken into pieces

1 bag of M&Ms

1 can peanuts (optional)

1 bag of square pretzels

Gently melt the chocolate in a double boiler or in the microwave. In a large bowl combine half of the cereal, M&Ms, peanuts and pretzels. Drizzle half of the melted chocolate over the mixture and stir to coat. Add remaining cereal M&Ms, peanuts and pretzels and pour remaining chocolate over it. Lay out several sheets of wax paper and pour mixture onto the wax paper and let dry. Break apart and enjoy!

Connie R.

Pecan Rolls

1 – 1 ½ cup chopped pecans

1 stick of butter, melted

1 small package of Jell-O brand Cook and Serve Butterscotch Pudding (NOT instant!)

½ cup brown sugar

1 tsp cinnamon

1 bag of Rhodes brand dinner rolls (they are small balls)

Spray a 9x3 pan well with no stick spray such as PAM. Pour chopped pecans into the pan. Place 12 of the rolls on top of the pecans and then sprinkle the pudding mix. Combine the brown sugar and cinnamon and sprinkle over the rolls. Pour the melted butter on top. Cover with a towel and let the rolls rise overnight. Preheat oven to 350 degrees and cook for 22 minutes. Put out and let sit for 5 minutes. Line a cookie sheet with aluminum foil and turn the pan of rolls over, onto the cookie sheet. Enjoy!

Connie R.

Cinnamon Chip Applesauce Coffee Cake

www.hersheys.com

I usually use a disposable foil pan so my husband does not have to worry about washing the pan and bringing it home from work.

Cake

1 cup butter

1 cup sugar

2 Eggs

½ tsp vanilla

¾ cup applesauce

2 ½ cups flour

1 tsp baking soda

½ tsp salt

1 (10oz) package cinnamon chips

1 cup pecan pieces

Topping

2/3 cup Bisquick mix

2/3 cup brown sugar

1 tsp cinnamon

4 TBS butter

Mix the Bisquick, cinnamon and sugar. Cut in butter until crumbly. Add pecans and may add more cinnamon if desired.

For cake:

Preheat oven to 350 degrees. Lightly grease a 13x9x2 pan. Mix flour, baking soda and salt. Set aside. Mix butter and sugar. Add eggs and vanilla. Mix. Add applesauce. Mix. Add flour mixture. Mix well. Add cinnamon chips and pecans and mix well. Pour into pan and top with the topping. Bake 30-35 minutes or until toothpick inserted comes out clean. Cool pan on rack.

Carolyn W.

Chocolate Cake

From www.tasteofhome.com

Cake:

2 cups flour

1 tsp salt

1 tsp baking powder

2 tsp baking soda

¾ cup cocoa

2 cups sugar

1 cup canola oil

1 cup brewed coffee

1 cup milk

2 eggs

1 tsp vanilla extract

Icing:

1 cup milk

5 TBS flour

½ cup butter, softened

½ cup shortening

1 cup sugar

1 tsp vanilla extract

½ block of cream cheese (added by Deb M.)

Sift together dry ingredients in a bowl, add oil, coffee and milk. Mix at medium speed for 1 minute. Add eggs and vanilla and beat 2 more minutes.

Pour into two greased and floured 9-inch round baking pans

Bake at 325 degrees for 25-30 minutes. Cool cakes for 10 minutes before removing and then finish cooling on wire racks.

Icing: Beat butter, shortening, cream cheese, sugar and vanilla until creamy. Add milk and flour and beat for 10 minutes. Frost cooled cake. Makes 12 servings.

Deb M.

Ella's Rhubarb Cake

1 ¼ cups sugar (plus ¼ cup and ½ tsp cinnamon mixed for topping)

1 stick butter

1 egg

1 cup sour cream

½ tsp salt

1 tsp baking soda

2 cups flour

2 cups rhubarb cut into ½ inch slices about 6 sticks

1 cup walnuts

Preheat oven to 350 degrees

Mix butter and sugar, add egg and sour cream. Mix flour, salt and baking soda separately and then add to sugar and butter mixture. Add rhubarb and walnuts. Spoon into (2) 8 ½ inch round pans. Top with the sugar and cinnamon mixture. Bake 40 minutes. Cool 10 minutes then use a plate to invert cake over a sink and then place right side up on a wire rack to complete cooling.

Ella N.

Banana Bread

American Home All Purpose Cookbook. Edited by Virginia T. Habeeb and the Food Staff of American Home The Curtis Publishing Company   1966

(My mother's old cookbook!)

A good recipe to use up over ripe bananas.

2 cups flour

2 3/4 tsp baking powder

½ tsp salt

3/4 cup sugar

½ cup butter

2 eggs

3 very ripe bananas mashed

3/4 cup chopped walnuts

1 package baking raisins. You may use 1 cup mini chocolate chips if you prefer.

Preheat oven to 350 degrees

In a small bowl mix the flour, baking powder and salt.

In a large bowl mix sugar and butter. Mix in eggs.   To this add ½ of the mashed bananas. Mix well. Add ½ of the flour mixture. Mix well. Add rest of bananas, mix then add remaining flour mixture and mix well. Add nuts and raisins or chocolate chips. Pour into a greased and floured 9x5 loaf pan.

Bake 60-70 minutes- until cake tester inserted in center comes out clean. Cool 10 minutes in pan on wire rack. Remove from pan and continue to cool on wire rack. Best if wrapped in foil and not eaten until the following day. This bread freezes well. Very good if sliced, each slice wrapped in Saran wrap and placed in a zipper bag in the freezer. To eat, remove a slice from Saran wrap, microwave a slice on a plate for 60 seconds on half power and another 10 seconds on full power if needed. The chocolate chips get soft and the banana flavor in the bread comes through when warm. It is delicious at room temperature too.

Carolyn W.

Banana Oat "cookies"

www.skinnytaste.com   February   18,   2013   Adapted   from
www.theburlapbag.com

This is a great recipe for using up bananas that are too ripe to eat as they are. It is also a healthy recipe but the inside of the "cookie" does not cook all the way and remains very very moist. You need to eat these "cookies" right away.

2 medium very ripe bananas

1 cup uncooked quick oats

¼ cup walnuts, chocolate chips or peanut butter chips or any other mix in of your choice. I used ½ cup walnuts and ½ cup chocolate chips.

Preheat oven to 350 degrees. Spray cookie sheet with non-stick spray or line with parchment. Mash the bananas well and combine them in a bowl with other ingredients. Place by Tablespoonful on baking sheet and bake 15 minutes or until cookies are firm and lightly browned. Remove and let cool completely on cooling rack. Makes approximately 16 cookies.

Carolyn L.

Snickerdoodles

2 ¾ cups all-purpose flour

¼ tsp salt

1 tsp baking soda

2 tsp cream of tarter

1 ½ cups sugar

1 cup butter or margarine, softened

2 eggs

For topping:

½ cup sugar

1 TBS cinnamon

In a bowl combine dry ingredients and set aside. In another bowl cream together the butter and 1 ½ cups sugar. Slowly add in the eggs. Mix in dry ingredients slowly. In a small bowl combine the remaining ½ cup sugar and the 1 TBS cinnamon. Take the dough and make balls and roll in cinnamon and sugar mixture. Place on an ungreased cookie sheet and bake at 350 degrees for 16-19 minutes.

Connie R.

Chocolate Chip Cookies

These cookies use less flour than traditional chocolate chip cookies. It makes the butter and brown sugar taste stand out versus a flour taste in traditional cookies. They don't puff up as much as traditional cookies but they taste a lot better.

2 cups flour

1 tsp baking soda

1 tsp salt

1 cup butter, softened

¾ cup sugar

¾ cup dark brown sugar, firmly packed

1 tsp vanilla extract (homemade and if not, do not ever us artificial but only pure vanilla extract)

2 eggs

1 (package chocolate chips), I use Ghirardelli 60% Cocoa bittersweet chocolate chips

1 cup walnut pieces, cut them yourself because the store bought pre- cut ones can be very tiny pieces. I break them with my hands into chunks.

Preheat oven to 375

Combine flour, baking soda and salt. Cream butter and sugars. Add vanilla and egg and mix well. Add to flour mixture and then add chips and walnuts. Drop on ungreased cookie sheet (I line my cookie sheets with foil for easier clean up.) Bake 9-11 minutes. Let cool on pan 1 minute and finish cooling on wire racks.

To make homemade vanilla extract, buy a jar of vanilla beans (expensive!) and cut up with kitchen scissor. Place in a jar with 1/3 – ½ cup vodka. Let marinate for a month or two in a cool, dry dark place. When using, the vanilla bean pieces will be on the bottom of the jar and you can pour off the top of the jar. Let beans stay in the jar as it will get more flavorful.

Carolyn W.

Quaker's Best Oatmeal cookies

Quaker Brand Oatmeal www.quakeroats.com

1 ¼ cup butter

¾ cups dark brown sugar

½ cup sugar

1 egg

1 tsp vanilla

1 ½ cups flour

1 tsp baking soda

½ tsp salt

1 tsp cinnamon

¼ tsp nutmeg (optional)

3 cups Quaker Oats

1 cup raisins or dried cranberries or mixed dried fruit chopped

Preheat oven to 375 degrees

Beat butter and sugars until fluffy. Add vanilla and egg. Beat. Combine flour, baking soda, salt, cinnamon and nutmeg, if using nutmeg. Add dry ingredients to wet and mix well. Add oats and dried fruit, whichever fruit you are using. Place on ungreased (I line my pan with foil for easier clean up) and bake 8-9 minutes for a chewy cookie and 10-11 minutes for a crisp cookie. Cool on pan one minute and then remove to cool on wire rack.

Carolyn W.

Cinnamon tortilla crisps

¼ cup butter, room temp

2 TBS sugar

2 tsp ground cinnamon

4 eight inch flour tortillas (found in the dairy section)

Mix butter, sugar and cinnamon. Spread on tortillas. Cut tortilla into eighths in pie shape... Place on foil lined baking sheet... do not crowd tortillas. Bake 400 degree oven for 7-8 minutes, until golden. Great just plain or serve with chopped strawberries and Kiwis and eat like Salsa and chips. Also great with ice cream.

Carolyn W.

Our Time With Our Fellow Wives Has Come to An End

It's come to the point in this book that we have to say our goodbyes. We welcome final thoughts from our participating LEOWs and we too, the authors, want to leave you with a few final thoughts.

Do you have any final advice or thoughts on your life as a LEOW that you would like to share?

I am proud to be the wife of a law enforcement officer. He loves his job, he takes it seriously and he is really good at it. I love the Thin Blue Line family that I have gained because of it too. I never imagined that I would be married to a cop... but I am so lucky that I am. I love him!

Meredith K.

I've had my share of ups and downs being married to a LEO. Sometimes I wish he'd be more of a husband emotionally and not give me a "its life, you need to get over it, things happen" type speech because sometimes I honestly just want someone to listen to me moan and groan and complain and not try to fix it. But, I also have to remember that after twenty three years in law enforcement, he's trained to be that way in most situations. I have to remind myself when things get hard that I chose to marry a LEO and while I would like normalcy sometimes, that's not the life I married into. I love my LEO more than anything in the world and all I want is for him to succeed and love his job and have a wife who is behind him and one that he can come home and vent to about his day and know that he won't be judged or made fun of at all. Be behind your husband and support him in whatever he decides to do and make sure you keep the lines of communication open. I've been blessed to find a man who wants to talk to me about anything that's bothering me so that we can work to resolve it together. We talk about money and even if we only spend a couple of dollars, we tell the other one so that we both know where our money is going. It may seem silly and insignificant but it really keeps our marriage open and truthful and strong. He can tell me anything that happens without me going nuts and accusing him of things and I can tell him anything and he is okay with whatever happens. Keeping communication open is the most important thing in your marriage to a LEO because it will truly help your marriage and help both of you cope with the stresses of life. Also, make time for couple time and time for just you, because you need it.

Patty R.

Communication is the key to a wonderful and happy marriage; jealousy has no place in a successful marriage; one must trust the other no matter what. I love the quote "Live, Laugh, Love" – that says it all!

Bjae K.

Be very supportive of your LEO. If he needs to talk, listen. If he wants space, give it to him. Be very understanding is my number one thing I would tell a new LEOW. There will be plans changed due to the duty calling so just know that ahead of time and remember your LEO is doing what he loves and the community needs him as much as you do.

Vicky C.

My advice for other LEOWs is to find a group of women who get the lifestyle. I am pleased to have in my circle many women who are married to local police officers. None of them are in my husband's department but they deal with the same stress in their own departments and can be a source of encouragement and problem solving help. It's great to get another point of view. It's also great to have "normal" female friends whose husbands have a normal job. They provide a great barometer of how different our lifestyles are and can give us the impetus to demand more balance in our marital relationships. I enjoy my time with non LEOWs as well.

Annemarie J.

A LEO shares her thoughts:

I have a son from a previous marriage and he is in his 20's. I also have a young son who is under ten, from my present marriage. Yes, quite an age difference but I have to say it has worked out well overall. My oldest was nine when I joined the police department. I was already divorced and trying to make a career for myself. I sometimes feel guilty because I wasn't able to give him the kind of attention he needed during my years as an officer. He too has a good father and I don't think he ever lacked attention but again, Moms love different. We give a more nurturing kind of love. I was so concerned about paying bills and keeping my head above water financially that I didn't take the time to enjoy watching him grow into the man he is now. I do regret that. I've come to realize that when you're a young parent, your priorities are different, make the car payment, rent, bills and take in a movie with your son... Now that I'm in my forties, I can't wait to get home and see my family. It's all I want to do. My job is important to me but my family comes first.

Lori T.

Wow, what a journey! We have so enjoyed getting to know our sisters in the Thin Blue Line family while writing this book. We have great respect and admiration for the women who contributed to this book. They opened up their lives to our readers in an effort to share their experiences and wisdom with fellow LEOWs. We come from many different backgrounds and our husbands work in many different law enforcement agencies but we all share in the life of a LEOW. We share the same difficulties, sorrows and obstacles of being a LEOW but we also share in the same joys.

There are many words in the English language... and the urban dictionary...used to describe law enforcement officers. Police, PoPo, 5-0, copper, pig, donut eaters and so many more unsavory terms that could probably make up a book all their own. To the people who love them however, they are simply, *son...daddy...husband...daughter...mommy...wife.* It's no secret that it takes a certain kind of person to be a police officer. Just about everyone can agree on that, despite their feelings about officers in general. To be the one running in when everyone else is running out is a deep rooted passion. Some may even say a calling.

To love a man, or woman of the Thin Blue Line is its own calling. I think this book has made that more than clear. We are a quirky bunch, we who love our cops. Strong and independent are two qualities that have come up over and over throughout this book. We are also nurturers, caregivers, emotional supporters...the *heart* behind the badge, one might say. We are proud of our spouses and the torch they carry, we champion for them and we love them unconditionally.

Not that all that is so easy. As you have seen throughout the book, we have our tough times. Ever try feeding a family of four on a civil service salary? Not so easy to do but we do it. How about cook a meal that has to taste good reheated or better yet...cold, in the front seat of a cruiser in between calls for service?

We love our cops with all our hearts and we are so very proud of what they do. That is why we do what we do. The reason we seek each other out for support and often as sounding boards for the many frustrations that accompany this life we love so much. That is what makes us a true sisterhood.

Enjoy and embrace the LEOW life! You will make some of the best friends you could ever have with LEOs and their wives. They will give you the shirt off their back and help you at any time of day or night, without question or hesitation. We were recently out to dinner with several other LEO couples and as I looked around the table, I thought about how blessed I am to know these wonderful people. The "job" brought them into our lives but who they are made them our friends. Our lives are so much better for knowing them.

Everyday LEOs retire and new ones take their place. As always, "The Times They Are A-Changin" but the basics of LEOW life cross time, boundaries and age groups. We are connected by the life we have chosen and we are truly family! We wish all a "safe tour."

LEOWs: We hope you gained some new ideas and wisdom and some "oh yeah" moments from the experiences of the women in this book. You are not alone in your crazy life! You have many sisters in the Thin Blue Line Family going through the same challenges and triumphs.

LEOW family members: We hope we have been able to give you new insight into the LEOW life. We hope this new insight will help you to better support your LEOW and have a little more admiration for all that she does. We truly need our family's support!

LEOs: Give your LEOW a giant hug. We hope you look at her with a new respect for all that she does to support you in your career. She is proud of you and hopefully you are proud of her. We hope this book will lead to many discussions in your home about how to best support each other.

Non-LEOW readers: thank you for giving us this opportunity to share our lives with you. It is our hope that we have given you a new perspective of our lives and perhaps the next time you see a LEO working, you will think of him as not just a man in uniform but as a husband and father who has a family at home loving him, missing him and making sacrifices so that you will be safe in your home.

Thank you for spending your time and treasure to share in our conversations with police wives. We hope you have enjoyed reading this book as much as we did writing it.

And finally, a salute to our sisters who are fire fighter and military wives. Our lives are different in some ways but we all love our men who would lay down their lives to protect the people of this country we love. We thank you for your service as well!

Resources and References

Throughout this book we have shared various resources that have been helpful to law enforcement wives. We have placed them along with other LEOW recommended resources together in the following pages to make them easy to find. It is by no means a complete list of available resources nor do we as authors vouch for their usefulness and we encourage you to do your own research for topics of interest to you. Many of our participating LEOWs are Christian and therefor some of the recommend resources have a Christian theme, however many may have useful advice to all faiths.

Cover Photography
www.facebook.com/bobbuchananphotography
www.bobbuchanan.com
www.bobbpsychicmedium.com
www.youtube.com/user/bobbybproductions/videos

Books

Marriage:

The Love Dare by Alex Kendrick and Stephen Kendrick. B&H Books; Revised edition (January 1, 2013) This book has a Christian / Bible based theme.

The 5 Love Languages by Gary D. Chapman   Northfield Publishing; New Edition (December 17, 2009)

The Divorce Remedy: The Proven 7-Step Program for Saving Your Marriage by Michele Weiner Davis Simon & Schuster (September 4, 2002)

Divorce Busting: A Step-by-Step Approach to Making Your Marriage Loving Again by Michele Weiner A Fireside Book (February 1, 1993)

Unglued: Making Wise Choices in the Midst of Raw Emotions by Lysa TerKeurst Zondervan (August 7, 2012)

His Needs, Her Needs: Building an Affair – Proof Marriage by Willard F. Harley Jr. Revell; Rev Exp edition (February 1, 2011)

Love & Respect: The Love She Most Desires; The Respect He Desperately Needs by Emerson Eggerichs Thomas Nelson; 1 edition (September 7, 2004)

Draw Close: A Devotional for Couples by Willard F. Jr. Harley and Joyce S. Joyce Revell (October 1, 2011)

A comparison of Law Enforcement Divorce Rates with Those of Other Occupations. Shawn P. McCoy   Michael G. Aamodt   Published online 20 October 2009 Springer Science + Business Media LLC 2009

Religious / Spiritual

Spiritual Survival for Law Enforcement by Cary A. Friedman Compass Books 2005

Just Enough Light for the Step I'm On: Trusting God in the Tough Times by Stormie Omartian Harvest House Publishers (January 1, 2008)

The Power of Prayer to Change Your Marriage by Stormie Omartian Harvest House Publishers (January 1, 2009)

The Power of a Praying Wife by Stormie Omartian Harvest House Publisher (January 1, 2007)

Because I'm Suitable: The Journey of a Wife on Duty by Allison P. Uribe WestBow Press (February 22, 2012)

The Noticer: Sometimes All a Person Needs Is A Little Perspective by Andy Andrews Thomas Nelson; 1 edition (April 12, 2011)

Lives Behind the Badge by Kristi Neace Create Space December 1, 2009 (Combines real life issues of police wives and Christian Devotionals.)

For Officers and wives:

Emotional Survival for Law Enforcement: A Guide for Officers and Their Families by Kevin M. Gilmartin. E-S Press (2002)

CopShock, Second Edition: Surviving Posttraumatic Stress Disorder (PTSD) by Allen R. Kates Holbrook Street Press; 2nd edition (September 1, 2008)

Police Suicide: Epidemic in Blue by John M. Violanti Charles C Thomas Pub Ltd; 2 edition (September 1, 2007)

On The Edge: Recent Perspectives on Police Suicide by John M. Violanti Charles C Thomas Pub Ltd (April 20, 2011)

I Love a cop, Revised Edition: What Police Families Need to Know by Ellen Kirschman PHD. The Guilford Press; Revised edition (December 16, 2006)

Bullets in the Washing Machine by Melissa Littles The Police Wife Life (September 23, 2011)

A Chip on My Shoulder by Victoria M. Newman Tate Publishing (November 8, 2011)

Films

Fireproof Starring Kirk Cameron Sony Pictures Home Entertainment A Christian themed movie which uses the book The Love Dare.

Courageous Starring Alex Kendrick Sony Pictures Home Entertainment A Christian themed movie about fatherhood.

Domestic Violence / Intimate Partner Violence

 The National Domestic Violence Hotline is a wonderful resource. 1800-799-7233.

Domestic Violence Statistics: www.domesticviolencestatistics.org

Women's health: www.womenshealth.gov

Findings from the National Violence Against Women Survey November 2000 available at the Center for Disease Control and Prevention website: www.cdc.gov

The Government Center for Disease Control and Prevention gives a hotline for child abuse: To report abuse or get help, contact the National Child Abuse Hotline at 1-800-4-A-CHILD (1-800-422-4453). The phone is staffed twenty four hours a day, seven days a week. All calls are confidential. The hotline offers crisis help, referrals, literature and support resources.

Suicide

24 hour /7 days a week "Suicide Prevention hotline: 1-800-273-TALK (8255)

www.cdc.gov

www.afsp.org The American Foundation for Suicide Prevention

www.nihm.gov National Institute of Mental health

www.policeone.com

Alcohol and suicide

www.safecallnow.org is a website that was started to specifically help Public Safety Employees, current and retired and their families with various issues including alcohol abuse and suicide. Their Mission Statement is: "Safe Call Now is a confidential, comprehensive, 24-hour crisis referral service for all public safety employees, all emergency services personnel and their family members nationwide." Their phone number is: 206-459-3020. They have confidential referral services for suicide, alcohol abuse or other substance abuse. You will speak with a police officer, retired police officer, Public Safety Officer and other mental health professional who understands the issues unique to the law enforcement officer

www.niaaa.nih.gov National Institute of Alcohol Abuse and Alcoholism www.badgeoflife.com

Recipes

Books

American Home All Purpose Cookbook. Edited by Virginia T. Habeeb and the Food Staff of American Home. The Curtis Publishing Company 1966

Fix it and Forget it Cookbook by Phyllis Pelman Publisher Good Books.

Food websites

www.skinnytaste.com

www.mixinajar.com

www.quakeroats.com

www.ohbiteit.com

www.allrecipes.com

www.food.com

www.tasteofhome.com

www.epicurious.com

Facebook Groups

National Police W

ives Association

Blue Line Life

Wives Behind the Badge

Law Enforcement Families Unite

The Thin Blue Line

Book group discussion questions

Questions for law enforcement wife book discussion groups

What surprised you most about being a Police wife?

What did the authors leave out of the book that you think they should have addressed?

How have your experiences been different than the women in the book?

What advice would you give to a newly married LEOW?

What parts of the book did you relate to the most?

If you had to do it over again, would you marry a LEO?

Were there particular women or answers that you could relate particularly well to?

Do you think your children worry about your spouse's job safety and have you talked with them about their worries?

Questions for non-law enforcement wife book discussion groups.

Has your opinion of police wives changed after reading this book and if so, in what ways?

What about a Police wife's life surprised you most?

What other jobs have similar stress and conditions to LEOs?

Were there any women or issues you most identified with?

What aspect of being a Police wife would you find hardest to deal with?

What support could you offer to a Police wife whom you know?

How has your spouse's career choice impacted your life?

How has your career choice impacted your spouse's life?

How are your children impacted by yours and your spouse's career choices?

Questions For non- LEO women:

Do you think LEOWs lives are that much different than your own?

In what ways would your life be different if you had married a LEO?

Are there ways your life might be harder than a Police Wife's life?

Some Final thoughts...

While both authors are married to police officers, author Carolyn Whiting also has the unique perspective being both a police spouse and a retired police officer. Her input to the book was twofold, offering advice to other spouses but with a special understanding of what the LEO in their life goes through on a daily basis. As was stated in the first few pages, the authors truly believe that being married to a LEO is a special calling. What they didn't necessarily realize is that others- civilians- recognize that as well. Please enjoy below, a few comments from the mothers of the authors.

From Carolyn L.'s Mother:

Being the wife of a police officer is not for everyone. Women (or men) who marry officers need to be the strong silent type for the survival of their family. I'm proud of my daughter for many reasons. She balances home life with work life. She stands behind what her husband needs to do to be successful at his job. She forfeits what she wants at times to bring peace and continuity to their home. She knows her officer husband needs a day of rest to transition from 'work' on the streets to life at home. She smiles when she hears a loud noise from the dryer - knowing it's only a bullet tumbling around and not a broken dryer.
I pray for them both often, that he comes home each morning and that she doesn't become a widow because someone else had a violent argument with their spouse. Whenever I think of such a situation, I say a prayer.
I love them both. And appreciate the things they both do to keep our area safe. They rock!

From Carolyn W.'s Mother:

When Carolyn was about six years old, her playmates said a girl couldn't be a LEO when she grew up. She didn't believe them and asked me. I said any girl could be anything she wanted to be and then I forgot about it. But she remembered.

When she graduated from high school, she said she wanted to be a LEO. I suggested college first, and she said OK. When she finished college she said she wanted to be a LEO. I suggested grad school first and she said OK. Midway through grad school she came home and said: "Mom, I quit grad school. I'm going to take the test for the Police Academy. I got a civilian job at the police department to earn money until I'm accepted. My mind is made up. It's what I've always wanted to do". At that moment, remembering all the way back to her question as a little girl, I knew it was my turn to say, OK, and I did, although reluctantly. I was scared and worried for her, knowing that she was choosing a sometimes dangerous career, but her decision was final and I had to accept it.

It turned out to be a good decision. She became a LEO, served several jurisdictions, married a wonderful LEO she met on the job, then retired after being injured on the job. As a LEOW, she has devoted herself to furthering her LEO's career objectives and helping him to mesh them with their growth as individuals and their joint life goals.

I'm glad she followed her heart, not my fears. Her life has been the richer for it, not in money, but in what matters most, self-respect and life satisfaction. I'm proud of her and the life course she has charted. Carolyn leads by example, demonstrating 24/7 that any girl can be anything she wants to be.

Fiction Titles Available From Author Carolyn LaRoche

Follow author Carolyn La Roche on Facebook for excerpts from other works and up to date information on future publications at:
https://www.facebook.com/pages/Carolyn-La-Roche-Author

ebooks available at amazon.com and barnesandnoble.com

Paperback copies also available at amazon.com

Double Jeopardy

When a murderer surfaces in the sunny resort town of Virginia Beach, Virginia homicide detective Jo Pratt is convinced it will be just another routine investigation. When the murderer turns out to be a serial killer with a preference for women who look just like they could be Jo's deceased sister, there is nothing routine about it. If the local rag sheet reporter would just quit interfering in the investigation and her partner confirmed bachelor Sam Jones could remember they were partners and not lovers, Jo might be able to figure out why the killer was fixated on her and take him down for good. Haunted by her dead sister's memory and the faces of the women who have died, Jo is bound and determined to find the man responsible and make sure he never does it again without losing her heart and soul to the one man she swore would never be right for her.

Four Lucy Fight Club

The way Susie Timmons saw it, the whole family was only one collection call away from living in a refrigerator box. If things didn't turn around soon her only option would be strutting her tired, worn out stuff on the nearest street corner. Things just couldn't get any worse. A drunk driver totals Susie's car and puts her in the hospital. She loses her pathetic sandwich making job and there are only so many double shifts her police officer husband can work before he has to actually sleep. There is absolutely no doubt that the Timmons family is in a total downward spiral. Ramen noodles become gourmet and that refrigerator box starts looking pretty good. If not for her good friends and co-conspirators Claire, Becca and Laura she might have actually thought twice about robbing that bank. Famed bank robber Willie Sutton once said he robbed banks because that was where the money was. Susie and her friends needed money. The banks had plenty. So what if Susie's husband was a cop.

Willie Sutton made them do it.
The defense rests....

CPSIA information can be obtained
at www.ICGtesting.com
Printed in the USA
BVOW08s0735040318

509630BV00028B/669/P